Why Do

WITHDRAWN

The first recorded English name for the make-up we now call *blusher* was *paint*, in 1660. In the 1750s a new word, *rouge*, displaced *paint*, and remained in standard usage for around two centuries. Then, in 1965, an advertisement coined a new word for the product: *blusher*. Each generation speaks a little differently, and every language is constantly changing. It is not only words that change, every aspect of a language changes over time – pronunciation, word meanings and grammer. Packed with fascinating examples of changes in the English language over time, this entertaining book explores the origin of words and place names, the differences between British and American English, and the apparent eccentricities of the English spelling system. Amusingly written yet deeply instructive, it will be enjoyed by anyone involved in studying the English language and its history, as well as anyone interested in how and why languages change.

R. L. TRASK was a world authority on the Basque language and on historical linguistics. He wrote both academic and popular books, notably on grammar, punctuation, and English style and usage. His publications include *Language: The Basics* (1995) and *Mind the Gaffe* (2001). At the time of his death in 2004, he was Professor of Linguistics at the University of Sussex.

The book has been revised by Robert McColl Millar, Senior Lecturer in Linguistics at the University of Aberdeen.

Why Do Languages Change?

R. L. Trask

Revised by
Robert McColl Millar

 **CAMBRIDGE**
UNIVERSITY PRESS

CAMBRIDGE UNIVERSITY PRESS
Cambridge, New York, Melbourne, Madrid, Cape Town, Singapore, São Paulo, Delhi

Cambridge University Press
The Edinburgh Building, Cambridge CB2 8RU, UK

Published in the United States of America by Cambridge University Press, New York

www.cambridge.org
Information on this title: www.cambridge.org/9780521546935

First published 2010

Printed in the United Kingdom at the University Press, Cambridge

A catalogue record for this publication is available from the British Library

ISBN 978-0-521-83802-3 Hardback
ISBN 978-0-521-54693-5 Paperback

For my wonderful Jan

Contents

Figures and tables

Figures

Tables

A few words before we start

This book is intended to give a sense of language change to interested laypeople of any age; it is not a textbook. I do hope, however, that it will act as a door into historical linguistics for some readers.

Because of its nature, I have made no assumptions about knowledge either of languages or, more importantly, of the techniques linguists use to describe language. If we are going to treat the subject in any depth or seriousness, however, I have found it necessary occasionally to use special terms and symbols in the text. I normally explain these, but I want to discuss some potential sticking points before we start. Readers may well find themselves coming back to this page occasionally.

The Roman alphabet used for English is not terribly effective, as we will see, in representing the sounds of English, never mind the potential sounds found in *all* the world's languages. Because of this, phoneticians and other linguists who work with sounds have spent a considerable amount of effort over the last hundred years and more developing an extended writing system, the International Phonetic Alphabet (IPA), which can describe *all* of these sounds. I will not use more than a handful of these symbols in this book, and only when necessary. Most of these symbols make sense to anyone used to the Roman alphabet: /p/ stands for <p>, for instance; /n/ for <n>. Sometimes, however, there is potential for confusion. IPA /j/ stands for the first sound in English *yes*; the <j> in *judge* is represented by /dʒ/ in IPA; IPA /y/ stands for the vowel in French *tu*. When potential headaches of this sort exist, I have highlighted them. It is worth noting that the vowel symbols in IPA stand for the 'continental' values associated with these letters. Thus /e/ stands for the vowel found in *bay*, if you are from Scotland and a few other places, not the vowel in *bee*. /a/ stands for the vowel in *cat* for most British people; while /æ/ is the vowel found in the same word in most North American accents (and some conservative upper-class varieties in southern England); /ɑ/ is the vowel found in words like *bath* in southeast England (other British varieties would have /a/).

You may have noticed that I have used the convention / / to surround sounds in most of the book, but [ ] for a few. This represents a subtle but important distinction in sound perception. All speakers have the ability to produce *all* sounds which can be produced by humans. By the time they have reached school age, however, the number of separate sounds speakers perceive from this variety depends upon what language they speak. For instance, German speakers can, of course, make the sound [θ], as found at the start of English *thing*; unless they are trained, however, they hear it only as a variant of a larger unit, /s/. For most English speakers, however, the initial sounds in *thing* and *sing* are absolutely separate; to a German speaker, they are variants of the same essential sound. These essential sounds are called *phonemes* and are represented by / /; all variants of these phonemes are called *allophones* and are represented by [ ]. The important thing to remember is that how phonemes are laid out over the range of potential sounds differs from language to language. Spellings, when necessary, are shown using < >.

Acknowledgements

I am indebted to Lyle Campbell, Richard Coates, Jan Lock, Tony Lock, Andrew Winnard and two anonymous readers for valuable comments on earlier drafts of some or all chapters. Many of the examples in Chapter 4 are taken from the scholarly publications of Richard Coates. Acknowledgements for examples taken from other people's writing are provided in the text.

For the origins of English words, I have relied chiefly on the *Chambers Dictionary of Etymology* (originally published as the *Barnhart Dictionary of Etymology*) and on the *Oxford English Dictionary*. In doubtful cases, I have consulted several other dictionaries and very many websites.

The map in Figure 1.1 is reproduced with permission from Walt Wolfram and Natalie Schilling-Estes, *American English* (Oxford: Blackwell, 1998). The BSL signs in Figure 8.1 are reproduced with permission from J. G. Kyle and B. Woll, *Sign Language: The Study of Deaf People and Their Language* (Cambridge: Cambridge University Press, 1985).

Any remaining shortcomings are my responsibility.

A note from the reviser

This book was left in an advanced state at the time of Larry Trask's death in 2004, since when it has passed through the editorial process at Cambridge University Press. When I took on the task of revising the typescript in Spring 2008, I made the decision that, unlike my treatment of Trask's *Historical Linguistics*, I would *not* stamp my own personality and views on *Why Do Languages Change?* When *I* is used in this book, therefore, it is Larry Trask who has chosen to do so. My task, as I saw it, was to do what Larry Trask would have done had he had the opportunity: 'cleaning' the text and ironing out inconsistencies. I hope that I have done so in as unobtrusive a manner as possible. My thanks go to my dear wife, Sandra, who helped with this work, despite the slight distraction of having a baby mid-way through the process.

I am very glad to answer queries on the material covered in this book. My e-mail address is r.millar@abdn.ac.uk.

Robert McColl Millar, November 2008

1   How do languages change?

All languages change

My grandparents didn't talk the way I talk. For example, my father's mother never used the words *at the end*. Instead, she always said *at the last end*: 'at the last end of the movie', 'at the last end of the game', and so on. My father said the same. But I have never said this, and even in childhood I considered it strange.

You too have very likely noticed that your parents or your grandparents speak or spoke a little differently from you. And, if you have children or grand-children, you have almost certainly heard them saying things that you would never say. Everywhere we look, we find differences in speech between the generations.

Each generation speaks a little differently because our language is always changing. And not just our language: *every* language is always changing. There is no such thing as a living language that fails to change. This is a piece of truth on which you can rely absolutely.

There's a widespread legend about a remarkable village, in the Appalachians or in Derbyshire or somewhere distant from London and New York, where the locals still speak pure and unchanged Elizabethan English. It doesn't exist. Nobody on earth has spoken Elizabethan English since the time of Queen Elizabeth I, around 400 years ago. There is nobody alive today who speaks English the way William Shakespeare spoke it, or the way Samuel Johnson spoke it, or the way Abraham Lincoln spoke it, or the way Queen Victoria spoke it. Apart perhaps from a handful of very elderly people, there is no one alive today who speaks English like Humphrey Bogart or Noël Coward (both born in 1899), or like Laurence Olivier or John Wayne (both born in 1907), or like Sir Donald Bradman or Bette Davis (both born in 1908). There aren't even many people around today who speak English like John F. Kennedy or Anthony Burgess (both born in 1917), or like Marilyn Monroe (born in 1926).

Watching English change

What do you call the coloured stuff that women sometimes put on their cheeks? The first recorded English name for this stuff is *paint*, recorded from 1660. In those days, both men and women of certain social classes painted their faces: you may have seen the garishly painted faces of the dandies in portraits of the time. In 1753, a new word appeared in English: *rouge*. The first writer to use this French word thought it necessary to explain to his readers that rouge was the same thing as paint. But *rouge* soon displaced *paint*, and it remained the usual English word for around two centuries. When I was a child, in the 1950s, *rouge* was the only word anybody ever used.

Then, in 1965, an advertisement coined a new word for the product: *blusher*. This word has gradually displaced *rouge*. When I recently heard a fashionable young woman call it *rouge*, I almost fell over with astonishment: I hadn't heard anyone use the word for decades, and associated it with styles which were already ancient when I was a child.

Few names of cosmetics are very old. Only in 1890 do we find the first mention of *mascaro*, a thick dark make-up used by (mostly male) stage actors to paint on eyebrows, so that their faces could be seen from the cheap seats. (The word derives from an Italian word for 'mask'.) And only in 1922 do we find the first use of the altered and presumably more feminine version *mascara* to label a slightly more subtle kind of eye make-up for women.

Fashionable items may be particularly given to linguistic change. Visiting my local cosmetics counter, I was startled to discover a sign inviting me to buy a certain product which, I was assured, was just the thing to 'fragrance your home or your car'. When I was just a little younger, English most emphatically did not permit me to 'fragrance' anything. Languages are always changing, and we older speakers find ourselves grumbling in the wake of the changes.

Sometimes, of course, the language changes because the world changes. When shiny little silvery discs began to appear a few years ago carrying recorded music, they had to be given a name, and so *compact discs* was duly coined – though it took English speakers the better part of ten minutes to shorten this intolerably long name to *CDs*.

This is just a very tiny sample of recent changes in English. Some have occurred within my lifetime; some have occurred very recently indeed. Consider Marilyn Monroe, who died in 1962. Marilyn never heard the word *compact disc* or *CD*. It is quite possible that she never heard *blusher*, since that word was not recorded in writing until shortly after her death. If she did hear it, it was a brand-new word, just beginning to be used in speech by Americans, but not yet found in print.

Since Marilyn's death, the language has acquired many new words. Here is just a tiny sample of the familiar English words that Marilyn Monroe never heard: *body-piercing, reggae, single mother, videotape, aromatherapy, G-spot, laptop, AIDS, miniskirt, jumbo jet, sex worker, designer label, downsizing, toyboy, trophy wife, sleaze, one-hit wonder, sound bite, bikini line, e-mail, Third World, GM food, microwave oven, smoking gun* ('hard evidence'), *into* ('deeply interested in') and *topless dancer*. In fact, the word *topless*, applied to a woman's attire, is not recorded until 1964, and Marilyn probably never heard it, even though *topless* is recorded from 1937 in connection with laws against such swimming costumes for *men*! Those were dear dead days indeed: the world has changed almost more than we can imagine, and the language has not lagged behind.

Social changes have introduced whole areas of vocabulary that Marilyn never heard. As a young woman, Marilyn didn't smoke, but she was obliged to learn to smoke for her role in the 1953 film *Niagara*, in which she played a Bad Girl. We have many candid photos of a more mature Marilyn smoking off-screen, and so it appears that her film smoking led her to take up smoking in real life. This meant that she had to learn the vocabulary associated with smoking although, surprisingly, given how many people smoked then, this was very limited. In the 1950s, smoking went unremarked almost everywhere, and tobacco companies were still claiming that doctors endorsed their products. Accordingly, Marilyn never heard the words *nicotine-free*, *passive smoking*, *smokeless tobacco*, *advertising ban*, *nicotine patch*, *smoke-free zone*, *health warning*, *anti-smoking laws* or even *low-tar*. She never even heard *smoking area*, since practically everywhere was a smoking area in Marilyn's day, and it was only the rare non-smoking areas that had to be labelled.

I must stress that the lists above do not contain even one-tenth of 1 per cent of the new words which have entered English since 1962 – even if I exclude the vast number of technical terms which have come into use in such fields as computing. There are so many thousands of words which we use every day, but which didn't exist in 1962, that we might almost begin to wonder what Marilyn Monroe talked about when she was off the screen.

Of course, Marilyn never found herself short of words, since the English of the 1950s already provided her with a rich vocabulary for talking about anything she liked. Among the new words that only entered English in the 1950s are *rock 'n' roll*, *sex kitten*, *coffee break*, *bikini*, *hardback* (book), *junk mail*, *press release*, *dreadlocks*, *shades* (sunglasses), *sunroof*, *economy class*, *hula hoop*, *hacker*, *software*, *the pill* (for contraception), *BLT* (sandwich), *stir fry*, *scuba diving* and *exotic dancer*, among many hundreds of others, so Marilyn's contemporaries were no slower than their successors in coining new words at will.

Language changes like fashion

Looking into word origins produces some surprises. I had always assumed, for instance, that *feminism* must be a very recent coinage indeed. But I was wrong: the word is first recorded in 1846! The word was never common, however, and gradually dropped out of use. The feminists of the 1960s called their movement *women's liberation*, later shortened to *women's lib*. But this name fell into disfavour in the 1970s, possibly because it became associated with radical posturing. The newly revived *feminism* gradually replaced it. Anybody who used *women's lib* today would get some pretty peculiar looks.

This last example illustrates one further point: words can disappear as well as appear. The formerly prominent *women's lib* is now gone, and few people now use *rouge*. In the 1960s, there was a *sit-in* or a *love-in* in the paper almost every week, but many younger readers probably don't even know what these things are. In the 1950s, everybody followed the *hit parade*. Any idea what that is? (We now call it the *charts*.) Do you know what a *B-girl* is, or a *carhop*, or a *flack*? (A female employee in a bar who encourages customers to spend money; a waiter in an eat-in-your-car fast-food restaurant; a public-relations person.) Can you remember *rabbit ears*? (A kind of indoor TV aerial.) Come to think of it, when was the last time you heard anybody talk about a *colour* television?

Only if you're acquainted with certain historical periods or topics are you likely to know what a *bustle* is, or a *flivver*, or a *Gibson girl* (A bizarre contraption for rearranging a woman's figure; a battered old car; a young woman epitomising the fashionable ideal of around 1900.) Most of us have come across *flivver* only from Aldous Huxley's *Brave New World*, where a future society has made Henry Ford, the car manufacturer, its God. One of the many clichés which has been altered to fit this new 'reality' comes out as 'Ford's in his Flivver: all's right with the world.'

As we move slowly back in time, the dead words we encounter become steadily more numerous, and perhaps steadily more obscure. You have to be an especially devoted fan of Victorian fiction to know what a *pocket pistol* is. (It's a hip flask.) Even this degree of devotion might not help you with *delope*. A duellist deloped by refusing to fire at his opponent, instead firing his pistol harmlessly into the air. With the disappearance of duelling, its associated vocabulary has evaporated, and only a handful of people with suitable historical interests now trouble to learn these antique words. For most of us they are as dead as the street slang of Pompeii.

Word meanings are slippery

What do you call the thing you sleep in at night? Unless you are a submariner obliged to sleep in a hammock, you probably call it a *bed*, like everyone else. This word has existed in English as long as English has existed as a distinct language, and in fact it was present in the ancestors of English earlier than that. Very likely future speakers will go on calling this object a *bed* for centuries to come. This is the way we expect words to behave. But our expectations are not always satisfied. Sometimes words do change their meanings, and sometimes those changes in meaning are breathtaking. For instance, today the word *bead* means 'small decorative ball with a hole through it', and beads are usually found strung together into necklaces or bracelets. But, a few centuries ago, the meaning of *bead* was utterly different: the word meant only 'prayer'. How could it change its meaning from 'prayer' to 'small ball'?

Well, if you know a little about medieval Christianity, you can probably guess at least roughly what happened. Medieval Christians were in the habit of counting their prayers, and for this purpose they used a string of beads – a *rosary* – to keep track of the number of *Hail Mary*s or other prayers that had been uttered. With each completed prayer, another bead was slipped along the string, and this activity was called *telling one's beads*. The word *tell* originally meant 'count' as well as 'relate', which is why the person who counts out cash in a bank is called a *teller*, and so the expression *telling one's beads* meant 'counting one's prayers' – which is what the praying person was doing.

However, since the person doing this *appeared* to be counting off the little balls on the string of his rosary, the expression *telling one's beads* came to be re-interpreted as meaning 'counting the little balls on the string'. As a result, *bead* shifted its meaning from 'prayer' to 'small ball'. In the context, this shift of meaning was natural and easy.

Slightly more complicated is the case of *grammar* and *glamour*. Though you may be astonished to hear this, *grammar* and *glamour* are the same word. But glamour is fashionable, sexy and utterly desirable, while grammar is just about the least fashionable and least sexy piece of the universe that non-linguists can think of.

So how did this happen? Well, the ancestor of the word *grammar* was coined in Ancient Greek and applied to the study of writing. This word was taken over by the Romans into their Latin, and from Latin it spread into much of Europe. Today we still use *grammar* to label the study of the structures of words, phrases and sentences. But things were a little different in the Middle Ages.

In medieval times, few people in Europe could read and write; literacy was seen as a rare, almost fabulous, achievement. Even fewer people could go beyond mere literacy to the extent of studying and understanding the writings of the great philosophers, scholars and scientists, particularly since these were generally available only in Latin. To most people, such a degree of book-learning appeared simply magical, and indeed book-learning, which was commonly referred to simply as *grammar*, was hardly distinguished from magic at all. In English, the variant form *gramarye* was an everyday word for 'magic' or 'conjuring', while in French the word *grammaire* was altered into *grimoire*, meaning 'a book of magical spells'; the word was later borrowed into English in this form and has recently become current again through the Harry Potter books.

Our story moves now to Scotland, where the word *grammar* underwent a small change of pronunciation to *glamour*, reflecting the awkwardness of having two instances of /r/ in one word. In Scots, this form *glamour*, often compounded as *glamour-might*, acquired the sense of 'enchantment', 'magic spell', and eventually it came to be applied specifically to a kind of enchantment upon the eye, so that the victim sees things differently from the way they really are. Until the early nineteenth century, this sense remained unknown outside Scotland, but then Sir Walter Scott, a native speaker of Scots, began using it in his poems and stories. Here is an example from Scott's poem *Lay of the Last Minstrel*:

> It had much of glamour might,
> Could make a ladye seem a knight;
> The cobwebs on a dungeon wall
> Seem tapistry in lordly hall;
> And youth seem age, and age seem youth –
> All was delusion, nought was truth.

The popularity of Scott's writings carried this formerly obscure Scots word throughout the English-speaking world. But the meaning of the word began rapidly to shift. In Scots, *glamour* was specifically a kind of supernatural enchantment. Outside Scotland, other writers began quickly extending the sense of the word to label any kind of seductive but false charm, the sort of charm you get from an unscrupulous but skilful manipulator who hopes to take advantage of you. At this stage, the word was an insult, and one that could be applied to both sexes.

In the late nineteenth century, however, *glamour* came to be applied more and more regularly and finally only to women, apparently in line with the Genesis view of women as dangerous temptresses out to seduce honourable and upright men away from the paths of righteousness. For a while, the label was still an insult, applied to a woman portrayed as a devious siren up to no good, but before long it lost its negative connotations entirely, possibly because of the more fictional allure peddled by the Hollywood dream factory. *Glamour* became a term of enthusiastic approval, as it still is today. When a gushing magazine describes a female celebrity as 'glamorous', the word expresses unqualified admiration, and there is no longer the slightest hint that the young lady in the picture is an unprincipled home-wrecker. Other words must be found for such an insinuation.

The writer Jeffrey Kacirk has uncovered a particularly interesting use of *glamour* in a late Victorian 'yellow' novel (a cheap and downmarket work), with the engaging title *Held in Bondage*: 'I know how quickly the glamour fades in the test of intercourse.'

This sounds a startling sentence to encounter in a Victorian novel, yellow or otherwise, and you might wonder how it slipped past the censors in a day when references to sexual intimacy, however discreet, were simply Not Allowed – and this one doesn't sound very discreet. The apparent suggestion that a string of eye-catching young ladies had grievously disappointed the narrator in bed does not sound at all like the sort of thing that would have amused Her Britannic Majesty. How could this happen?

Well, of course, we are looking at another change of meaning. In English, as with most languages, speaking about the act of sex has always proved difficult. At any given moment, we can usually choose between obscure medical terms that will scarcely be understood, and words so blunt and coarse they will get our faces slapped in some circles. As a result, we struggle desperately to find some clear but delicate way of talking about sexual congress. Polite expressions come and go in this domain at a brisk pace, since no word can remain wholly delicate for long.

The word *intercourse* has existed in English since about 1450, but for centuries it meant no more than 'dealings between people'. This sense persisted into the nineteenth century. That very genteel novelist Jane Austen could write of her exceedingly genteel characters Miss Anne Elliott and Captain Wentworth that 'they had no intercourse but what the commonest civility required'. All that Jane Austen meant was that Anne and the Captain barely exchanged a word beyond a grudging 'good morning', but a modern reader cannot avoid at the very least a snigger at the clear suggestion that minimal courtesy in Georgian England required rather more than it does now.

Why has this happened? In our never-ending quest for polite ways of talking about sex, somebody coined the clumsy but suitably decent expression *sexual intercourse*. But English speakers are not celebrated for their love of cumbersome polysyllabic expressions, and it was no time before this coinage had been shortened to *intercourse*. As a result, the word *intercourse* today is understood as meaning sex and nothing else, and the word cannot be used in any other way. Occasionally an unwary writer tries to recover the lost meaning of the word by turning out something like: *The Serbs and the Croats have resumed normal intercourse*. But the result is always surprising, and the older sense of the word is probably gone for good – or at least until another euphemism for naming the 'unmentionable' is found.

What words we use, what words we consider fashionable, can change from day to day. The variation involved can appear particularly fickle. With other linguistic features – grammar, sound, and so on – change appears much slower; yet when it happens, it can still be very striking.

Changes in grammar

Language change is easiest to see in vocabulary, since new words are coined in their hundreds every year, and since reading old prose will usually turn up a few dead words. But it is not only words that change: in fact, *every* aspect of a language changes over time. Pronunciation changes. Word meanings change.

And, of course, grammar changes. Let's look at a few recent changes in the grammar of English.

A good place to start is the *progressive passive*, as in *My house is being painted*. This form seems wholly unremarkable, but in fact it is a recent introduction into English. Until only a few generations ago, this form did not exist and could not be used. A speaker had to say instead either *My house is painting*, a form which now seems strange or worse, or *My house is painted*, which exists for us but has an entirely different meaning.

In 1662, Samuel Pepys wrote in his famous diary *I went to see if any play was acted*. The intended sense is ... *was being acted*, but this form was impossible for Pepys. About 1839, Charles Dickens wrote in his novel *Nicholas Nickleby: [H]e found that the coach had sunk greatly on one side, though it was still dragged forward by the horses*. The intended sense is ... *still being dragged forward*, but Dickens, who *would* have known the new usage, obviously could not bring himself to use it. Indeed, we know that many people of the time considered it 'vulgar'.

Far more commonly, though, we find the other choice. For example:

[T]he King's statue is making by the Mercers Company. (The sense is *is being made*.) (Pepys's diary, 1660)

At the very time that this dispute was maintaining by the centinel and the drummer – was the same point debating betwixt a trumpeter and a trumpeter's wife. (Laurence Sterne, *Tristram Shandy*, around 1760)

Whilst the Anthem was singing I was conducted by the Virger to the Pulpit... (James Woodforde's diary, 1784)

A code is preparing for the regulation of commerce (J. C. S. Abbot, *Napoleon*, 1854)

This construction began to recede in the nineteenth century, but it did not die out, and examples are not rare in the twentieth century:

...his canoe, which was towing behind the long-boat... (Joseph Conrad, *Lord Jim*, 1900)

Bramante's palace was still building until 1565. (C. N. Parkinson, 1957)

Today, however, this traditional construction seems strange or impossible, and we have to say instead *is being prepared*, *was being towed*, *was still being built*, and so on. The construction *My house is painting* is probably impossible for everyone, though a few speakers will still accept it with a handful of verbs. For example, in place of *My book is being reprinted*, some people are happy with *My book is reprinting*. Indeed, the linguist David Denison, from whose writings almost all of my examples are taken, found the following in the British newspaper *The Guardian*, 22 March 1983: *Inside the... room more than a dozen television cameras were setting up on an elevated stand*. I would consider this construction to be impossible, and I require *were being set up*, but you may take a different view.

In spite of the presence of a few lingering traces of the old construction, it is now effectively dead, while the new construction is now for most of us the only possibility. This is just one example of recent change in English.

By the way, this change did not pass without comment. Until well into the nineteenth century, many educated and careful users of English regarded *My house is painting* as the only possibility in standard English. When a few innovating speakers began writing things like *My house is being painted*, these linguistic conservatives could not contain their fury. Veins bulging purple from their foreheads, they attacked the new form as 'clumsy', 'illogical', 'confusing' and 'monstrous'. But their efforts were in vain: all the people who hated the new form grew old and died, until eventually the only speakers left alive were those who had grown up with the new form and considered it normal.

For some centuries now, English has had a construction called the *perfect*. Very often, the perfect is constructed by placing the auxiliary *have* in front of the verb. Examples: *I have finished dinner*; *Susie has written a book*. However, with intransitive verbs (those taking no object), earlier English frequently used, not *have*, but *be*. The common forms were therefore as follows: *Susie is arrived*; *My notes are disappeared*.

For example, Shakespeare's play *Much Ado About Nothing*, written about 1599, has this: *...yet Benedicke was such another, and now is he become a man*. This form has for several centuries been gradually receding in favour of the *have* perfect, but the process was slow. Even as late as 1849, we find Charlotte Brontë writing this in her novel *Shirley*: *As it cleared away he looked again for the soldiers, but they were vanished*.

Forms like *she is arrived* and *they are vanished* are effectively dead for most English speakers today, at least in ordinary speech (although this may be hidden by pronunciation) and writing; the sole exceptions being Shetland dialect and a few other remote varieties. But you will doubtless recognise such usages in archaic English, perhaps most obviously in religious texts, where the archaic construction is sometimes maintained for solemn effect, as in *He is risen*. A few literary writers may occasionally write something like *they were vanished* for effect, though such archaising styles seem to enjoy little popularity among today's streetwise novelists.

But there is one special case. Even though nobody says *She is come* any more, everyone is happy to say *She is gone*. This fossilised form is confined to the single verb *go*, and is now functionally distinct from the regular perfect with *have*: *She is gone* does not mean quite the same as *She has gone*. And note that the form with *is* cannot be extended: we can say *She has gone home*, but not *She is gone home*. Today, *She is gone* is just another way of saying *She's not here*, and that's it. Once again, English grammar has changed.

Changes in grammar, like all linguistic changes, are happening all the time. At every moment, including this moment, every language is in the middle of a number of grammatical changes. Take a look at a few examples, and decide what you think of each:

(1) *I recommend you to take the job.*
(2) *He demanded that the agitators were arrested.*
(3) *This is just between you and I.*
(4) *Due to the rain, we had to cancel the picnic.*
(5) *This paper was written by Susie and myself.*
(6) *Please come between eight a.m. to six p.m.*
(7) *If he'd've played, we would have won.*
(8) *He makes tedious jokes about mother-in-laws.*
(9) *Having said that, there is no feasible alternative.*

Every one of these examples was formerly impossible for all speakers, but every one of them is now perfectly normal for many speakers today – though not for all speakers. Every one represents a grammatical form or construction which was formerly absent from the language but which is now frequent and prominent in many or all parts of the English-speaking world. In each case, we are probably looking at a grammatical change in progress, and it may be only a matter of time before each is accepted by practically everyone as normal English grammar.

Of course, if your tastes are conservative, you may consider some of my examples to be unspeakably slovenly and ignorant. I don't much care for most of them myself. But remember what happened to all those conservatives who railed against *My house is being painted.*

On the other hand, we should realise that not all of these changes are recent ones. The constructions illustrated in examples (3) and (7) above have been recorded in writing for centuries, and they have apparently been frequent in speech for at least as long. So far, however, they have not been accepted as part of Standard English – that is, they are not considered to belong to that set of forms, usages and constructions which all educated people agree are appropriate in the most careful styles of speech and writing.

I will close this section by mentioning one of the most dramatic changes in English grammar of recent years. The construction is so new that it doesn't yet have an accepted name, but I'll call it the *I'm like* construction. This novel construction has recently appeared in the speech of young people; it seems to have originated in the USA, but it can now be heard in almost every English-speaking country. It is a way of relating narratives, and it is rather different from more traditional ways of doing this. An example: *Well, I'm standing there, like 'What's going on?', and he's like 'Can I put my arm around you?', and I'm like 'Yuck! What a pig!'*

I was raised in the USA, and I don't think I ever heard this construction used before I reached the age of twenty-five or so. Today, I can't get through a day without hearing it. It seems likely that this innovation will outlive us all, and become a regular part of the grammar of spoken English, at least.

The changing sounds of the language

The pronunciation of English has been changing steadily and ceaselessly for as long as the language has existed. Quite apart from the difficulties of vocabulary and grammar, the pronunciation of English in the past would be wholly unintelligible to us, if we could hear it. We could no more understand the pronunciation of King Alfred the Great (died 899) than we can understand modern Norwegian, and the pronunciation of the poet Geoffrey Chaucer (died 1400) would not be a lot easier. William Shakespeare (died 1616) is quite a bit closer to us in time: we have little trouble reading what he wrote, but nevertheless many specialists believe we would not be able to understand his speech, if we could hear it: his pronunciation was just too different from modern ones.

After English was carried across the Atlantic to North America in the seventeenth century, pronunciation, like every other aspect of the language, continued to change on both sides of the water. By the early nineteenth century, both Americans and Britons were commenting on the prominent 'accent' used by the people on the other side of the Atlantic. When Hollywood movies with sound were first shown in Britain in the 1930s, British audiences found them hard to understand: most Britons had never heard American accents, and they were bewildered by their first exposure to American speech. Americans, of course, do not find British accents any easier at first encounter, not even BBC accents.

Our archaic spelling system gives us a few clues about earlier pronunciation. Take the word *knight*. Why does it have such an eccentric spelling? Because it was formerly pronounced just as this spelling suggests: it began with a /k/ sound, followed by an /n/, followed by the vowel of *sit*, followed by a breathy consonant like the one spelled <ch> in the Scottish word *loch*, followed by a /t/. The spelling therefore made perfect sense – once. But, since then, two of the consonants have disappeared completely, while the vowel has changed its nature greatly.

Let's look at just a few of the recent changes in English pronunciation, starting with /r/-dropping.

Until relatively recently, all English speakers pronounced a consonant /r/ in every position in which our spelling has the letter <r>. So, not only was /r/ present in *red* and *cream*, it was also present in *far*, *arm*, *dark* and *bird*. But then, in the seventeenth or early eighteenth century, some people in the southeast of England began to 'drop' their /r/s whenever those /r/s were not followed by a vowel. As a result, in this style of speech, /r/ was retained in *red* and *cream*, but it disappeared from the other four words. In such /r/-dropping speech – which is known technically as *non-rhotic* speech – *farther* sounds just like *father*, and *star* rhymes perfectly with *Shah*. In many non-rhotic varieties (though not in all), *court* is further pronounced just like *caught*.

This new style of pronunciation arose among working-class speakers in the metropolitan London area, and for a long time it was condemned as substandard and ignorant: educated speakers were careful to retain their /r/s in all positions, and to refrain from the vulgar habit of dropping them. Writers on language inveighed against this sloppy habit of dropping one's /r/s. John Keats (1795–1821), who rhymed non-rhotically, was accused of being a 'Cockney' by his contemporaries.

In spite of such condemnation, this /r/-dropping continued to spread – not only horizontally, into new territory, but also vertically, up the social scale, possibly because it was considered fashionable or perhaps even a little daring. With increasing frequency, the dropping of /r/ could be heard in the speech of posh people who prided themselves on their elegant speech. Finally, the condemnation ceased, and /r/-dropping came to be fully accepted as a feature of elegant speech in England. In fact, for several generations now, it has been essential to drop your /r/s in England if you want to sound elegant. If you pronounce all your /r/s, as many people still do, especially in the southwest of England, then you will sound quaint and rustic, and perhaps even comical.

This newly fashionable dropping of /r/s has spread into the English of Wales and of the Southern Hemisphere countries. It has failed to spread into Scotland or Ireland, both of which retain the historical /r/s in all positions. To some extent, /r/-dropping managed to spread to the east coast of the United States, but most Americans and Canadians continue to pronounce their /r/s, and /r/-dropping is now losing ground on the east coast, where it is beginning to be perceived as vulgar.

Vowels change even faster than consonants. In fact, English vowels have been so unstable during the last few centuries that I might pick out any of a very large number of stories to tell. Here's one.

By about 1700, the assorted dramatic developments that had been affecting the English vowel system for some 300 years had brought about a peculiar and uncomfortable state of affairs. There were two vowels in the language which were linguistically different but which were phonetically almost identical. The first vowel appeared in such words as *cot* and *don*, while the second appeared in *caught* and *dawn*. The phonetic difference between the two vowels was minute – and a minute difference between two vowels that are supposed to be distinguishing pairs of words like *cot* and *caught* is not comfortable. We might therefore suppose that something would happen to relieve the discomfort.

And something did happen. Today there is perhaps no variety of English anywhere in the world in which the vowels of *cot* and *caught* are still distinguished only by the tiny difference that existed 300 years ago. Inevitably, however, different regional varieties of English found their own solutions to the problem, and those solutions were often quite different.

In much of England, the solution adopted for keeping the vowels of *cot* and *caught* apart was to move the vowel of *caught*. This vowel was moved upwards in the mouth, away from the vowel of *cot*, so that *caught* began to sound quite different from *cot*. So far, excellent, but now we have another problem: the vowel of *caught* begins to sound quite a bit like the vowel of *coat*, especially as it is still pronounced in Scotland. Confusing another pair of vowels is not progress, and so further steps are necessary. In England, the obvious solution was adopted: the vowel of *coat* was *also* moved, this time so as to take it away from its former phonetic value, now being encroached on by the incoming vowel of *caught*.

So far, then, we have *caught* moving away from *cot* and towards *coat*; and we likewise have *coat* moving away in turn, to get out of the way. But this further movement has a further consequence, as you've probably surmised: the vowel of *coat*, in moving, has to move towards some other existing vowel. That vowel is the vowel of *Kate*, and in fact *coat* has been moving towards *Kate* in England, though it has so far moved only part way towards the latter.

So, the Londoners have solved the problem of the tiny distance between the *cot* vowel and the *caught* vowel, and they have done it while keeping all their vowels distinct. The price they have paid is that they have been forced to change the pronunciations of two vowels, the vowel of *caught* and the vowel of *coat*, and that they have wound up with the vowels of *coat* and *Kate* much closer together than they used to be.

These changes are very noticeable to the ear of an English speaker who has not participated in them. Take an American speaker, since none of this has happened in American English. When an American listens to an Englishman, he hears some surprising vowels. The Englishman's *cot*, which has not changed much, sounds to the American rather like his own *caught*, for reasons to be explained shortly. The Londoner's *caught*, of course, sounds to the American like his own *coat*, and the Londoner's *coat* sounds to the American uncomfortably like *Kate*.

In most varieties of American English, the solution adopted to the original problem was entirely different. The vowel of *caught* did not move at all, and therefore there was no need to move the vowel of *coat*, either, and so this did not approach the vowel of *Kate*. The American solution was to move the *other* of the original two problem vowels: the vowel of *cot*. In American pronunciation, the *cot* vowel was moved away from the *caught* vowel and actually merged with the vowel of *cart*. In other words, Americans abandoned the historical difference between the vowel of *cot* and the vowel of *cart*, a difference which is still retained today in England.

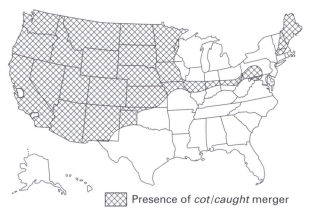

Presence of *cot*/*caught* merger

Figure 1.1 The *cot*/*caught* merger

But *cot* did not become identical to *cart* for Americans, because Americans still pronounce their /r/s, and so *cart* differs from *cot* in containing an /r/. Nevertheless, an American's pronunciation of *cot* sounds strikingly like an Englishman's pronunciation of *cart*.

So, speakers in England solved the problem by moving the vowel of *caught*, while Americans solved it by moving the vowel of *cot*, in both cases with further consequences. But there was a third resolution to the original problem, which was adopted in both Scotland and Canada. That solution was the simplest one possible: the Scots and the Canadians simply abandoned the effort of trying to keep the two vowels distinct, and they merged the two vowels into one. As a result, a Scot or a Canadian pronounces *cot* and *caught* identically, and likewise *don* and *dawn*, and all other such pairs. For native speakers of these varieties no particular problems have been encountered by this merger, interestingly.

All other areas of the English-speaking world have adopted one of these three solutions, and so you might think that the problem was solved and gone. But there is a complication in the United States. Several generations ago, Americans solved the problem of keeping the two similar vowels apart by moving the *cot* vowel to a new position. That, you might think, should have been that. But not so. Just in the last few years, there has been a new development with these vowels in the USA: many speakers have suddenly opted for the Canadian solution, and lost the difference between *cot* and *caught* altogether. This new type of pronunciation – new in America, that is – has already taken over the entire western half of the USA, apart from metropolitan San Francisco and Los Angeles, where the distinction is retained, and now the new style is spreading rapidly across the Midwest into Pennsylvania. The map in Figure 1.1 shows the spread of the new pronunciation a few years ago; by now it has doubtless extended into further territory.

Another recent change in vowels is a rather elaborate set of changes which are now happening in northern American cities like Chicago, Detroit, Cleveland and Buffalo. This set of changes has been dubbed the *Northern Cities Shift*, and it is an example of a *chain shift*, in which the changing sounds follow one another. Six vowels are involved. The vowel of *cat* is shifting towards the vowel of *kit*. Likewise, *cot* is shifting towards *cat*; *caught* is shifting towards *cot*; *bud* is shifting towards *bawd*; *bed* is shifting towards *bud*; and *bid* is shifting towards *bed*.

As a result of all this vowel-shifting, a speaker who has undergone the shift can be quite hard to understand for another American speaker who has not undergone it, and mishearings are frequent. When a non-shifter listens to a shifter, *Ann* sounds like *Ian*; *socks* sounds like *sax*; *chalk* sounds like *chock*; *bus* sounds like *boss*; *steady* sounds like *study*; and *hid* sounds like *head*. Naturally, it can be quite a challenge for the listener to decipher something like this: *Ian bot some sacks at the Mahl, but she luft 'em an the boss.*

Of course, it is not only American English which is busily rearranging its vowels at the moment. A number of vowel changes are also going on in British English. Here is just one example.

In England, the most prestigious kind of accent has for more than a century been *Received Pronunciation*, or RP. RP is a minority accent, but it is the accent traditionally used by the royal family, by Oxbridge professors, by senior army officers and churchmen, and by barristers and High Court judges. RP is currently undergoing several vowel shifts, and one of these poses potential problems: the vowel of *cat* and the vowel of *cut*, which are historically very different, and still are in most accents, are moving very close together – so close together that they can be almost indistinguishable in an RP accent.

Pronunciation change, like all language change, happens in even the most elegant and prestigious varieties of a language. No language is immune to change, and no variety is immune.

Changes in pronunciation can happen with considerable speed. Consider /hw/. Historically, English had a number of words beginning with the sequence of consonants /hw/, curiously spelled <wh> since the Middle Ages. This sequence was pronounced very differently from plain /w/, and so *whine* sounded different from *wine*, *whales* from *Wales*, *which* from *witch*, *where* from *wear*, *wheel* from *weal*, and so on.

But then the sound /h/ began to be lost from /hw/, which was therefore reduced to plain /w/. As a result, *whine* began to sound just like *wine*, and so on, for all the other pairs. This change happened first in England. By the end of the nineteenth century, there were very few people in England who were still making a difference in pronunciation between *whales* and *Wales*. Nevertheless, there continued to be a kind of dim folk-memory that making the difference was elegant, and teachers of elocution in England continued to try to teach their charges to make the difference until well into the twentieth century – even though there were perhaps no speakers left alive in England who had made the distinction in childhood.

This new style of pronunciation was exported to the Commonwealth, and particularly to the Southern Hemisphere countries. According to the most recent work I have seen, /hw/ is now completely gone in Australia and in South Africa, and it is found among no more than a handful of speakers on the South Island of New Zealand.

In great contrast, the sequence /hw/ is still rock-solid in Scotland and in Ireland, and all Scottish and Irish speakers distinguish pairs like *whine* and *wine* clearly and consistently. Or at least all adults do. A couple of years ago, a linguist reported on an electronic list that he had heard several Scottish children who appeared to lack /hw/ altogether, even though they otherwise had conspicuously Scottish accents. Only time will tell whether this observation was an oddity or the thin end of the wedge. Belfast, in northeastern Ireland, is unique on that island in having /w/ in <wh> words. This is a working-class rather than English-initiated change: teachers, often from the counties around the city where the distinction continues to be made, vainly attempt to reinstate the split.

In North America, the situation is more complicated. When I was growing up in a rural part of the USA, in the 1950s, practically everybody retained /hw/. I learned it in childhood; I grew up with it; and I still have it today. But no sooner had I acquired it for life when it began to disappear as something children learned. All of my younger siblings lack /hw/ entirely, and they pronounce *whine* just like *wine* – which I cannot do. My mother noticed this change, and she described it as 'sloppy'. But, sloppy or not, the loss of the /h/ in /hw/ has spread across the United States with astounding speed, and today there is practically no one in that country under the age of fifty or so who still retains the difference between *whine* and *wine*.

I still have the difference, but having it marks me out as almost unspeakably old-fashioned. Recently my university department appointed another American, a couple of decades younger than I am. She tells me that she finds the use of /hw/ 'pretentious'. In the space of my own lifetime, I have gone from being a perfectly normal speaker, indistinguishable from everybody else, to being a pretentious old fossil.

As I write these words, I am only in my fifties, but already slightly younger people are finding my speech strange. No doubt, in twenty years time, people who speak like me will sound bizarre to young people. I'm not doing anything much to my speech, but the language is changing relentlessly away from the English I grew up with. And that is why old people talk funny.

This looks like a logical place to end the chapter, but I can't resist adding a section on one more recent change in English, one which is so striking and dramatic that everybody has noticed it, and one that has seemingly come out of nowhere to take over the world in the space of a few years.

I suppose you speak uptalk?

Traditionally in English, as in most languages, the pitch of our voice falls at the end of a statement but rises at the end of a question. For example, if I say *You're going out tonight*, with falling intonation, this is a statement. However, if I say *You're going out tonight?*, with rising intonation, this is a question, even though I haven't bothered with any of the formal paraphernalia of questions, as in *Are you going out tonight?*

That's the way things have been practically for ever. But, in the last few years, we have suddenly come face to face with a stunning new pattern: the use of rising intonation in statements. In this new style, an utterance like *I bought a new skirt?*, with strongly rising intonation, is a simple statement, and not a question, even though it sounds like a question.

This rising intonation in statements has been dubbed by linguists *high-rise terminals*, or *HRT*. But, since this initialism is unfortunate for people acquainted with hormone replacement therapy, I will call it by its zippy informal name: *uptalk*.

Uptalk is especially prominent in the USA, Australia and New Zealand, but it is now far from rare elsewhere, and it seems to be spreading rapidly. It has only attracted attention from journalists and the general public in the last few years, though academic linguists were already writing about it in the 1980s, and there is one report of it from as early as 1965, though that report describes it as an aberration produced by nervous speakers in interviews.

The oldest uptalking speakers so far discovered were born in the mid to late 1950s, and so uptalk is often thought to have come into existence shortly after this time – perhaps in the 1960s. But few uptalkers are this old. Most are much younger, and the great majority of them are teenagers.

Nobody knows where uptalk began. Some people think it started in California, where it is certainly extremely prominent. Others think it began in Australia, where it is just as conspicuous. One person has even suggested Ireland as the source. But, wherever it started, it has spread like the proverbial wildfire. Uptalk is very noticeable in American TV shows like *Friends* and in Australian soap operas like *Home and Away*, and quite a few people think these popular programmes have been helping to spread uptalk – though not everyone is convinced that features of speech can be so easily acquired from television shows.

But acquired easily it often is. The British journalist Matt Seaton, writing in *The Guardian* (21 September 2001), described what happened when he took his children on holiday to the USA. Both had been raised in London, and both spoke only the vernacular London form called 'Estuary English', with no trace of uptalk. After only several days at an American summer camp, his daughter was responding to 'So what did you do today?' as follows. 'Well, we went canoeing on the lake? Which was, like, really really fun? And then we had storytelling in the barn? And we all had to tell a story about, like, where we're from or our family or something?'

In short, his daughter had acquired and mastered uptalk almost instantly, along with several other features of American speech. In great contrast, Seaton's son never acquired uptalk at all. This is consistent with the observation, often made, that uptalk is far more prevalent among females than among males – though there are certainly some males who have it.

The linguist Deborah Tannen has suggested that uptalk is largely a teenage phenomenon, a feature adopted by teenagers as a badge of identity but then abandoned after adolescence is over. Perhaps, but it is clear that not all speakers abandon uptalk upon reaching maturity. I recently heard a lecture by a North American academic in her forties who had the fiercest case of uptalk I have ever heard. She didn't just raise her voice at the end of a sentence: she raised it at the end of each *phrase*. As a result, her lecture sounded rather like this. 'I've been making a study? of the use of connective words? like *however* and *though*? in informal conversations?' And so on. It took me quite a while to adjust my ears to this, so that I could take in the content of her talk.

It is too early to tell what the fate of uptalk will be. Perhaps it is a passing fad which will die out. Perhaps it will hang around in the language as a feature of adolescent speech, or as an idiosyncrasy of certain people. Or perhaps it will become the norm in English, and the English teachers of the future will have to teach it to foreign learners who want to sound as much as possible like native speakers. Already, Matt Seaton tells us, the British actor Kate Lock, who has a sideline in recording English language-teaching tapes, is finding herself asked to produce tapes with uptalk built in.

The conclusion for this chapter is a simple one: **languages are always changing**. A dead language – a language which has died out and is no longer used – does not change any more. But a living language – a language which is still being learned by children – is always changing. In this book we will discuss many of these processes in greater depth, developing our understanding of what factors cause and channel each change.

2   Why are languages always changing?

Some myths

We saw in the last chapter that languages are always changing. A rather more complex question is: 'why?' People have been speculating about this for about as long as they have been aware of language change. Some ideas are unlikely, perhaps even absurd, however. Sadly these regularly turn up in popular discussions of language change.

One idea is that languages change because their speakers have particular physical characteristics: short tongues, or thick lips, or gappy teeth, or something else in this vein. This is of course nonsense: the size of your tongue has no more to do with the way you speak than has the size of your feet. But that doesn't stop people making this kind of argument.

Several decades ago, an enthusiastic scholar named L. F. Brosnahan became obsessed with dental fricatives: the hissing and buzzing noises produced by putting the tongue onto or between the teeth. There are two dental fricatives in English, both spelled <th> the one in *thin*, for which the phonetic symbol is [θ], and the one in *this*, for which the symbol is [ð]. In contemporary Europe, dental fricatives occur in only a few languages, all of them curiously spread out around the watery margins of the continent: Icelandic, English, Welsh, Castilian Spanish, Albanian and Greek. In addition, these sounds were formerly present also in the ancestors of German, Dutch, Norwegian, Swedish and Danish, in Irish and Scottish Gaelic, among others.

Brosnahan observed that the edges of Europe are, on the whole, the areas in which type O blood is most frequent. So, he put forward his big idea. He suggested that type O blood makes it easy to pronounce dental fricatives, while types A and B blood make dental fricatives very hard to pronounce. In his hypothesis, then, ancient Europe was full of people with type O blood, speaking languages rich in dental fricatives. Over time, however, waves of immigrants poured into Europe from Asia. These immigrants had blood of types A and B, and so, as their blood types began to swamp the earlier type O, dental fricatives began to disappear from the languages of Europe, until today these sounds survive only in a few languages along the edges, where the percentage of the earlier type O blood is still high enough to permit the existence of dental fricatives.

This correlation may look impressive at first. But there is a problem. The living language which has beyond question been spoken in western Europe for longer than any other is Basque. And the Basques, it was discovered long ago, have the highest percentage of type O blood in Europe and perhaps the highest in the world. Accordingly, we should expect the Basque language to be particularly full of dental fricatives.

But Basque has no dental fricatives at all, and the evidence suggests that it has had no dental fricatives for thousands of years. Moreover, when native speakers of Basque have in the past learned to speak the neighbouring language Castilian Spanish, they have found themselves unable to pronounce the dental fricatives of that language, representing them with the /s/ and /z/ sounds English speakers associate with the accent of a French speaker who says *I sink zat ...* when trying to produce *I think that ...*

This appears to be an insuperable problem for Brosnahan's exciting hypothesis. But he didn't see it that way. In his book, he dealt with it in surprising fashion, appealing to the logical technique that mathematicians call 'proof by intimidation': he simply declared firmly that the Basque language *did* have dental fricatives after all, and carried on presenting his case, a case which was fatally flawed. This view is only intensified by our awareness that the English of the United States of America – spoken by people of almost every ethnic origin imaginable – is as likely to have dental fricatives as the varieties of English still spoken on the European periphery. Like shoe size, blood type has no effect on anyone's language, and pursuing the linguistic consequences of blood types or of nose shapes is a waste of time at best. At worst, it can easily become offensive and even dangerous.

Another myth holds that certain kinds of terrain or weather favour certain kinds of structural features in languages, and so languages tend to change in order to conform better to their location.

A prominent example of this kind of thinking concerns the nasal vowels of French. Unlike most western European languages, French has a set of distinctively nasalised vowels: four in conservative, three in less conservative accents. The traditional four nasal vowels are represented in *un bon vin blanc*, 'a good white wine'. French is a direct descendant of Latin, which had no nasal vowels, and most of the closest relatives of French today lack nasal vowels. So why does French have them?

Several popular books put forward the following suggestion: Standard French developed in the region of Paris, and Paris is famously damp and foggy. Because of the damp, foggy climate, French speakers suffer constantly from head colds; head colds make the victims' speech more nasal; and so the damp French climate caused the nasal vowels to appear in French.

Well, I really don't know if it's true that Paris is damper or foggier than anywhere else. Certainly the English city of Brighton, where I live, seems to have enough damp, foggy weather to compete for any championship that may be going, and yet the English of Brighton contains no nasal vowels. However, the argument is even more worrying than this.

To start with, it is simply not true that a head cold makes your voice more nasal. This widely held but badly confused view is in fact the very opposite of the truth: a head cold makes your speech *less* nasal than it normally is. When you have a head cold, you have difficulty in pronouncing nasal sounds like [m] and [n], and a word like *men* comes out sounding quite a bit like *bed*. This 'explanation' of the French nasal vowels, therefore, actually predicts that French should acquire no nasal vowels at all, and if anything that French should lose its nasal consonants – which of course it has not done.

But whatever may be the truth about the Parisian climate, it is a fact that another modern descendant of Latin has also acquired nasal vowels. This is Portuguese, spoken in warm, dry Portugal, where there is little hope of appealing to fog or dampness.

All such appeals to geography are likewise doomed. There is absolutely nothing that is generally true of the languages spoken in mountains, or on islands, or in the tropics, or in dry areas, or in any kind of terrain or climate you can think of. Pick a linguistic feature, and you will find that it occurs in languages in every kind of terrain. For example, astounding clusters (sequences) of consonants are found in Georgian, spoken in the rugged mountains of the Caucasus, but also in several languages spoken in the coastal plain of British Columbia. Pick a kind of terrain, and you will find that the languages spoken in that terrain have nothing special in common. For example, some languages spoken in deserts have grammatical gender, while others do not.

A third myth is *stadialism*. According to stadialism, each human culture must move step by step through a rigid series of stages, and the language of each culture at each moment must reflect the stage of culture which it has so far reached. This idea was popular in nineteenth-century Europe, where it was commonly assumed that every culture, and every language, was striving for perfection – a perfection which had so far been achieved, of course, only by European cultures and languages. In this view, anybody who was different from Europeans was *ipso facto* inferior to Europeans, and still had a long way to go. Since stadialism is transparently no more than a version of racism, I will not pursue it further here, except to warn you against taking stadial ideas seriously if you happen to come across them. Stadialism is grossly false, and there is no observable tendency for languages to change in one direction rather than in another.

You may doubt this. Perhaps you are one of those people who believe that languages which undergo change must become 'simpler' as a result. Perhaps you are aware that Ancient Greek, Classical Latin and Old English all had batteries of complicated grammatical endings, while their modern descendants have fewer and simpler endings. This observation *is* broadly true for these particular languages, but it is not generally true that language change implies simplification – far from it.

To start with, grammatical endings are only one aspect of linguistic structure. English and French may have fewer endings than their ancestors, but both of them have pronunciations which are much more complicated and difficult than what was present in the ancestors. And the syntax of Modern English exhibits complex constructions which had no parallel in the English of a thousand years ago. Just ponder an example like this one: *The amphora, around the inside of the rim of which mysterious markings have recently been found to have been inscribed with some kind of metal tool, will be taken apart in order to be examined with suitable instruments.* There is nothing in *Beowulf* of this level of syntactic complexity, although the building blocks of Old English were more complex.

In fact, it is not even true that languages always lose grammatical endings, or simplify their endings. Finnish and Hungarian, for example, are descended from a common ancestor spoken several thousand years ago. Both of these languages have acquired a very large number of grammatical endings which did not exist in their ancestor, and these endings have moreover acquired quite a variety of complications in their forms. A reference grammar of Hungarian is obliged to devote large amounts of space to listing the profusion of grammatical endings and the several forms that each ending can assume, and to writing rules for the use of all these things – practically all of which have appeared in Hungarian since its ancestor separated from the ancestor of Finnish several millennia ago. In fact, languages acquire new endings just as often as they lose old ones, and they acquire complications in their endings just as often as they simplify.

If this were not so, then we would have to believe that the first languages ever created by our earliest human ancestors, perhaps 200,000 years ago, must have been staggeringly complex monstrosities, far more Byzantine in their structures than anything we can hear on the planet today, and that 2,000 centuries of human existence have been devoted to simplifying these first grotesque attempts at language. This is preposterous. As we will see in Chapter 8, languages which are newly created by people are – just as you would expect – simple and highly regular, with a distinct lack of unnecessary complications.

All these proposals are bad ideas. But is it possible to develop satisfactory explanations for language change?

Changes in the world

As we saw in Chapter 1, all languages are constantly changing because of changes in technology. We didn't, for instance, need a word for 'television' until one was invented. Given the speed of technological development in the last two centuries, it is unsurprising that change of this type has been particularly prevalent. Given human ingenuity, however, it is probable that this has always been the case – back to the wheel and beyond.

But the world is not changed only by engineers. Not so many years ago, hardly any English speakers knew the words *cappuccino* and *latte*, but today many of us can't imagine getting through the day without these words. Most of us make room in our lives (and stomachs) for *ciabatta*, and *vindaloo*, and *tiramisu*, and *crème caramel*, and *tzatziki*, and *sushi*, and *döner kebab*, and *osso bucco*, and *sangría*, and *dim sum*, and countless other items of food and drink which I assure you my parents never heard of.

In fact, in order to accommodate changes in society, English speakers are happy to accept useful words from wherever they can find them. Among our recent borrowings are *ombudsman* from Swedish, *salsa* from Cuban Spanish, *intifada* from Palestinian Arabic, *sauna* from Finnish, and *karaoke* from Japanese, joining such earlier ones as *savoir-faire* from French, *kindergarten* from German, *intermezzo* from Italian, *kiosk* from Turkish, and *hurricane* from the Taino language of Haiti.

So: culture changes; the way we order our lives changes. And language has to change with them. But this cannot be the *sole* explanation for change.

Laziness?

It is widely suspected by the general public that a great deal of language change comes about because of sheer laziness, or, if you prefer, that all-too-familiar human habit of sloppiness. Well, it is true that we humans are rather impatient creatures, and we often prefer briefer expressions to longer ones. We saw in the last chapter that *compact disc* has been shortened to *CD*, for instance. In similar ways, *telephone* has been shortened to *phone*, *gymnasium* to *gym*, *influenza* to *flu*, *British Broadcasting Corporation* to *BBC*, *situation comedy* to *sitcom*, *human beings* to *humans*, and so on. Much of this is easy to understand. Who in their right mind would prefer to work through the longer forms all the time? Does anybody really want to say *Federal Bureau of Investigation* more than about twice in a lifetime, when *FBI* is available? And how many people can remember that the full name of the insecticide *DDT* is the mouth-filling *dichlorodiphenyltrichloroethane*?

Words and phrases which we use constantly are particularly likely to be shortened in one way or another. The former *God be with you* has been irreversibly reduced to *good-bye*, and the equivalent French *au revoir* is often abbreviated to *'voir*. The Germans and the Italians often give up on their own *auf Wiedersehen* and *arrividerci*, and introduce the new, shorter *tschüss* and *ciao* instead. English speakers shorten the original *goodbye* to *bye!* in essentially the same process.

Words which acquire a grammatical function are particularly likely to be reduced. Consider English *will*. Formerly, this was an ordinary verb meaning 'want', and an utterance like *I will go to Paris* meant literally 'I want to go to Paris'. But in the course of the Middle Ages the word gradually lost its sense of 'want', and it became merely a grammatical device for marking future time in certain types of contexts – and the result has been that *will* is now commonly reduced to *'ll*, as in *I'll go to Paris*. Very many of the grammatical endings in English and in other languages were once independent words, but their reduction to grammatical functions caused them also to be reduced in bulk to mere endings. A splendid example from English is the adverbial ending *-ly*, as in *slowly* and *happily*, which was originally the word *like*. Early English speakers said, literally, *She did it slow-like*, but we have long since reduced this to *She did it slowly*.

So, we can point to our natural impatience as a reason for the shortening of longer words and expressions which become everyday items or grammatical devices. But this explanation can account for only a small number of shortenings, and not for anything more. There are also long-term examples of survivals, such as the use of the plural *men* for *man*, which argue against this viewpoint. Are there any other simple explanations for change?

Emphasis and clarity

An important point about language change is that very often the occurrence of one change makes another change more likely. This can happen for several reasons.

More often than not, changes in pronunciation make words shorter than they used to be. Old English *hlaford* and *hlæfdige* have developed into modern *lord* and *lady*, and Old English *heafod* has become *head*. Rather more dramatically, Latin *Augustus* 'August' has been reduced in French to something which is spelled *août* but which in fact is pronounced just /u/ – one vowel, and nothing else. And Latin *aqua* 'water' has likewise turned into a French word written *eau* but pronounced /o/ – again with a solitary vowel, and no consonant sound to be heard.

It would appear that we are in some danger of allowing our words to be reduced to nothing. If every word in the language is eventually reduced in pronunciation to something like /u/ or /o/ then we will no longer be able to understand one another's speech – and choosing to write these tiny words with silent letters will not help. What can be done?

One obvious solution is to reinforce our words when they become unappealingly short. Let's look at an example, also from French.

In early Latin, 'today' was expressed by the phrase **hoc die*, literally 'on this day', where the asterisk shows that this form is not recorded but has been reconstructed by linguists. By the time of Classical Latin, this phrase had coalesced into a single word, *hodie*, with the loss of one consonant in the process.

By the time of the first Roman emperor, no Latin speaker was pronouncing aitches any more. *Hodie* was now being pronounced *odie*, even though educated people kept on writing the aitches because of the prestige of earlier writers.

In Paris, there were further changes in pronunciation, and in particular more sounds were lost. In *hodie*, the sound /d/ disappeared, and after a while speakers of the Parisian variety of Latin, which was beginning to be called 'French', were writing their word for 'today' as *hui*, though that <h> was only an act of obeisance to the 'mother' language, and what people were really saying could have been written *ui*.

It appears that speakers of French were getting a little uncomfortable uttering such a small noise to say 'today'. So, they responded by creating a more substantial way of expressing that concept. What they came up with was the orotund phrase *au jour d'hui*, which is literally 'on the day of today'. This certainly solved the problem, and people began using this heavy expression more and more often, until finally nobody was saying just plain *hui* any more at all. Today the only possible way of saying 'today' in French is *aujourd'hui*, which is now written as a single word, and the former *hui* is dead and buried. Almost inevitably, this word can be reduced to something like *dwee* in colloquial speech.

Very likely you know somebody who is constitutionally incapable of uttering the little English word *now* and who replaces it on every occasion with the mouth-filling sequence *at this moment in time*. So far, this remains a pompous piece of bureaucrat-speak, inveighed against by usage handbooks everywhere, but there is no guarantee that it will not one day displace its shorter equivalent altogether, much as has happened in French.

Sometimes this quest for clarity has been resolved in more dramatic fashion. Old English had the two verbs *lætan* 'permit, allow' and *lettan* 'hinder, obstruct'. After some routine changes in the pronunciation of the language, both these verbs wound up being pronounced identically, as *let*. This, of course, was problematical: permitting something is practically the opposite of obstructing it, and any speaker who used one of these verbs was in grave danger of being badly misunderstood. From the fifteenth century on, therefore, speakers took steps: they simply stopped using the verb *let* meaning 'obstruct', and they used only *let* meaning 'permit'. The verb meaning 'obstruct' disappeared from the language altogether, thus solving the problem. Today this ancient verb survives only in the form of its related noun *let*, in the legal phrase *without let or hindrance*, the now archaic *French Letter* for 'condom' and as a technical term for a replayed point resulting from an obstruction in the games of tennis and squash.

This desire to avoid ambiguity can bring about all sorts of intriguing changes. Among the pronouns in Old English were *he* 'he', *heo* 'she' and *hi* 'they'. With the passage of time, the typical English weakening of final syllables made these three pronouns uncomfortably similar in pronunciation. Speakers of English a little less than a thousand years ago took steps to resolve this.

On the one hand, the form *heo* was replaced by a different form, the one that has come down to us as *she*. The origin of this innovation is obscure, but is likely to have developed via the pronunciation of *hie*, the 'accusative' form of the word, by Norse speakers in the north of England during the Viking period. While Old English had 'falling' diphthongs, with the stress on the first element (/i/ on this occasion), Old Norse had 'rising' ones, with stress on the second (/e/ on this occasion). The original /hi/ therefore became /hj/, as found in words like *huge* and *Hugh*. You may have noticed that most people do not pronounce the /h/ and the /j/ independently of each other; instead, a sound represented as [ç] by phoneticists, a buzzing and hissing noise pronounced with your tongue near your hard palate, is produced. There are a number of English speakers today – most notably from western Scotland – who find this sound almost impossible to pronounce at the start of words. Instead, they use /ʃ/, a similar sound found in words like *sheep*. In these dialects, people called *Hugh* are regularly called *Shughie* or *Shug*, for instance. There is evidence that a similar change took place in northern England about a thousand years ago. Over time, the *she* form spread into central and southern England. Remnants of the original form can be found, however, in the traditional dialects of the midlands and south of England, where 'she' is still represented by forms such as *oo* and *a*.

On the other hand, the native word *hi* was almost entirely lost in favour of a new form *they* – with its inflected forms *them* and *their* – which is not native English at all but taken from the Old Norse speech of the Vikings who settled in northern England. It is unusual for one language to take a pronoun from another language, but the Anglo Saxons apparently saw good reason to do this. Today the ancient native pronoun *hi* retains only a marginal presence in English: its former dative form *hem* still clings to life as the item we spell *'em*, as in *Give it to 'em*.

Politeness

Most of us, most of the time, are eager to avoid giving offence, and avoiding offence can require some manipulation of the language. As we saw in the last chapter, English speakers have been struggling for generations to find delicate and polite ways of talking about copulation, but no solution seems to remain wholly delicate for long. The coy six-syllable creation *sexual intercourse* was promptly shortened to *intercourse*, and already this word is beginning to sound rather blunt and graphic to many ears: perhaps even legal and scientific, particularly in comparison to other coinages such as *making love* and *sleeping together*, which still draw a hazy veil over just what the participants are up to. Soon, no doubt, *intercourse* will come to seem almost as coarse as the terms it was invented to avoid, and we'll have to scramble for yet another euphemism.

Sex, excretion and death are the topics that most plainly call for euphemisms and weasel words, and hence for innovations in the language, but there are many other areas in which a desire for politeness can bring about changes in the language. For generations, English obliged women to declare their marital status publicly on every occasion, with *Miss Johnson* or *Mrs Wilson*, while no such obligation was laid on men. Only in the middle of the twentieth century did this linguistic discrimination come to be seen as outrageously sexist and patronising. Having realised this, English now has *Ms* in the language for any women who want to use it – and very many of them do.

Somewhat different is the case of country names. As a rule in English, the name of a country takes the article *the* only if this word is required for structural reasons: *the United States*, *the United Kingdom*, *the Philippines*, *the Netherlands*. But most country names lack the article: *Cuba*, *Russia*, *Italy*, *Wales*, *Brazil*. However, for various historical reasons, there are a number of countries whose English names commonly took the article until very recently: *the Sudan*, *the Lebanon*, *the Gambia*, *the Ukraine*, and a few others. But the article has now disappeared from all these names in careful writing, where we find only *Sudan*, *Lebanon*, *Gambia* and *Ukraine*.

This is done to avoid giving offence. Citizens of these countries are often deeply offended when the name of their country gets the article. They point out indignantly that country names do not normally take the article, and that the article is usual only in the names of vaguely defined geographical *regions*, such as *the Kalahari*, *the Midlands*, *the Arctic* and *the Midwest*. To a Ukrainian, then, writing or saying *the Ukraine* suggests that Ukraine is not a proper country at all, but something less – perhaps no more than a renegade region of Russia. Removal of the historical article from these names is therefore necessary to avoid giving unintended offence.

Misunderstanding

Some changes derive from simple misunderstanding. In the last chapter, we saw how the expression *telling one's beads*, originally 'counting one's prayers', was reinterpreted as meaning 'counting the little balls', with the result that *bead* changed its meaning from 'prayer' to 'little ball'. Such misunderstandings are perhaps more frequent than you might suppose. Consider the *be going to* construction.

Normally, I can only say *I'm going to bed* if I am actually on my way to bed, or at least on the very point of getting out of my chair and heading for the bedroom. It would be seriously abnormal for me to say *I'm going to bed* when I have no intention of leaving my chair for another two or three hours.

The same used to be true of sentences like *I'm going to visit Mrs Pumphrey.* Until the early nineteenth century, such a thing could only be uttered by someone who was actually on her way to Mrs Pumphrey's house, or at least on the very point of setting off. But then something happened. People hearing things like *I'm going to visit Mrs Pumphrey* from speakers just getting ready to set out took the speakers to mean, not 'I'm on my way', but rather 'I *intend* to visit Mrs Pumphrey.' As a result, the once-obligatory sense of immediate movement was 'bleached out' of the construction, which was reanalysed as no more than an expression of intention at some unspecified future time.

Today we can happily say *I'm going to see the new Spielberg film* while we are curled up cosily in our chairs with no intention of moving for hours and no plans to see the film for days. We can even say things like *I'm going to finish this book tonight*, in which no relevant movement is even conceivable.

Other problems with interpretation are also present in all languages, however.

Long ago, English had a word *guma*, meaning 'man'. This word formed part of a compound, *brydguma*, literally 'bride-man', and applied to a man getting married. But then the independent word *guma* gradually dropped out of use and vanished from the language. This loss left the second half of *brydguma* isolated and opaque. English speakers hearing *bride-goom* understood the *bride* part without difficulties, but the *goom* was a complete mystery. Trying to make some sense of it, they altered *bridegoom* into *bridegroom*. Speakers would have been aware that *groom* was a real English word that they were familiar with. Of course, it didn't have much to do with weddings: a groom is simply somebody who looks after horses. But at least a groom was a kind of man and so speakers happily altered the mysterious *bridegoom* into the slightly more intelligible-looking *bridegroom*. This kind of rearrangement of an opaque word is called *folk-etymology*.

Another example of change through misinterpretation: English has long had a word to express the sense of 'lucky'. In Old English, that word was the native English word *silly*, but, after this word changed its meaning rather dramatically, another word, *lucky*, was adopted, apparently from Dutch or Low German (the name given to the dialects, more like Dutch than Standard German, spoken in northern Germany, which were once the lingua franca of northern Europe) via gamblers' argot. So, there has always been a way of expressing this range of senses. Nevertheless, after the Norman Conquest of England, the word *fortunate*, with the same meaning, was taken over from Norman French. For centuries these two words have existed side by side in English: the plain, workaday *lucky* and the more formal and elevated *fortunate*.

Continuing with the sense 'lucky': English also has a word *fortuitous*. This word, until recently elevated and rather rare, means 'accidental', 'happening by chance'; it does not mean 'lucky', and it is only very distantly related to *fortunate*. But, in recent years, some people have stumbled across the unfamiliar word *fortuitous* in reading; not being familiar with it, they surmised that it must be an even fancier word for 'fortunate'. As a result, more and more people are now writing and saying *fortuitous* when they mean to express only the meaning of 'lucky'. This formerly uncommon word has become decidedly frequent, and those who use it almost without exception use it meaning 'lucky', and not 'accidental'. The word *fortuitous* is now well on its way to a change of meaning: its traditional sense of 'accidental' is disappearing, and its unexpected new sense of 'lucky' is taking over. Within a generation or two, it is very likely that there will be no speakers left alive still using the word in its older sense, and the shift of meaning will be complete.

Why has this happened? On the face of it, we are looking at nothing more than an ignorant blunder. A speaker of pedantic outlook might put it like this: 'A few ill-educated oafs stumbled across this word, didn't know what it meant, and made a wild wrong guess; now they're being followed in this ignorant howler by other ill-educated oafs, and the proper use of the word is being forgotten.'

This may be true, but there's another point at issue here. Since English has always had a plain word to express 'lucky' (although different words at different times), why did our ancestors bother to take over the word *fortunate* from French in the first place? After all, it is unlikely that French *pain* 'bread' or *voiture* 'car' or *chemin* 'road' will be borrowed and used frequently, so why *fortunate*? The answer can be summed up in one word: prestige.

Prestige and pretentiousness

After the conquest of England by the French-speaking Normans, Norman French enjoyed enormous prestige in England, where it was the language of the king, the court and the aristocracy, while English remained only the everyday language of ordinary people, with no prestige at all. The native upper classes, and those who had hopes of joining the upper classes, learned to speak French. Having learned it, they did not fail to show off their command of this prestigious language by dropping French words into their English. By definition, French words were more refined and elevated than our crude and clumsy English words, and so French words poured into English, in many cases displacing their native English equivalents. In fact, specialists estimate that between 60 and 80 per cent of the native English vocabulary disappeared in the centuries after the Norman Conquest, as we can see in Table 2.

The torrent of Norman words flowing into English eventually dried up, but French influence on English was far from over. From about the sixteenth

Table 2.1 *Old English words and their modern equivalents*

Native	French
berg	*mountain*
ea	*river*
here	*army*
andwlita	*face*
swamm	*mousseron* (now *mushroom*)
wuldor	*glory*
æwnung	*marriage*
swæsende	*feast* (and later also French *banquet*)
gewrit	*document*

century onwards, France was generally perceived as the leading European nation, and French culture was everywhere regarded as the pinnacle of civilisation. As a result, French words flooded into the other languages of Europe, and no other language was more receptive than English. Among the hundreds of new arrivals were *armistice, coup de grace, picnic, cigarette, crusade, clique, champagne, ragout, roulette, courtesan, soirée, crochet, garage, ballet, pastel, café, demi-monde, tutu, cognac* and the more unexpected *turtle*. Turtles aside, these few but typical examples demonstrate that French borrowings from the sixteenth to the early twentieth century were associated with a way of life that was cosmopolitan, sophisticated, urbane, prosperous and, by strait-laced standards, a little sinful.

Since at least 1945, the prestige of French has been declining, but its former cachet has not entirely disappeared. You may know someone who cannot resist spattering his English speech with Gallicisms like *au contraire* and *naturellement*. When long French-style loaves of crispy bread were first introduced into British supermarkets a couple of decades ago, they were called *French sticks*, but this blunt English label has not survived, and today nobody in Britain calls them anything but *baguettes*.

Today, however, the shoe is mostly on the other foot. English is now the most prestigious language on the planet, and English words are enthusiastically taken into Spanish, German, Japanese, Greek – and French. The French authorities take great offence over the countless English words streaming into French, and the French language police work concentrate on inventing 'genuine' French equivalents. The august *Académie française* issues firm instructions to eschew *le weekend* in favour of *le fin de semaine*. It commands loyal Frenchmen and women to avoid the horrible English word *le bulldozer* and to trot out the stoutly French creation *le bouledozeur*. In practice, however, most French speakers pay little attention to the Academy's rulings and say whatever they like – and what they like is often a piece of English. So fond are today's French speakers of English that they even invent 'English' words and use those in French, like *le footing* 'jogging', *le jogging* 'tracksuit' and *le brushing* 'blow-dry' – not to mention *le shampooing* 'shampoo'.

To be fair, the Academy has enjoyed some successes. While just about everybody else in Europe is happy to buy a *computer* with *software*, a French speaker must buy an *ordinateur* with *logiciels*. Originally, the well-known English computing term *to debug* was taken bodily into French as the awkward *débugger*, which is hardly even pronounceable. The authorities demanded, and got, a rearrangement of this into *déboguer*, which at least looks like French. This verb naturally gave rise to a derivative *débogage* for 'debugging', but the 'language police' were still not happy. The wonderful creation *déverminage*, the word given in the latest French dictionaries, has become the preferred choice.

It is not easy to decide just when succumbing to prestige lapses into pretentiousness. But there is no doubt that prestige is an immensely important force in language change.

Structural reasons

Human speech has to be produced by the human vocal tract, which has a complicated and irregular shape. The shape of the vocal tract is sometimes a factor in producing language change, especially changes in pronunciation.

English has a sound unit /k/, which is variously spelled <c>, <k>, <ck>, <q>, and occasionally in other ways. This sound occurs at the beginning of the word *car*, and also at the beginning of the word *key*. But try pronouncing *car key* several times. You will quickly notice that the /k/ in *key* is pronounced very differently from the /k/ in *car*. In particular, the /k/ in *key* is pronounced with the tongue much higher and further forward in the mouth. In our technical terminology, we say that the /k/ in *key* is *palatalised*, and we can represent this palatalised /k/ by the phonetic symbol [kʲ].

In terms of its tongue position, however, this [kʲ] is really not very close to the 'plain' /k/ in *car*, and it is in fact much closer to the consonant /tʃ/ which occurs at the beginning of the word *cheese*. Try saying *car – key – cheese* in sequence, and you will notice that the tongue positions are quite far apart for the /k/ in *car* and the /k/ in *key*, but rather close together for the /k/ of *key* and the /tʃ/ of *cheese*.

Why does this happen? It results from the effect of the following vowel. In *car*, the vowel is /a/ or /ɑ/, which is pronounced with the tongue held low in the mouth and, for most speakers, in the middle or towards the back of the mouth. In *key*, however, the following vowel is /i/, which is pronounced with the tongue held high in the mouth and pushed forward about as far as it will go. English speakers, like speakers of all languages, find it unnatural and difficult to make the /k/ sound with the tongue pulled back and down, and then to hurl the tongue dramatically forward and up to make the vowel /i/. Try it: you will find it difficult, and, if you manage it, you will produce something that doesn't sound like English. In practice, it is easier to push our tongues forward and up while we are still pronouncing the /k/ sound, so that we have our tongues in perfect position to do the vowel when we get to it. It is this raising and fronting of the tongue that constitutes *palatalisation*.

The consonants /k/ (as in *car* and *key*) and /g/ (as in *go* and *give*) are technically known as *velar* consonants, because they are pronounced with the back of the tongue against the velum, or soft palate, towards the back of the top of the mouth. Vowels pronounced with the tongue pushed to the top and the front of the mouth, like /i/ in *key*, are called *high front vowels*. When a velar consonant is immediately followed by a high front vowel, as it is in *key*, humans find it almost impossible to avoid palatalising the consonant: we just naturally push the consonant forward in our mouths onto the (hard) palate to get ready for that vowel.

But, once we start doing this, it is very easy to exaggerate the palatalisation ever so slightly. If this happens, our palatalised [kʲ] sound quickly slips into the sound [tʃ] or something similar. Exactly this happened some centuries ago in English. All the words *chin, cheese, child, chaff, chicken* and *chalk*, among many others, used to start with the consonant /k/ followed by a front vowel. But early English speakers slightly 'overdid' the palatalisation, and so the original /k/ (phonetic [kʲ]) turned into /tʃ/, the sound we usually spell <ch> in Modern English. German is a language that shares a common origin with English, as we will see later in the book; compare German *Kinn* 'chin', *Käse* 'cheese', *Kind* 'child', and so on. The German /k/ in these words is still the palatalised [kʲ], but German speakers have so far managed to resist the temptation to push the palatalisation just a bit further.

Structural factors are not important only in pronunciation. Grammatical structures and semantic structures (meaning structures) can also play a part in language change. Consider an example from Basque, a language spoken at the western end of the Pyrenees. Among the several Basque colour terms is *urdin*, which means 'blue' and nothing else. However, there is a kind of mushroom which has a striking bright-green cap, and this mushroom is called in Basque a *gibel-urdin* – literally, it would seem, a 'blue-back' (*gibel* means 'back'). Why isn't it called something more sensible, like perhaps *gibel-berde* 'green-back'?

The answer can be found in the ways that the Basque language has changed. Some centuries ago, Basque had fewer colour terms than it has today, and *urdin* was the Basque label covering all of green and blue, as well as the lighter shades of grey. The mushroom was therefore named *gibel-urdin*, because *urdin* was the ordinary Basque name for its colour.

But Basque speakers eventually noticed that their Spanish-speaking neighbours had two different words for 'green' and 'blue', as well as a third word for 'grey'. They then took over Spanish *verde* 'green' as *berde*, which became their new word for 'green', and they also took over Spanish *gris* 'grey' as *gris* 'grey'. And what happened to *urdin*? It remained in the language, of course, but its range of application shrank. *Berde* took over the job of labelling the green part of *urdin*, while the other new word *gris* took over the grey part of *urdin*. Consequently, the native word was left with only the blue part of its former meaning. Today, therefore, *urdin* just means 'blue', and the once-sensible name of the mushroom has become puzzling.

This kind of change results from structural factors: the colour term *urdin* was part of an integrated system of colour terms, and, when the new colour terms *berde* and *gris* were introduced into the system, the value of *urdin* was forced to change in order to accommodate the new words.

Exactly the same thing has happened in English, several times, as our system of colour terms has been expanded. Consider the word *orange*.

The fruit we call the orange is native to Asia, and until rather recently it remained an exotic rarity in Europe. But knowledge of the fruit slowly spread, and its name, taken from Sanskrit, an ancient language of India, passed through Persian, Arabic and French before finally reaching English. The first mention of the fruit in English is recorded in 1387, but only the richest people would have seen oranges in medieval England. Yet the brilliant and distinctive colour of the fruit attracted attention, and after a while English speakers began using the expression *orange-colour* to label this sort of colour on the few occasions when they needed such a label. Only in 1600 do we find unmodified *orange* recorded as the name of the colour, but this use remained rare, and it only started to become common in the 1780s.

Today, of course, it is perfectly clear to English speakers that *orange* is just as basic a colour term as *red*, *yellow* or *green*. While *crimson* and *scarlet*, for example, are clearly only varieties of *red*, *orange* is not a variety of *red*, nor a variety of anything else. So, thanks to the introduction of this vividly coloured Asian fruit, English now has a basic colour term which it formerly lacked, and this term can be applied to anything of a suitable colour.

Before they became acquainted with the fruit, no one had any reason to worry about what colour it was. But people must occasionally have bumped into things that we would unhesitatingly describe as 'orange', so what colour term did they apply – say, to one of the newfangled orange carrots which were beginning to displace the traditional white ones? Well, they could not say 'orange', because no such term existed, and there was no equivalent word. So, anything which lay somewhere between bright red and bright yellow in colour had to be either 'red' or 'yellow'. Or it might be 'yellow-red', a word recorded from before the Norman Conquest. Or the speaker might exhibit a little imagination, and call the object 'apple-yellow' – also recorded before the Conquest – or words to that effect.

Another recent addition to the English set of colour terms is *pink*. Since the 1570s, *pink* has been the name of a garden flower whose petals have distinctive zigzag edges. These flowers are found in several colours, but their most frequent colour is pale red. Around 1720 the name of the flower began to be used as a descriptive label for anything having a pale red colour, much as we might describe something today as 'primrose' or 'magnolia' because of its colour. Oddly, however, the word *pink* was nowhere recorded independently as the name of a colour until it appeared in Noah Webster's famous American dictionary of 1828 – and even there it was given only as an artists' colour.

So, *pink* is a very recent addition to the English colour-term system, but this term too is now regarded as basic, and most English speakers do not think of pink as a kind of red. In a manner that seems almost haphazard, the way English lays out colour boundaries has once again changed, and all because of the former popularity of a garden flower whose existence most of us are hardly aware of.

Structural factors can lead to changes in a language, and changes in a language can have consequences for its structure.

Analogy

There is one kind of structural reason for change that is so important it deserves its own section here. This is the phenomenon linguists call *analogy*.

Suppose I tell you (truthfully) that each of the obscure English words *ziff*, *zo* and *zax* is the name of something that can be counted. What do you suppose their plural forms are? *Ziffs*, *zos* and *zaxes*, of course. You managed to create these plural forms instantly, and you can even pronounce them without difficulty, even though – if you listen carefully – the plural ending is pronounced somewhat differently in each of the three words according to a consistent rule.

How can you do this? How can you instantly create the correct plural form of a word you've never seen before? Well, you do it by analogy. You have learned that there is a regular pattern for constructing English plurals, as in *cats*, *dogs* and *foxes*, and you can readily extend that pattern to any new words you come across. Generally this works well.

Of course, not always. Standard English does not permit the plural forms *foots*, *childs*, *sheeps*, *mouses* or *radiuses*, and we all have to memorise the unpredictable plurals *feet*, *children*, *sheep*, *mice* and *radii*. But there aren't *that* many of these, and creating plural forms by analogy works very well most of the time.

Table 2.2 *Old English plurals*

Singular	Plural	Gloss
sunu	*suna*	'son'
nama	*naman*	'name'
cild	*cildru*	'child'
cyning	*cyningas*	'king'
stede	*stede*	'place'
scip	*scipu*	'ship'
spere	*speru*	'spear'
glof	*glofa*	'glove'
cwen	*cwene*	'woman'
heorte	*heortan*	'heart'
ende	*endas*	'end'
here	*herias*	'army'
wealh	*wealas*	'foreigner'
fot	*fet*	'foot'
dæg	*dagas*	'day'

In fact, we human beings adore analogy. Every one of us is eager to see patterns in the world, and language is no exception. And this desire to find patterns can lead us innocently into changing our language.

The past tense and the participle of the verb *work* used to be *wrought*, but this verb has been attracted by analogy to the common pattern illustrated by *love, loved*. Now the verb goes *work, worked*, by analogy, and the old form *wrought* is confined, except in traditional Scottish dialects, to a few fossilised expressions like *wrought iron*, no longer even associated with *work*. In fact, very many formerly irregular English verbs have been made regular by just this kind of analogy. But analogy can also work in the other direction. The past tense of *catch* was formerly the regular *catched*, as in *I catched a cold*. But this verb was re-formed by analogy with *teach, taught*, and today, if we want to sound educated, we must say *I caught a cold* – a form that would have sounded ridiculously ignorant 500 years ago. And, in much of the northeastern United States, the verb *dive* has likewise been re-formed by analogy with the several verbs like *drive, drove*, and Americans from this area now say *I dove into the water*. Analogy does not always bring about regularity and simplicity.

Given enough time, analogy can transform the shape of a language. Let's return to English plurals. The English spoken before around 1150 – Old English – was, like Modern German, a language with a large number of ways of constructing plurals. Table 2.1 shows a sample of some Old English plural forms.

This table by no means exhausts all the complications encountered in forming plurals in Old English, but it gives you an idea of the amount of work involved (for Modern English speakers, naturally: it was second nature to the Anglo-Saxons) in learning to pluralise nouns in that language.

English retains only a little of this former complexity. But again this simplification results from analogy. Early English speakers seemingly no longer kept track of so many different plural forms, and they began to extend some of the plural forms analogically to words which had previously not taken these plural forms.

The pattern which has finally won out is the one represented in Old English by *cyning, cyningas* 'king' in the table. But this <-s> plural did not take over the language in one go. The extension of plural <-s> to nouns which had not formerly had it began in the Old English period. During the Middle English period (from around 1100 to 1500), the <-s> plural slowly but steadily attracted ever more nouns to itself. Even so, Middle English texts reveal quite a few nouns with other plurals, most conspicuously the <-n> found with Middle English *name, namen* 'name': *shoon* 'shoes', *eyen* 'eyes', *eyren* 'eggs', *kine* 'cows', and lots of others. Today, however, the <-n> plural has been analogised completely out of the language, except in the uncommon *oxen* and the strangely formed *children*. This last word is really a double plural: the Old English plural *cildru* became Middle English *childer*, but this form appears to have been perceived as insufficiently clearly marked as a plural, and so the formerly prominent <-n> was tacked onto it to produce the modern form. Some Modern English speakers from the north of England still use *childer*, however, while many English Catholics call the Feast of the Holy Innocents in January *Childermass*.

Today this particular struggle is largely over. When the Italian word *pizza* came into English, there was no agonising over whether its plural should be *pizze* or *pizzen* or *pizzaru*. The plural was instantly *pizzas*, and there was no discussion. It might have been different if *pizza* were a learned Greek or Hebrew term. Even here distinctions can be made, however. The plural of *cherub*, the Hebrew word for the angels of fire who surround the presence of God, is *cherubim*, with an authentic Hebrew plural. When *cherub* is used to describe the chubby infant angels shown on Christmas cards, however, the plural form is the native *cherubs*.

Group identity

Politeness, prestige, misunderstanding, analogy – all these things and others play a part in language change. But there is one more factor which, we linguists have finally realised, is of immense importance. That factor is *group identity*.

Every one of us wants to belong to a group of people, to be accepted by the other members of that group as one of them, to be recognised by outsiders as a member of that group. And we linguists have gradually realised, although only really since the 1960s, that one of the most powerful ways of maintaining and displaying membership in a group is language.

A group may perhaps be identified by its members' clothes, or hairstyles, or accessories, or favourite hangouts. But just about every group can be readily identified by the speech of its members.

Consider a motor mechanic in London. He speaks the kind of English which is usual among working-class people in that city, the kind commonly known as 'Cockney'. If you ask him what he thinks about his English, he will very likely describe it as 'not very good'. This response is typical of working-class speakers in London and elsewhere.

From an objective point of view, it is perfectly clear that Cockney speech is not the sort of English which is generally regarded as prestigious in London. Instead, prestige attaches itself to the educated English spoken by television newsreaders, stockbrokers, barristers, university professors, and other members of the middle and upper classes. That being so, why doesn't our motor mechanic adjust his speech towards the English used by those television newsreaders and by his more prosperous customers? After all, he hears this kind of English often enough, so why doesn't he try to adopt it himself?

Just imagine for a moment that he tried to do this. Suppose he tried hard to abandon his Cockney speech and to speak instead with the best approximation to middle-class English that he could muster. What would happen?

For a few seconds, his family and his friends would assume he was making some kind of joke, and they would laugh. But only for a few seconds. Before long, they would become distant, annoyed and perhaps even hostile. He would no longer be welcome in the circles in which he was formerly a valued member.

Why is this? Prestige is not a simple notion. The mechanic belongs to a group of people with whom he shares background, circumstances, tastes and values. And it is the members of this group upon whom he relies for his social life, for support in times of difficulty, and in general for his sense of self-respect, for his sense that he has a place in society, for his sense that he is a valued person.

But how does he maintain his all-important place in this social group? One of the most powerful ways of maintaining and exhibiting membership in a social group is *language*. Every social group has its own way of speaking, a style of speech which serves as a badge of membership in that group. So, if our motor mechanic wants to retain his place in the group, then the one thing he must do above all else is to *speak the way the others speak*.

Doing so carries a clear message: 'I regard myself as a member of your group.' But, as soon as our mechanic begins to speak in some other way, then he is announcing in the clearest way possible 'I no longer regard myself a member of your group.' If he persists, the others will quickly get the message, and he will indeed find himself excluded from the group.

This is true of every social group. For purposes of group membership, it makes no difference at all whether the group's speech is regarded, by the members of the group or by outsiders, as good or bad, as prestigious or as vulgar. All that matters is to speak the way the others speak, because only by doing this can anybody maintain a place in the group.

And that means accepting whatever changes become current in the chosen speech variety. The vernacular speech of London has undergone a number of rather distinctive changes in pronunciation. For example, a Londoner's pronunciation of *time* sounds like *tsoim*; a Londoner's *paint* sounds like *pint*, while a Londoner's *pint* sounds like *point*; and a Londoner's *water* famously sounds like *woh'ah*, with a glottal stop in the middle. There are distinctive London words, like *loaf* for 'head', and distinctive London locutions like *blimey* for surprise and *dun I* for reinforcement, as in *I drives a van, dun I?*. Any working-class Londoner who wants to fit in must accept and use these forms, because these are the forms which express membership in the group. The use of these forms represents what linguists call *covert prestige*, in contrast to the *overt prestige* associated with educated middle-class norms.

So the maintenance and expression of group identity is an important force in language change. In Chapter 8 we will see some further striking cases of deliberate language change in pursuit of a distinct identity, including the most spectacular example so far uncovered.

A final thought

In this chapter we have considered some of the central mechanisms of language change: prestige, analogy, cultural change and 'ease'. These forces are so powerful that they are at work constantly on every living language. Normally in subtle ways, occasionally in very striking ways, the language we hear (and to an extent use) in old age is different from what we heard and spoke as a teenager.

In the rest of this book, we will consider these forces in relation to separate features of language change, each of which will be approached as a series of questions. In the next chapter, we will investigate the vexed question of word origin.

3   Where do words come from?

The romance of word origins

Every language has thousands of words, and every one of those words must have an origin of some kind – that is, it must have come from somewhere. Words can have all kinds of origins, but mostly they come from other words, in the same language or in other languages. The study of word origins is called *etymology*, a laborious and exacting business requiring considerable erudition. You have practically no chance of uncovering the origin of any word unless you have an almost encyclopaedic knowledge of the history of every language (and its speakers) that might possibly be relevant to your task – and even then you won't get far unless you know how and where to locate dusty and forgotten documents buried in out-of-the-way archives, and how to use those documents.

This is not obvious when you consult a reference book giving word origins. There are several large scholarly etymological dictionaries of English, each of them soberly reporting everything that has so far been uncovered about the origins of thousands of English words, and there are many more popular books on word origins which typically present some of the more engaging word origins. And word origins can certainly be engaging. Who is not delighted to learn that *bikini* takes its name from that of a Pacific atoll where some early atomic bombs were tested, on the ground that the effect of the new costume was comparably 'explosive'? Or that the drug *heroin* gets its name from the super-human delusions it induces in its user? Or that *ramble* originally meant 'wander about like a randy ram looking for ewes to copulate with'? Or that *work* and *orgy* are historically the same word? And only the most inflexible teetotaller can fail to be impressed by learning that *whisky* derives from Gaelic *uisge beatha* 'water of life'.

Generations of etymologists have worked their way slowly and painfully through the vocabularies of English and other languages, establishing for example that *garlic* descends from Old English *gar-leac* 'spear-leek' (because of its pointy cloves), that *shampoo* derives from the Hindi order *cāmpo!* 'press it!' (used as an instruction to massage a patron in a Turkish bath), and that *nightmare* has nothing to do with horses but contains the obsolete English word *mære*, a kind of evil spirit or goblin which was thought to sit on sleepers' chests and give them bad dreams. Very few of these conclusions are obvious, and almost every one of them required dozens or hundreds of hours of painstaking investigation to establish the facts.

Non-specialists do not always realise this, often assuming that finding the origin of a word consists of nothing more than finding another word somewhere which resembles it, more or less. But, as always in linguistic work, resemblances are almost always worthless, and etymologists must work with more reliable procedures to establish correspondences. It is far from obvious, for example, that English *head* and French *chef* are historically the same word, but that both languages have changed the pronunciation greatly (the original was roughly **kaput*), while French has also changed the meaning. This sort of conclusion – and this one is established beyond dispute – cannot be obtained from a mindless search for lookalikes.

Are English *ear* (of corn) and *ear* (on the head) historically the same word or not? No; they are not related at all, although it is only painstaking scholarly work which has established this (and it has to be recognised that the similarity in appearance had led speakers to assume a connection between the two for centuries). Is English *bimbo* 'sexy but dim-witted young woman' related somehow to Italian *bimbo* 'child'? Yes, it is, but the connection is far from simple: the Italian word was first taken into English as an informal word for 'fellow', 'chap', and the shift in sex is still not entirely understood. Languages do strange and unexpected things. Is there any connection between *flower* (a rose or a buttercup) and *flour* (for making bread)? Yes; they are actually historically the same word. This conclusion could hardly be less obvious. Few people would have guessed it in advance, but once again scholarly work has established this as a fact beyond dispute. Is *spring* 'the season after winter' the same word as *spring* 'a place where water rises out of the ground'? Yes; the first is a metaphorical use of the second. Is *blackmail* related to *mail* 'post' or to *mail* 'armour'? No; it is related to neither. It contains the otherwise obsolete English word *mail* 'tribute, rent', derived from *mál* 'speech, agreement' in Old Norse, the language of the Vikings who once settled parts of Britain. In the sixteenth century, unscrupulous Scottish chieftains ran what we would now call a protection racket, and the money they extorted from their victims in return for not killing them or beggaring them came to be called *blackmail*.

Word origins can be decidedly peculiar. Where do you suppose the word *gorilla* might come from? Names of non-European animals are often taken from the local languages spoken where the animals are found, as has happened with *skunk*, *raccoon*, *okapi*, *yak*, *kangaroo*, *wombat* and *kiwi*. So, we might suppose that *gorilla* is simply the name of the animal in a local African language. But the truth is very different.

In the fifth century BC, the Carthaginian explorer Hanno reported that he had encountered, somewhere in West Africa, a tribe of wild hairy people, whose females, according to an interpreter, were called *gorillas*. And that is where the word stayed for about twenty-four centuries, until European scientists first became aware of the huge African apes. In 1847, the American scientist Thomas Savage, who apparently had a sense of humour, applied Hanno's ancient word to these creatures, and within a few years *gorillas* had become their accepted name.

After generations of scholarly toil, we now know the origins of most English words – but not of all of them. Among the English words whose origins are still wholly unknown today, in spite of immense efforts, are these: *yo-yo, zebra* (English took this from Spanish, Portuguese or Italian, but nobody knows where these other languages got it from), *sleazy, gourmand, ricochet, bauble* (these last three are taken from French, of course, but the origins of the French words are mysterious), *slender, baste* ('moisten roasting meat with fat'; the origin of *baste* 'sew loosely' is well understood), *rickrack* (the zigzag decoration on clothing), *bridge* (the card game) and the British word *loo* 'toilet'. There is still a lot of work to be done, although the origins of some of these words are probably beyond recovery, for lack of evidence. Remarkably, *yo-yo* is not recorded before about 1915, and *loo* not before the 1920s, yet even so scholars have not been able to find any clear evidence of their origins: both words just seem to have dropped out of the sky. (Some dictionaries will tell you that *yo-yo* originated as a trade name, but in fact the trade name *Yo-Yo* was filed only in 1932, seventeen years after the name of the toy was recorded; the explanation that *loo* is derived from pronunciations of French *l'eau* 'the water' in Renaissance Edinburgh is problematical because the word was first recorded in the twentieth century.)

Such cases are not rare at any period. At the beginning of the thirteenth century, the word *brim* seemingly dropped out of the sky into English, originally in the sense of 'edge'. There is no whisper of the word in the written English of the several centuries preceding its appearance, even though the word looks for all the world like a native English word, and even though obviously related words for 'edge' are found in other Germanic languages. So what happened? Nobody supposes that there was a vast conspiracy among English writers to avoid putting the word down on paper for several centuries. Many of the more vulgar English four-letter words appear in writing only very late precisely because nobody wanted to write them down, but it hardly seems possible that the inoffensive *brim* could be a candidate for such treatment.

But we can't be sure. Consider *occupy*. This was taken into English in the fourteenth century, either from Latin *occupare* or from that word's Old French descendant *occuper*. For a couple of centuries it remained an ordinary and unremarkable English word. Then, in the sixteenth and seventeenth centuries, the word almost disappeared from written English, because it had become a common slang term for 'have sex with' ('as King Edwin occupied Alfgifa his concubine', recorded in 1546), and, as always in such cases, writers were reluctant to use the word in its harmless sense for fear of inducing vulgar laughter. Shakespeare puts this protest into the mouth of Doll Tearsheet in *King Henry IV, Part II*: 'A captain! God's light, these villains will make the word 'captain' as odious as the word "occupy", which was an excellent good word before it was ill sorted.' Eventually, however, the sexual sense of the word dropped out of use, and *occupy* was restored to good standing in our lexicon.

A famous mystery word is *penguin*. A favourite story sees the source as Welsh *pen gwyn*, which means 'white head'. *Pen gwyn* is indeed perfect Welsh, and it's a perfect source for the English word as far as the pronunciation is concerned. But penguins don't have white heads: they have black ones. This looks a fatal shortcoming, but things, as usual, are more complicated. Originally, the word *penguin* was not applied to the Antarctic bird at all, but to a quite different bird, the now-extinct great auk of the North Atlantic. Only later was the name transferred to the vaguely similar-looking southern bird. But the great auk didn't have a white head either. It is hard to imagine English ships loaded down with Welsh sailors boisterously shouting *Whitehead!* in Welsh every time they saw a big bird with a black head. It seems, therefore, that we are stuck.

There is a school of thought which holds that any story is better than none at all, but most etymologists are reluctant to embrace this view, and they prefer to have no explanation rather than one that looks deeply dubious.

The origin of the word *butterfly* demonstrates that we must strip away the connotations the being or thing has – in this case, that it is beautiful – to find the often pedestrian origins of a word. In English and in other languages, the butterfly is a byword for inconstancy, and European names for the insect are likewise unstable. Names come and names go at a brisk pace. Among the recent names are Albanian *flutur*, Bulgarian *peperuda*, Czech *motel*, Danish *sommer-fugl* and *skurvefugl*, Dutch *vlinder*, Estonian *liblikas*, Finnish *perhonen*, French *papillon*, Scottish Gaelic *dear badan-de* and *seillan de*, German *Schmetterling*, Greek *petalóvda*, Hungarian *pillango*, Icelandic *fithrildi*, Irish *feileacan*, Italian *farfalla*, Latvian *tauriuö*, Lithuanian *peteliöke*, Norwegian *sommerfugl*, Polish *motyl*, Portuguese *borboleta*, Romanian *fluturi*, Russian *babochka*, Serbian and Croatian *leptir*, Slovenian *metulj*, Spanish *mariposa*, Swedish *fjäril*, Turkish *kelebek*, and Welsh *pili-pala* and half-a-dozen other words. Basque, spoken only in a circumscribed area, has more than twenty-five names for the creature, including *tximeleta*, *inguma*, *pinpirina* and *jainko-oilo*.

Against this background, English *butterfly* is a rock of stability. This word has been used as long as English has existed as a distinct language: it occurs in Old English in the form *butorfleoge*. The same word is recorded in some of the continental Germanic languages: we have a Dutch word *botervlieg* (from earlier *botervlieghe*) and a regional German name *Butterfliege*. But why 'butter-fly'? What has the insect to do with butter?

Of course, there are speculations. One idea is that the bright yellow butterflies now called 'sulphurs' are commonplace in Europe, and that these butter-coloured varieties were taken as the stereotypical butterflies. Another proposal is that there was once an old wives' tale that butterflies stole butter from kitchens. Maybe, but there is no trace of such a story. A third possibility is a little less romantic. Butterfly excrement is oily and yellowish, and so perhaps the insects take their name from the appearance of their droppings. This time we have a small bit of supporting evidence, since we have a record of another Dutch name for the creature, *boterschijte*, which means what it looks like.

Another puzzling word is *nipple*. Nobody is sure about the origin of this one, but many people point to the Scottish and northern English word *neb*, which means 'anything which projects' and is applied to a bird's beak, a nose or a snout. These people suggest that *nipple* originated as a diminutive of this word, and hence as 'little thing that sticks out'. This is not a bad guess, but it's a guess: there is no hard evidence to support it, and a diminutive of *neb* wouldn't normally have the form *nipple*; instead, it would be *nebble*.

However, perhaps the greatest outstanding etymological puzzles in English are the origins of two humdrum but common little words: *boy* and *girl*.

The one thing that is certain about *boy* is that it cannot be a native English word. No native English word ever contains the sound /ɔi/ (except in words like *find* or *tie*, if the speaker is Cockney, Australian or from New Zealand, or from some of the island communities in the Chesapeake Bay in the United States), and any English word containing it has been taken from another language. This is a tiny example of the kind of knowledge which professional etymologists must have at their fingertips. Most of our words containing <oi>, like *oil, coin, boil, noise, coy* and *destroy*, have been taken from Norman French, in which the sound was common, but sadly Norman French has no such word as *boy*. So where can the word come from?

Scholarly ingenuity has not been lacking. Some scholars have proposed that the English word derives from a word *boi*, meaning 'young gentleman', in Frisian. (Frisian is a Germanic language spoken in the north of the Netherlands and in some islands off the northwest coast of Germany.) This idea looks superficially good, but it is practically unknown for a Frisian word to be taken into English. And there's another problem.

English *boy* is recorded from 1225, but its original sense was 'servant'. Only later did it shift its meaning to the modern one. This is bad news for the Frisian conjecture. So, other scholars have turned back to Norman French, and they have found the Norman French verb *embuier* 'put (someone) into fetters'. They therefore surmise that this verb gave rise to an unrecorded participle **embuié* 'fettered', and that this word came to be applied to a servant boy in English, followed by irregular reduction to the attested form *boy* 'servant'.

Neither the Frisian conjecture nor the French conjecture is supported by anything much in the way of evidence, and neither looks obviously satisfying. Most specialists, therefore, continue to record English *boy* as being 'of unknown origin'.

Girl is even less well served. This word is also first recorded in the thirteenth century, but curiously it originally meant 'child' (of either sex), and it retained this meaning for centuries. In the middle of the fifteenth century, we find examples like *knave-gerlys* 'boy children' (English *knave* originally meant 'boy', but it has gone down in the world). Eventually *girl* came to be specialised to meaning '*female* child', but that is no help in finding its origin. The closest possible relatives that anyone has ever managed to find are Low German *gör(e)* '(naughty) child' and a dialectal Norwegian word *gurre* 'lamb'. This gives you an idea of how desperate the specialists are with this word. There is no evidence, and we are stuck.

A mostly successful case

More often than not, however, the efforts of the etymologists have been crowned with success. In this section, I'll present the story of a family of words practically all of which derive from the same ancient source. This is mostly a success story, although a few of the details still remain obscure.

Latin had a verb *battuere*, meaning 'beat, hit, strike'. This does not appear to be a native Latin word. Nobody really knows where it came from, though several scholars have suggested that it was taken from Gaulish, the very sparsely recorded Celtic language of what is now France. The sole evidence for this conjecture, and very scanty it is, is the observation that Gaulish is known to have had a word *andabata* for a certain kind of gladiator.

However, the Latin verb certainly existed, and it survived into Old French in the form *battre* or *batre*. After the Norman Conquest, this verb was taken into English as *batter*, meaning 'hit heavily and repeatedly'. And this, of course, is the source of the first part of *battering ram*, the name of an instrument for knocking down doors. From its verb, Old French derived a noun *bateure*, meaning 'a beating', and this word was curiously taken into English as *batter* and applied to the semi-liquid stuff used to make pancakes or to coat food to be fried. So, kitchen batter is so called because it is beaten (*beat*, by the way, although similar in shape and meaning to *batter*, is not related to it).

The same Old French verb formed a participle *batant* 'beating', and this word then came to be used as a noun meaning 'something which is pounded'. In the form *batten*, this noun passed into the English nautical vocabulary, where it designated a wooden cover used to hold something in place. This noun then came to be used as a verb meaning 'cover with a batten', and the result is known to every landlubber in the expression *batten down the hatches*.

From their verb the French derived yet another noun, *baterie*, which also meant 'a beating or pounding'. This was also dutifully taken into English, in the form *battery*. The original sense of 'beating' survives only in the legal phrase *assault and battery*. In other senses, however, the word *battery* has flourished.

Quite early, *battery* was applied to a set of metal articles that had been fashioned by hammering, a sense which is now obsolete. Then the word was applied to a set of heavy guns firing together in combat, although there is some disagreement among the specialists as to how this shift of meaning occurred. Some etymologists believe that *battery* was shifted directly from 'set of metal objects' to 'set of guns'. But others think that *battery* was applied first to the pounding effect which the guns produced on their targets, and was then transferred to the instruments of this pounding, the guns. At present, the evidence appears too scanty to allow us a confident conclusion on this detail.

Now we come to electricity. The first practical device for storing electricity was the Leyden jar, and physicists discovered early that a set of Leyden jars could be connected in sequence to produce a satisfyingly large discharge of electricity. This arrangement was quickly dubbed a *battery* by English-speaking scientists, but again there is a difference of opinion among etymologists as to why. One view holds that, since *battery* already meant 'group', the application of the word to a group of electrical cells was straightforward. The other view, however, observes that the function of the early batteries was to provide a discharge of electricity, and therefore holds that this use of *battery* resides in a shift from 'discharge of guns' to 'discharge of electricity'. Whatever the truth, English has extended the use of *battery* from a collection of cells to a single cell, and these days we buy a *battery* (a single cell) for a camera or a calculator.

The word *battery* has gone on to be applied to all sorts of things. Most often, it has the 'group' sense, as in expressions like *a battery of tests* and in the chiefly British term *battery hens*, meaning hens raised in large numbers in small, confined cages. In baseball, however, the *battery* is the pitcher and the catcher taken together. The baseball lexicographer Paul Dickson concludes that this use is a military metaphor, since these two players, the counterparts of the bowler and the wicketkeeper in cricket, were perceived in the early days of the game as the team's principal strike force in the task of mowing down the opposing batters.

Back now to Latin. From their verb *battuere* 'beat', the Romans coined a noun *battualia* 'military or gladiatorial exercises'. In popular speech, this was altered to the unrecorded *battalia, and its meaning was strengthened to the sense of real fighting. In Old French, the word developed into *bataille*, and this of course was taken into English as *battle*. The Italian form of the same word was *battaglia*, and from this the Italians coined a derivative *battaglione*, meaning 'a fighting unit'; this formation passed into French and from there into English as *battalion*.

Moving on: I've already mentioned baseball and cricket once: does the *bat* used in these sports go back to the same source? Did the Normans have yet another derivative of the form *batte*, meaning 'club'?

Yes: the Normans did have a word *batte*, and it did mean 'cudgel', and it was derived from their verb *batre*. It looks as if we have an obvious source for English *bat*, but there's a problem. The English word *batt* 'club, cudgel' is recorded in the late Old English period, *before* the Normans reached England. Apparently this word has a somewhat more complicated origin after all. Some specialists suggest that the English word may be of Celtic origin. (I'm afraid some etymologists have a bad habit of saying 'possibly of Celtic origin' whenever they run into a difficult word: the ancient Celtic languages are almost wholly unrecorded, and so they *might* have been a source for almost anything.)

Nevertheless, it seems likely that Old French *batte* at least played a part in establishing the form and meaning of English *bat*, but it can't be the whole story, however. It might be worth noting that a very small number of Norman French words – most notably *pride* – actually entered English before the Conquest, however.

A less successful case

There is probably no American contribution to world civilisation which is more important than jazz. While the origins of jazz music are obscure, it seems certain that this music developed out of the earlier ragtime music sometime around 1900, and virtually certain that it developed in the American south. But the origin of the word *jazz* is almost entirely unknown: we simply do not know where the word originally came from. It is first recorded in writing in 1909 (as the name of a dance) and in 1916 (in its modern sense). But it was very likely used in speech for at least a few years before then, and perhaps a bit further back. It is impossible to say.

Naturally, such a prominent word has attracted a great deal of attention. Here are just a few of the proposals which have been put forward.

- The word derives from Arabic *jazib* 'one who allures'.
- The word derives from *jaiza*, a term meaning 'distant drums' in some unidentified African language.
- The word derives from Hindi *jasba* 'ardent desire'.

Unfortunately these proposals are practically worthless, since they are nothing more than miscellaneous lookalikes in arbitrary languages, and, if you have learned anything from reading this book, you have learned that miscellaneous lookalikes are worthless.

In fact, it is not even certain that these suggested source words exist at all. Take *jaiza*. There are perhaps 2,000 distinct languages spoken in Africa, and attributing a word to an unidentified African language is as useful as assigning it to an unidentified Martian language. Moreover, why on earth would the name of a kind of music that developed in the south of the United States around 1900 be taken from such a faraway and implausible language as Arabic or Hindi? How many people in the American south in those days knew a single word of these languages? And why would speakers of English choose a word from such a remote and improbable language to label something which they liked quite a lot?

Other proposals include:

- The word is taken from the name of a dancing slave called Jasper, who performed in New Orleans in the 1820s.
- The word is an alteration of the name of a Mr Razz, who was a bandleader in New Orleans around 1904.
- The word is an alteration of the name of a popular Mississippi drummer of the 1890s named Charles Washington but commonly called *Chaz*.
- The word derives from the name of a Chicago musician called Jasbo Brown.
- The word is an alteration of the name of Charles Alexander, the bandleader who made *Alexander's Ragtime Band* famous. His name was always written on programmes as *Chas.*, and so people called him *Chazz*, and they shouted *Come on, Chazz!* when the music got exciting.

Are these any better than the first set?

Well, at least they are set in the United States, at something like the right period (except for the first one), and at least they involve people in the music business. To that small extent, they are better than the first lot.

However, they are really nothing more than wild guesses, backed up by no evidence at all. It has not even been demonstrated that all of these fascinating people actually existed, let alone that any one of them had anything at all to do with the creation of jazz. (It is also not demonstrated that these people were black, an observation whose importance will become obvious below.) Moreover, trying to derive the word *jazz* from something like *Chas.*, or even *razz*, has an air of desperation about it. I'm afraid these proposals too are likely to be worthless.

In order to make any progress in identifying the source of the word *jazz*, we first need to find out as much as we can about the origins of jazz music. These origins too are somewhat cloudy, but there is one thing that is utterly clear and beyond dispute: jazz was created by African Americans.

Since this much is not in doubt, we should obviously be directing our investigations towards the speech of black Americans around 1900. Frustratingly, this is not a topic on which we have much information. The African Americans of the day practically never bothered to write down their everyday speech, and the people who *were* writing things down were usually paying no attention to black speech. As always in historical linguistics, the absence of records that could easily have been kept, if only someone had been interested, is an infuriating obstacle to our investigations. Furthermore, it is now too late to find anyone who was alive at the time and who could tell us interesting things about the black southern speech of the day. If only a linguist had been interested enough around 1930 to ask a few black people about the origins of the word *jazz*, we would probably now have the full story.

However, the usual painstaking investigation by linguists in our own day has turned up one fact which is clearly of central importance. In black American speech, the word *jazz* has existed for a long time as a slang word meaning 'vigorous activity', and most particularly 'sexual intercourse'. Although little used by white American speakers (but certainly understood), this word has been so prominent for so long in black speech that we cannot reasonably doubt that it is the *direct* source of the name of the music.

Indeed, when in 1919 the first concert by a jazz band was announced in Columbia, South Carolina, there was thunderstruck horror among the city's white and mostly sternly Baptist population, since they had never heard *jazz* used in any sense other than 'copulation'. Such reports appear to confirm the conclusion that the music takes its name directly from a common but obscene name for sexual activity.

I mentioned above that no linguists were asking questions about the word *jazz* in the 1930s. But a historian of music named Herbert Asbury was in fact inquiring into the origins of the music at that time. Asbury was not especially interested in the name, but he nevertheless turned up some possibly valuable information. According to Asbury, the first known jazz band was a group formed in New Orleans about 1895 and calling itself the *Razzy Dazzy Spasm Band*. Still according to Asbury, around 1900 a second band booked an appearance at a dance hall using the same name, which provoked some hostility from the original group. Fearing trouble, the owner of the dance hall altered his posters to read *Razzy Dazzy Jazzy Band*, and this, Asbury tells us, was the first use of *jazz* in print. Asbury tells us that we can be sure of these things because he managed to interview two surviving members of the original band. Perhaps, but these details are not very informative.

So where did this slang word *jazz* come from to start with? Nobody knows. It is notoriously difficult to trace the origins of slang words even in highly literate societies – and southern American black society in the decades after the Civil War was not especially literate. Naturally, several linguists have suggested that the word *jazz* might have been taken from one of the West African languages spoken by the Africans carried as slaves to the American south before the Civil War. This is not impossible. But we happen to know quite a bit about the languages spoken by those slaves, and no such word as *jazz* has so far been found in any of them: the closest thing anybody has found is Mandingo *jasi* 'act out of character' or Temne *yas* 'be energetic', of which the first has a useless meaning and the second has an unhelpful form. Moreover, apart perhaps from one or two names of foods, there is as yet no certain case of a word of West African origin surviving in the speech of African Americans after the Civil War. It appears that the destruction of African culture and language brought about by enslavement was so complete that even individual words of the original languages did not survive.

Another possibility is French. While nobody knows exactly *where* jazz music originated, the favourite guess of musical historians is the city of New Orleans, with its great musical traditions, with its known early jazz bands, with its celebrated degree of sexual licence, and of course with its French-speaking culture. A verb *jaser* is apparently recorded in New Orleans French, with the senses 'speed up', 'chatter' and 'make fun of'. This does not look especially helpful, even though the meaning of 'speed up' is vaguely applicable to jazz music, some forms of which give the impression of speeding up during the performance of a piece. But the seemingly required sexual sense is absent from this word.

More interesting is the French word *chasse*, whose central sense is 'chase, pursuit, hunt' and whose Old French ancestor is the source of English *chase*. French dictionaries report that this word also has various sexual senses, including 'chasing' sexual partners (as in English *chasing women* and *skirt-chasing*) and 'being on heat' (of a female). In addition, the famous *Robert* dictionary tells us that, in the French of New Orleans – of all places – *chasse* has the obscene slang sense of 'sexual intercourse'. This is an intriguing possibility, especially since some sources report that *jazz* was sometimes written *jass* in the earliest days.

So, we can conclude that the word *jazz* was coined by English-speaking African Americans, either before or – more likely – after the Civil War, almost certainly in the American south. It may well have been coined in New Orleans, and it may well have been taken from the reportedly obscene local French term *chasse*, but we cannot be at all sure about either of these things. For a long time the word was mainly an obscene sexual term, but, eventually, when an exciting new form of music developed out of the earlier ragtime, some time around 1900, the word was for some reason applied to this music. Some scholars speculate that jazz music originated in the brothels of New Orleans, which we know provided patrons with music and dancing, as well as with the more obvious services; this idea provides an instant explanation of the name 'jazz music', but we have no evidence to confirm it.

The connection between obscene sexual terms and music among African Americans (and others) is hardly confined to this one item. Other musical terms with sexual origins include *boogie-woogie* (originally 'syphilis'), *swing* (originally 'copulate'), the *juke* of *juke box* (a *juke house* was a brothel in the south), and possibly also *gig* (an old term for the female sexual organs, but this etymology is far from certain). In addition, the famous early jazz musician Ferdinand Joseph La Menthe 'Jelly Roll' Morton – who once claimed to have invented the name *jazz* for the music – took his nickname from *jelly roll*, a longstanding slang term for the female sexual organs. The names of later popular musics derived from African American culture, such as *rock 'n' roll* and *funk*, appear also to have had strong sexual connotations.

All this is fascinating, but, sadly, it doesn't add up to a complete account of the origins of the word *jazz*. We may never know.

A pretty story: that dratted moth

In early 2000, Mr Joe Trela was a contestant on the American edition of the TV quiz programme *Who Wants to Be a Millionaire?* He did well and reached the final round. For one million dollars, he was asked this question: 'What insect shorted out an early supercomputer and inspired the term "computer bug"?' Mr Trela replied 'A moth', and claimed his million dollars.

The story behind this question is well known. In 1947, a group of US Navy technical staff were working on an early computer romantically named the Mark II. The Mark II was hardly a supercomputer: though very large, it was mechanical and clunky, and less powerful than the calculators given away today in boxes of corn flakes. One day the machine mysteriously broke down, and at first no one could figure out what had gone wrong. Eventually one member of the group opened the machine up and peered inside. Spotting something odd, he reached in with a pair of tweezers and pulled out the frazzled remains of a moth. That moth had crept inside the machine and into an electrical relay, shorting out the machine and frying itself to death.

Afterward, the story was told and retold by another member of the group, a navy officer named Grace Murray Hopper. Dr Hopper was a brilliant mathematician and a pioneering computer scientist; she was one of the designers of the computer language Cobol; and she reached the rank of rear admiral before she retired. Her story was eloquent. 'From then on', she said, 'whenever anything went wrong with a computer, we said it had bugs in it.'

There is hard evidence to back up her story. The US military is nothing if not meticulous, and the remains of that deceased moth were taped into the group's logbook, together with an account of the incident, dated 9 September 1947. The logbook is now in the Smithsonian Institution's Museum of American History, and it still contains what is left of the unfortunate insect – rather more substantial evidence than word historians can usually hope to uncover.

Without a doubt, this account of the origin of the computer term *bug* is one of the most wonderful stories in all of English etymology. Unfortunately, however, it is not true.

The moth was real enough, and so was its demise inside the Mark II. But this was not, in fact, the origin of the word *bug*. Specialists have demonstrated, in their usual painstaking way, that the term *bug*, in the sense of 'obscure fault in a machine', was in use long before that moth met its maker inside a US navy computer.

To start with, you will not be surprised to learn that the Mark II computer had been preceded by an earlier machine named – wait for it – the Mark I. The Mark I had been set up by IBM engineers in 1944, and those engineers were already using *bug* for a computing fault. In fact, the term *bug* is recorded as early as 1889, when the British magazine *Pall Mall Gazette* published an interview with the American inventor Thomas Edison, in which Edison remarked that he had found 'a bug' in the phonograph which he was then inventing. The *Gazette* went on to explain helpfully that the word *bug* was 'an expression for solving a difficulty, and implying that some imaginary insect has secreted itself inside and is causing all the trouble'.

Furthermore, examination of Admiral Hopper's papers, also stored in the Smithsonian, shows that she and her colleagues had been using *bug* in the same sense for several years before the incident with the moth. Very tellingly, the logbook entry accompanying the deceased moth is labelled 'first actual case of bug being found' – confirming that *bug* was already familiar to the navy group, and that they were amused by the coincidence of finding that a bug had been produced, for once, by a real insect.

So, in spite of what you will read in innumerable books and on countless websites, the world's most famous moth had nothing to do with the origin of the computing term *bug*. We are looking at an example of a pretty story destroyed by some ugly facts. How, then, did this word originate? Nobody knows.

A not-so-pretty story: pregnant chads

During the American presidential election of 2000, almost every English speaker suddenly learned a new word: *chad*. As everybody now knows, the state of Florida was using voting machines which recorded a vote by punching a hole in a card – and the little bit of material punched out of the card is a chad. Much of the kerfuffle in Florida had to do with chads which failed to let go of the card but which clung on resolutely, bulging or dangling in some fashion. But where does the word *chad* come from? Once again, nobody knows, but the investigation so far has been interesting.

To begin with, punched cards have been used for decades for storing information and for controlling machines. The giant American multinational IBM, best known today for its computers, in fact built much of its early success on manufacturing card-punching machines, before computers were invented.

The floor under a card-punching machine soon becomes covered with a thick layer of little bits of card that have been punched out. I don't have to imagine this, because I'm old enough to remember the 1960s, when computers were programmed with boxes full of punched cards, and an essential step in doing anything at all with a computer was punching out a box or two of cards.

There were several names for the refuse on the floor. It was called (*keypunch*) *droppings*, *confetti* or *chaff*. This last word is identical to the name of the metal confetti dropped by warplanes to confuse enemy radar. At some point, however, the stuff came to be called *chad*. Originally, this word was uncountable, like *sawdust*: you could speak of 'the chad on the floor', just like 'the sawdust on the floor', but you couldn't say 'a chad' any more than you can say 'a sawdust'. But, somewhere along the line, the word changed its grammatical behaviour, and a single punched scrap became *a chad*.

Most dictionaries agree that *chad* in this sense is nowhere recorded in writing before 1959. One dictionary claims 1947, but gives no citation. But these are citations in writing, and we may reasonably suppose that the word was in spoken use for some time before it came to be written down.

Five proposals exist to explain the origin of the word.

Proposal one sees *chad* as an alteration of the more familiar word *chaff*, which of course has the same sense. This is not crazy, but a change of /f/ to /d/ is unusual, to say the least.

Proposal two derives the word from a Scottish dialect word *chad*, meaning 'gravel'. Scottish dialect words are not well recorded in most dictionaries, and even my Scottish dictionary doesn't have this one, but I'm prepared to believe that *chad* means 'gravel' somewhere in Scotland. However, the word we are interested in seems to be chiefly American, and why should an obscure Scots word be picked up by Americans, long after the main migration of Scots speakers from Scotland and Ireland to North America in the eighteenth and nineteenth centuries? And why should a word for 'gravel' be applied to fluffy bits of card? The stuff on the floor is really not very much like gravel, and this idea is only a desperate wild guess.

Proposal three sees *chad* as an acronym, derived from the initial letters of the expression *card hole aggregate debris*. People are always dreaming up these acronymic stories, and they are almost always fairy tales. Maybe you've seen the story that *posh* derives from the desire of well-heeled ship passengers to travel 'port out, starboard home'. Hardly. Acronyms were very rare in English before the second half of the twentieth century, and anyway the earlier form of the word was *push*, with *posh* not recorded before 1918. If we want to, we can invent one of these for just about any word. For example, since English came into existence as the newly introduced language of southern England, I can interpret *English* as 'emerging new Germanic language in southern hills'. This took me the better part of three minutes to construct, and very likely you can do better.

Proposal four is more complicated. Someone has discovered that there once existed an American card-punching machine which did not punch any material out of the card: instead, it merely incised a U-shape in the card, and the material inside the U had to be bent back to produce a hole. And this device was apparently called the *Chadless keypunch*. The guess is that this odd device must have been invented by a certain Mr Chadless, who named it after himself. The operators who used it noted that, unlike other machines, it produced no confetti. Since the thing was called a 'Chadless' keypunch, they assumed that the intended sense must be 'without chad', and they therefore concluded that *chad* must be another word for 'confetti'.

But the problem is that no US patent has ever been issued to anyone called Chadless, and indeed there seems to be no record of a single individual with this name anywhere in the USA at any time. Moreover, the US Patent Classification calls the machine a 'chadless keypunch', with a small C. We must therefore presume that this machine was so called because it produced no chad, and that our word *chad* is therefore older than this machine.

There remains proposal five, which is the least explicit of all. Long ago, the US Army was one of the principal users of card-punching machines. It seems inevitable that the Army's military users would have coined one or two robust slang terms for the mess these machines left on the floor, quite possibly slang terms involving the notion of 'droppings'. It may be that *chad* started life as a cleaned-up version of one of these slang terms. Sadly, the vulgar slang terms used by a closed group of people are hardly ever documented in writing. Maybe there's an ancient American soldier out there who remembers what he and his buddies were calling the stuff around 1935, but, if so, we haven't yet tracked him down.

A scholarly blunder

In linguistics, as in other subjects, scholarly work is not infallible. Sometimes scholars commit blunders which then have to be recognised and painfully repaired by later scholars. Here is an example.

English has a word *bizarre*, meaning 'very strange'. The same word is found with the same meaning in French, where the form is *bizarre*, and in German, where the form is *bizarr*, and in Italian, where the form is *bizzarro*. The Spanish form is *bizarro*, but the word has a rather different meaning in Spanish: the sense there is 'valiant', 'brave'.

The English word is recorded from 1648. Since the French word is recorded somewhat earlier, in 1533, no one doubts that English has taken the word from French. But where did the French get it?

In 1607, the Basque writer Baltásar de Etxabe put forward the first-ever etymological proposal for this word. Etxabe suggested that Spanish *bizarro* 'valiant' must have been taken from the Basque word *bizar*, which means 'beard'. His idea was that a beard is a sign of manliness, and therefore of gallantry and bravery. So, the thinking went, Spanish soldiers, who were normally bearded in those days, came to be nicknamed *bizarros* 'beards' as a reflection of their bravery.

This doesn't seem implausible, but how did the French acquire the word and assign it such a different meaning? Etxabe didn't consider this, but somebody else proposed that the clean-shaven French soldiers were so startled by the appearance of the bearded Spanish troops – Spain and France were frequently at war during the period – that they borrowed the Spanish word in the sense of 'strange, weird'. And, of course, it was the French sense that was later borrowed into English, German and Italian.

Etxabe's proposal leads therefore to the following outline of the history of the word *bizarre*:

> Basque 'beard' > Spanish 'valiant' > French 'strange' > English, German, Italian 'strange'

Many scholars have found this account persuasive. One who certainly did was the German linguist Friedrich Diez, who almost single-handedly founded the comparative study of the Romance languages. Diez embraced Etxabe's idea and championed it in his publications. As a result of Diez's influence, this account of the origin of *bizarre* has been accepted by scholars for generations. It is presented as gospel in any number of dictionaries and reference books, including some of the most serious scholarly publications, and it is repeated in many popular books on words and word origins. Up and down Britain, pub quizmasters have for years been asking 'From what language does the word *bizarre* come?' and demanding the answer 'Basque'. Just recently, the weekly quiz in the *Guardian* newspaper asked the same question and insisted on the same answer. The Basque origin of *bizarre* has become for many people just one more piece of truth.

Engaging as this story is, however, it contains not a grain of truth. In the 1960s, two Spanish linguists became suspicious of the standard story and began to look into the evidence. In particular, they looked at Italian, which had been rather neglected in the standard account. According to the standard account, Italian must have taken its word *bizzarro* from French. But such a route means that the word must have existed in French earlier than in Italian. That turned out not to be the case.

The first record of the word *bizarre* in French dates from 1533. But Italian *bizzarro*, which is supposed to be later than the French word, is in fact very much earlier. The Italian word is recorded from the thirteenth century onward; it even occurs in Dante's classic fourteenth century work *The Divine Comedy*, and it is also found in the works of his younger contemporary, Boccaccio.

Words are, of course, commonly recorded in writing only after they have been in use in speech for some time – perhaps a few weeks or months, perhaps a hundred years or more. The first record of a word in writing is unlikely to represent its first use in the language. Nevertheless, something is badly wrong here. The Italian word *bizzarro* is recorded in writing nearly three hundred years earlier than the first record of French *bizarre* (in 1533) or of Spanish *bizarro* (in 1528). Moreover, the word is recorded repeatedly and frequently in Italian during the three centuries in which there is no trace of the word in French or Spanish. This evidence suggests *strongly* that the word existed in Italian long, long before it existed in French or Spanish or any other language, and therefore that the standard account of the word is wrong. It looks as if the word originated in Italian and spread from there to the other European languages.

Of course, the three-century gap doesn't quite *prove* that the word originated in Italian, but it certainly makes any other story awkward and difficult to maintain. Moreover, the Italian word has an identifiable Italian source: the Italian word *bizza*. This word is recorded from the thirteenth century in the sense 'quick flash of anger'. The word still exists in modern standard Italian, in the slightly different sense of 'tantrum'. Italian *bizzarro* is clearly derived from this *bizza*, since, in its earliest occurrences, Italian *bizzarro* means 'tending to quick flashes of anger', 'irascible'. Over time, the word gradually shifted its meaning in Italian, roughly as follows: 'tending to quick flashes of anger' > 'unpredictable' > 'eccentric' > 'strange, weird'. In the last few centuries, the Italian word has meant 'weird', and this is the sense in which the word was taken into French, and from French into English. (Italian also has another derivative, *bizzoso*, which means 'irritable', 'wayward', 'strange', but this word has not been taken into any other languages.)

That leaves the odd Spanish sense unexplained. We still aren't sure why or how the word *bizarro* acquired its quite different sense in Spanish. But in regional varieties of Italian *bizzarro* is recorded in favourable senses like 'spirited', 'frisky', and, in the dialect of the northern Italian city Genoa, even just plain 'good'. Probably one of these regional Italian senses was taken into Spanish.

How did scholars manage to get this story so wrong for so long? After all, the Italian evidence is abundant and decisive, and the writings of Dante and Boccaccio are anything but obscure. I surmise that the explanation lies in the familiar human frailties. Somebody had already told a story about *bizarre*; that story looked good on the page; it had been endorsed by eminent philologists and it appeared in all the best reference sources. The word had apparently already been dealt with satisfactorily, so why worry about it when there were so many other problems awaiting urgent attention?

A genuine Basque word in English

As a rule, if you name a language, you can find at least one word which has been taken into English from that language. English has *geyser* from Icelandic, *ski* from Norwegian, *smorgasbord* from Swedish, *sauna* from Finnish, and so on right across the globe. But Basque is something of a challenge.

We have seen that, in spite of the reference books, the word *bizarre* is not of Basque origin. Several people have suggested that the curious word *jingo* in the expression *By jingo!* might derive from Basque *jinko* 'god', but this wild guess has been disposed of by the philologists, who have demonstrated that *By jingo!* originated as a piece of conjurors' mumbo jumbo, like *abracadabra*. The

American word *chaparral* 'dense, shrubby and thorny vegetation' derives from Spanish *chaparra*, which may in turn be taken from Basque *txapar*, of somewhat similar meaning, but the history of these words is murky and uncertain.

An English word that does derive from Basque is *jai alai*, the name of the sport – a member of the squash family – in which each player catches and flings the ball with a long wicker basket strapped to his arm. But there's something strange about this borrowing: the name *jai alai* is not used in Basque.

The Basques are a plain and blunt people who care little for airs and graces. The Basque word for 'ball' is *pilota*, borrowed from Spanish *pelota*. And the game of jai alai, a Basque invention and the Basque national game, is just called in Basque *pilota* – or 'ball'.

In the late nineteenth century, the Basque Romantic writer Serafín Baroja found himself mulling over the observation that the Basque national game was known in Basque by a foreign name. He resolved to create a native Basque name for the sport, and the name he came up with was *jai alai* – from Basque *jai* 'festival' and *alai* 'happy, merry' – and therefore literally 'merry festival'.

This coinage met no enthusiasm among the Basques, who continued to call their game *pilota*, as they still do today. Oddly, though, the new name *jai alai* gained a foothold in Spanish, and from Spanish it passed into American English. Today jai alai is an important sport, not only in the Basque Country but also in much of Latin America and in parts of the United States, especially Florida. The game is always called *jai alai* in English, and so this is an English word which has been taken from Basque, but a rather strange one, since this 'Basque' name is not used at all in Basque.

If you visit a large Basque town with a jai-alai court, you will find that the local people call the game *pilota*, just as a jai-alai player is called a *pilotari*. Nobody calls the game *jai alai* in Basque. However, there is one more thing. Somewhere within fifty yards of the jai-alai court you will certainly find a bar called *Bar Jai-Alai*. But that's as far as it goes.

Putting aside the rather peculiar case of *jai alai*, there is still one familiar English word which is beyond question of Basque origin, though the English meaning bears no relation to the Basque meaning and results from an accident. It is most unlikely that you could ever guess the identity of the one English word which derives indisputably from Basque: it's *silhouette*. This will take a little explaining.

Basque has two different kinds of S sound, distinguished by two slightly different positions of the tongue. The two sounds are spelled Z and S in Basque orthography, although the sound spelled Z is the one that is more similar to the sound /s/ in English. This sound occurs in the word *zulo*, which means 'hole'.

This word occurs as the first element in a surname whose second element is the extremely common suffix *-eta*, which means '(place with) lots of'. So, the surname *Zuloeta*, often pronounced and spelled *Zulueta*, means 'the place with lots of holes (in the ground)'.

On the north side of the Pyrenees, the French Basques pronounce the word for 'hole' slightly differently: their form is *zilho*. The surname just mentioned accordingly appears in northern Basque as *Zilhueta*. This name was taken into French in the form *Silhouette*.

Étienne de Silhouette was an eighteenth-century French politician of some note. Silhouette was of Basque origin and bore a Basque surname, but he spoke no Basque at all, and considered himself a Frenchman. In the 1750s, Silhouette served the French government as minister of finance. In this post, he soon acquired an unenviable reputation for penny-pinching and cheese-paring. And then something else happened: Silhouette's surname became a popular label for an artistic representation of the bare profile of a face.

Nobody is sure just why this happened, and proposals are numerous. Perhaps the sketchy and unfinished appearance of a silhouette reminded people of Silhouette's financial skimping. Perhaps Silhouette himself made a hobby of constructing such drawings. We will probably never know, but there is no doubt at all that, during Silhouette's term in office, *silhouette* became the ordinary French word for an outline drawing of a face in profile. By 1785 this French word had been taken into English as the name for such a drawing intended as a minor work of art, although it was not until about 1870 that the English word came to be applied more generally to anything seen in outline.

So, a Basque surname meaning 'the place with lots of holes' has passed via French into English as our everyday word for something seen only in outline. All this is the result of a series of accidents that took place in France in the eighteenth century. If Silhouette had borne a different name, our word meaning 'silhouette' would now be something completely different, while, if Silhouette had merely had a different policy, we might not have a word meaning 'silhouette' at all. Who knows?

Making up our own words

Not all English words derive from Anglo-Saxon, Latin or Old French (or, indeed, from any language directly). Recall from Chapter 1 the huge number of words which have entered English since the Second World War. New words pour into English every year, so many that some publishers bring out annual volumes of last year's new words.

These new words are of every kind. Many are technical and formal. A few years ago, for example, scientists discovered that radon gas was seeping out of the granite bedrock in Cornwall and into houses built on the rock. Since radon is radioactive, its presence can make the people in an affected house sick, and so the medical scientists have coined the new word *geopathic* – literally 'involving earth-illness' – as a label for such illnesses. But many of our new words arise in far more informal ways.

Around the beginning of the eighteenth century, there arose something of a fashion in England for shortening long words: for example, *reputation* was shortened to *rep*, and *positively* to *pozz*. This fashion was roundly condemned by Jonathan Swift and other linguistic conservatives of the day, and it soon died out with few lasting consequences. But one of these new short forms has survived to our own day. The Latin phrase *mobile vulgus*, 'the fickle crowd', was used in English as a label for the mass of ordinary people, seen by the upper classes as irresponsible and untrustworthy. The fashion for shortening converted this into *mob*, and *mob* has remained in the language, although its sense has generally shifted to that of an unruly or violent crowd.

Linguists call this process *clipping*, the extraction of a short part of a longer word or phrase in order to obtain a new and shorter word of the same meaning. The eighteenth-century taste for clipping did not long survive, but a new enthusiasm for clipping has arisen in our own day. We now clip our words far more eagerly than Swift's contemporaries ever did, and we pay no attention to any critics who may inveigh against our practice.

(Incidentally, the word *mob* has undergone some remarkable developments in Australia. First, it has become the ordinary group noun for kangaroos: Australians speak of *a mob of roos*. Second, it has acquired the new sense of 'group of people'. This sense is especially common in Aboriginal English, as in *My mob lives Yuendemu way*. Finally, I am told by a colleague in Australia that the word, in the assimilated form *mapa*, has been taken into several native Australian languages as a plural marker for nouns!)

We have clipped *brassière* to *bra*, *violoncello* to *cello*, *gymnasium* to *gym*, *telephone* to *phone*, *influenza* to *flu*, *refrigerator* to *fridge*, *alligator* to *gator*, *crocodile* to *croc*, *hippopotamus* to *hippo*, *rhinoceros* to *rhino* and of course *omnibus* to *bus*.

And we seem to be always on the lookout for a chance to clip something else. We now often see *magazine* clipped to *mag*, *bisexual* to *bi*, *cigarette* to *cig*, *university* to *uni*, *difference* to *diff* (as in *What's the diff?*), and *promotion* to *promo*, to name just a few.

Occasionally we decorate our clippings with a diminutive suffix *-ie* or *-y*. This gives us *budgie* 'budgerigar', *hankie* 'handkerchief', *barbie* 'barbecue', Australian *umpy* 'umpire' (but compare American *ump* and British nothing), British *telly* 'television', *granny* 'grandmother', Australian *Uey* 'U-turn', and British *Corrie* for *Coronation Street*, the name of a soap opera. Several decades ago, the exciting new word *transistor radio* was rapidly clipped in Britain to *tranny*, but advances in technology have already made both forms obsolete (not helped, perhaps, by the development of the identical clipped form used for *transvestite*).

Sometimes a different suffix is preferred. The Australians have something of a taste for *-o*, as in *arvo* 'afternoon', *milko* 'milkman', *reffo* 'refugee', *garbo* 'garbage collector', *ambo* 'ambulanceman, paramedic' and the amazing *Seppo*

'American'. This word is very widespread, and young Australians use it without knowing where it comes from: it's a clipping of *septic tank*, old rhyming slang for *Yank*. Upper-middle-class British English is inordinately fond of *-ers* and *-er*, as in *champers* from *champagne*, *Roller* from *Rolls-Royce*, the celebrated cricket commentators *Blowers* and *Johnners* (*Henry Blofeld* and *Brian Johnston*), *rugger* from *rugby football*, and the now fossilised case of *soccer* from *association football*. Popular British English likes *-s*, as in *turps* for *turpentine* or as in *Becks*, from *David Beckham*, a prominent soccer player.

Clippings can be more complex with the extraction of multiple pieces, as in the clipping of *science fiction* to *sci-fi*, of *biographical picture* to *biopic*, of British *methylated spirits* to *meths*, or of British *mathematics* to *maths* (compare American *math*). And, of course, the TV series *Absolutely Fabulous* has seldom been known as anything but *Ab Fab*.

The meaning of a clipped form is generally the same as that of its source, but the shorter form is often much more informal. The informal nature of *hippo*, *hankie*, *fridge* and *telly* should be obvious, while *prez* for *president* and *tache* for *moustache* are very informal indeed. On the other hand, the originally clipped forms *cello*, *bus*, *mob* and *bra* have entirely lost their earlier informal status and become the ordinary words for what they denote. On occasion, a clipped form can be dismissive. For example, *lesbian* has the clipped forms *lez* and *lezzy*; my dictionary labels both of these 'informal', but in my experience they are offensive (and aggressive) more often than not.

A rare example of a clipped form which has shifted its meaning is *varsity*. This started life as a clipping of *university*, and it reflects a now-obsolete pronunciation of that word. But the meaning of the word has drifted away from that of its source: it is now mainly applied to sports teams, and in American English it has lost almost all connection with universities, and is chiefly used of high-school sports teams.

Observe that clipped forms are real words, and not merely abbreviations. They behave like other words. First, clipped forms can be inflected just like other words (*gyms*, *fridges*, *crocs*, *buses*). Note the interesting case of the clipped form of *disrespect*, coined in the 1980s. This is *diss*, also spelled *dis*, and it started life as a noun, as in *The shock jocks are filling their air time with diss*. But it was quickly converted to a verb, and it instantly acquired all the inflected forms of a verb, as in *He was dissing me* and *It ain't no brother that disses us like that*.

Second, clipped forms can form compounds like other words (*gym shoes*, *fridge magnet*, *croc handler*, *bus stop*). Indeed, while a *gym* may still be a *gymnasium* in some contexts, it is scarcely possible to speak of *gymnasium shorts* or *gymnasium shoes*. And nobody would dream of referring to the American baseball player *Hippo Vaughn* as *Hippopotamus Vaughn*.

Third, clipped forms are entered as words in good dictionaries; and they are legal in tournament Scrabble™. If you check the Scrabble™ dictionary which is official in your country (different English-speaking countries use different ones), you will find almost every one of my examples entered, though one or two of the most recent and informal coinages will probably be absent.

Clipping is just one of a number of engaging techniques used in recent years to create new English words from existing resources, without appealing to foreign languages. Another is *blending*, in which pieces of two existing words are combined to create another. Familiar examples include *smog* (*smoke* plus *fog*), *brunch* (*breakfast* plus *lunch*), *motel* (*motor* plus *hotel*), *guesstimate* (*guess* plus *estimate*) and *Paralympics* (*paraplegic* plus *Olympics*). Blends are greatly favoured by advertisers and promoters trying to draw attention to their products, and such coinages as *sexsational*, *infomercial* and *rockumentary* have now achieved at least a marginal foothold in the language.

Yet another procedure is *back-formation*, in which an *apparent* affix is removed from a word. Unlike my other processes, back-formation is not always deliberate. English used to have the words *pease* for a kind of vegetable and *cherries* for a kind of fruit; both of these were singular, but they happened to end in what *sounded* to English speakers like a plural ending, and so this non-existent 'plural' ending was removed to create new singulars, *pea* and *cherry*, which had not previously existed.

Our word *sculptor* is taken straight from Latin. It happens to end in what sounds like the familiar agent suffix -*er*, as in *singer* and *painter*, and as a result this non-existent suffix was removed to produce the new verb *sculpt*. This is now what sculptors do: they sculpt. Latin *editor* and French *burglar* have likewise led to the verbs *edit* and *burgle*.

Different again is *reanalysis*, in which a word is broken up into pieces which do not at all represent its original structure. A familiar case is provided by *hamburger*, which is taken from German, in which it consists of the city name *Hamburg* and the German suffix -*er*, meaning 'from'. A Hamburger is therefore someone from Hamburg, just as a Frankfurter is from Frankfurt and a Wiener is from Wien (Vienna). As well as being applied to citizens of these places, these adjectives can also be applied to their products. In the case of Frankfurt and Vienna, the added -*er* is normally associated with a particular type of sausage (the *Berliner*, on the other hand, is a type of doughnut). Strangely, the beef patty named the hamburger is *not* the native sausage of the north German city of Hamburg, however. A long debate continues on how the product came to be called this, but it isn't important for this discussion: the word-formation pattern is the same.

English speakers in North America, however, came to reanalyse the word. Because a hamburger contains meat, and *ham* is the name of a kind of meat (even though it's the wrong meat), the word began to be broken down as though it were *ham* plus *burger*, and as a result we now have cheeseburgers, vege-burgers, chickenburgers, and who knows how many more. In Britain, things have gone so far that the original article is now called a *beefburger*.

Remember the word *bikini*, which was taken from the name of the Pacific atoll where some early atomic bombs were tested, because of the 'explosive' effect of the new outfit at a time when women's bathing costumes normally covered a great deal more skin than they do now. When an even more shocking costume was introduced a couple of decades later, consisting only of the bottom half of a bikini, a new name was clearly called for. Some wag noticed that the first syllable of *bikini* was, entirely by chance, *bi-*, which looks like the element meaning 'two', as in *bifocals*, *bilateral* and *bisexual*. That wag therefore 'replaced' this 'prefix' with the element *mono-*, meaning 'one', as in *monosyllabic*, and came up with *monokini* for the scandalous new costume. This name has remained rather marginal in English, but it has become fully established in French, where it is so familiar that it has already undergone clipping: today no fashionable young French woman wears anything at the beach other than *le mono*.

A somewhat different case of reanalysis is provided by that now unavoidable prefix *mini-*. English has long had the words *minimum* and *miniature*. These words are not connected in any way, and the resemblance in form is purely by chance. But both words happen to have meanings involving 'very small'. Around 1960, somebody seized upon this observation, extracted a new prefix *mini-*, meaning 'very small', and used it to coin that pioneering word *miniskirt*. (If you can remember the earlier *knee-peeper*, you have seen a few fashions come and go.) Since then, this entirely new prefix has exploded across the language: nothing is *miniature* any more, and hardly anything is even *small*. Instead, we have *mini-books*, *mini-series*, *mini-cakes*, *mini-courses*, and even, for all I know, *mini-wars*.

The rarest way of obtaining new words in English is to construct them out of thin air. Yet this does happen occasionally.

On the back of almost every book – probably including this one – there is a paragraph telling you how wonderful the book is and why you absolutely have to buy it. This paragraph formerly had no name, but publishers have to talk about it, and so they needed a name. In the early years of the twentieth century, a publisher invited the American humorist Gelett Burgess to coin a name. Burgess's inspired proposal was *blurb*: he coined this word out of thin air, but ever since his day this has been the name for that paragraph on the back of a book.

Another example comes from mathematics. The number ten to the power one hundred – written in digits as one followed by a hundred zeros – is not mathematically special, but it engages the imagination of us human beings. In the 1930s, the American mathematician Edward Kasner asked his nine-year-old nephew to coin a name for this number. What Kasner got was *googol*, and mathematicians have used this label ever since in their popular writings, though they seldom use it among themselves. The word has even given rise to a derivative, *googolplex*, the name for the unimaginably huge number written as one followed by a googol of zeros.

A final example of coinage from thin air comes from chemistry. In the 1930s, chemists managed to synthesise a new polymer with remarkably appealing properties, including the capacity to provide the sheerest and sexiest women's stockings ever worn. Needing a name for their wonderful stuff, the chemists came up with *nylon*, a name again coined from nothing because of its agreeable sound. (Some popular books will tell you a pretty story about New York and London, but sadly this is fiction.)

It is even possible for new words to be created by mistake. English has long had a word *darkling*, meaning 'almost dark', and formed historically by adding to *dark* the suffix *-ling*. Encountering this word, the Romantic poet Lord Byron (1788–1824) misunderstood it. He took it to be the *-ing* form of a supposed verb *darkle*, and so he extracted this item in all innocence and began using it in his poems as a verb meaning 'get dark'. Several other nineteenth-century writers picked up the new word from Byron and used it in their own writing, and in fact the word *darkle* enjoyed some currency in Victorian literature before finally dropping almost entirely out of use. It is rather as though Byron had encountered the phrase *my darling wife* and concluded that my wife darls a lot.

A word created by mistake has been dubbed a *mumpsimus*, and another English mumpsimus is the now rather old-fashioned *helpmeet*, meaning 'a companion who gives assistance'. English used to have an adjective *meet*, meaning 'suitable', 'proper'. In the King James Bible of 1611, Genesis 2:18 tells us that God created Adam's future wife as 'an help meet for him' – that is, suitable for him. But, in a seventeenth-century printing of the Bible, this phrase was mistakenly put on the page as 'an help-meet for him'. As a result, many readers took *helpmeet* to be a single English word, and they assigned to this word the obvious meaning. But, since the second part of the new *helpmeet* seemed mysterious, the word was altered by some writers in the eighteenth century to *helpmate*, which seems to make more sense.

One last example is the fabric name *tweed*. The original form was *twill*, which still exists in English. In Scotland, the local form of this word was *tweel*. Then, in 1831, this Scots word appeared in the catalogue of a Scottish cloth manufacturer, where it was either misprinted (according to one account) or misread by a London hatter (according to another account) as *tweed*. This mistaken form seems to have been reinforced by the existence of the *Tweed*, the river separating Scotland from England.

Runcible

I will close this chapter with a word whose origin troubled people for a long time. The Victorian nonsense-writer Edward Lear's most famous poem is probably *The Owl and the Pussycat*. In that poem we read that the two title characters 'dined upon mince, and slices of quince, which they ate with a runcible spoon'. A good dictionary will tell you that this gadget is in fact a bizarre combination of a fork and a knife with a spoon-like shape: it is a fork, usually with three sharp prongs, the whole curved like the bowl of a spoon, with the outer edge of one prong sharpened like a knife.

But where did this odd-looking name come from? Lear's is the earliest known mention of the name, so it appears that he invented it, long before the gadget itself was invented: an unusual case of a thing being invented to go with its name. Proposals were varied. Perhaps the name comes from the obsolete English word *rouncival*, the name of a kind of large pea. Or perhaps Lear based the word on the name of Robert Runcie, who was the Chief Under Butler at Knowsley Hall, near Liverpool, where Lear was employed for a while by the owner, the Earl of Derby. Why Runcie? Because it was his responsibility to clean the silver spoons. Then again, perhaps Lear was making fun of his friend George Runcy, who held 'advanced' views about raising children and who had designed a new kind of angled spoon that allowed very small children to feed themselves. These appear to be deep waters, and we are in danger of testy scholarly exchanges.

But recall the importance, in etymological work, of scrutinising *all* the evidence. In this case, the most useful material to examine is the whole corpus of Lear's nonsense verses. When we do that, we discover that Lear used the word *runcible* on several occasions, and applied it to all sorts of things. For example, the Pobble's Aunt Jobisa possessed a *runcible cat*, with crimson whiskers, and elsewhere Lear writes of a *runcible hat*, a *runcible goose* and a *runcible wall*. We may safely conclude, I think, that Lear coined the nonsense word *runcible* out of thin air, because he liked the sound of it. If *we* think only of runcible spoons, that is probably only because *The Owl and the Pussycat* is the one piece of Lear's that most of us have read.

Conclusion

This chapter has demonstrated that, while definite patterns underlie word formation and word origin, the ways in which they are employed often appear random, and are definitely fickle. In the next chapter we will consider a particular type of word formation which is, if anything, even more eccentric and often has considerable time depth: place names.

4 Skunk-Leek – my kind of town: what's in a name?

Names are peculiar

Far more than ordinary words, names develop historically in ways which are complicated, unexpected and downright peculiar. Names are subject to all sorts of local and idiosyncratic changes, and we usually cannot predict how one name will behave by watching what happens to another one.

For example, I live in the English city of *Brighton*. What is the origin of this name? The ending looks familiar enough: there are hundreds of settlement names ending in *-ton*, which represents the Old English word *tūn* 'enclosed piece of land', 'homestead', later 'village'. But this leaves us apparently stuck with *bright*, certainly a good English word, but one that would be singular in its construction for all English names from that period. Often we find *-ton* attached to a personal name, as in *Edgbaston*, from the Old English personal name *Ecgbald*, and thus meaning 'Ecgbald's homestead', or to the name of a geographical feature, as in the common *Stratton*, whose first element is Old English *strǣt* 'Roman road', so that the whole is 'village by a Roman road'. The use of an adjective like *bright* in this context would be otherwise unknown, however.

The study of names depends absolutely upon the scrutiny of documents, and in this case we are lucky enough to have documentation of the history of the name. The earlier form of Brighton, our documents reveal, was *Bristelmestun*, or *Brighthelmston*, a perfectly ordinary and transparent name meaning 'Brighthelm's homestead'. The name has simply been rearranged over the centuries into the shorter modern form. Such drastic shortening is seldom observed in ordinary words, but, when it comes to names, almost nothing is out of bounds, and we must rely on our documentation to clarify the origins of names.

Nobody knows who Brighthelm was, since he makes no appearance in historical records. Presumably he was a local magnate of some standing. In any case, it appears that a village springing up on his land was the origin of modern Brighton, famous resort town, favourite of the Prince Regent, home of the Royal Pavilion, setting for the novel and the film *Brighton Rock*, overrun each summer by tourists and English-language students, renowned as the gay capital of Britain, site of one of the oldest nudist beaches in Britain, and home to two universities, at one of which I work. I wonder what Brighthelm would make of all this.

The branch of etymology dealing with the origins of names is called *onomastics*, and onomastics, even more than most etymological work, calls for some rather special talents and techniques. For example, if you are trying to uncover the original form and meaning of an opaque town name, and your preliminary investigations lead you to suspect an ancient compound meaning 'heather-valley', then you need to establish at least two things pretty quickly before you can usefully continue this line of investigation. First, the town must be located in a valley, or at least in something that might pass muster as a valley. Second, there must be heather growing in the area, or at least there must be evidence that heather formerly grew there in some abundance.

These requirements are often not obvious to non-professionals. Many non-professionals are completely happy to accept a name meaning 'heather-valley' without scrutiny, even if the town bearing this name is located on top of the only hill in the middle of a vast plain with no heather growing within hundreds of miles in any direction. Many non-professionals, in other words, are happy to believe that logic as we now analyse it did not exist in the past.

True, such wholly inappropriate names really are conferred once in a while. Around a thousand years ago, Eric the Red, an exile from Iceland, discovered a large expanse of land to the north and west of his homeland. He promptly named this island *Greenland*. I have flown over Greenland in an airliner, and I can confirm that, apart from a few dark smudges of bare land along the coast, Greenland is uniformly a brilliant white, because it is buried beneath one of the greatest unbroken masses of ice on the planet.

So why did Eric name the place *Greenland*? It appears that he had a political agenda. He was hoping to establish a settlement, and to attract settlers to populate it, and so he needed an appealing name. Something like 'Grim Expanse of Unbroken Ice' would probably have pulled in few settlers, and so Eric manufactured *Greenland* out of his unassisted imagination, hoping that the very name would attract settlers from Iceland – which, in spite of its name, is in fact much less icy than Greenland.

Such shenanigans are not unknown in our own day. The developers of a new town are very likely to give the place a name like *Cedar Valley* or *Palm Springs*, hoping to attract eager buyers, even though the first people to move in may find nothing more than a few houses sitting in a sea of bare mud decorated with building rubble.

And occasionally we find a name conferred for undeniably sarcastic reasons. In the eighteenth century, there was in a certain area of London a public facility of the type then delicately called a *laystall*. This was a place where citizens could dispose of their waste – in the blunt modern American phrase, a city dump. By one means or another, this pile of rotting rubbish acquired the label *Mount Pleasant*, and this name stuck. Today the site is occupied by the Royal Mail's principal sorting office in London, and the Mount Pleasant Sorting Office must be one of the few places in the world with a name commemorating the former existence of a pile of garbage.

As a rule, however, eccentric names of this type are not conferred by people who actually live in the places with the names, and the traditional names of settlements always made perfect sense to the settlers who gave those names.

It is important to realise that names make sense when they are conferred, even though later changes may render those names entirely opaque to us. Consider the town of *Bridgwater* in Somerset. At first glance, this name is obvious: it's *bridge* plus *water*, end of discussion. But, if you think about it a moment, you will realise that such a name makes little sense. Why on earth would anybody name a place 'bridge-water'? Surely almost all bridges do just that.

Once again, we must turn to the documents. The Domesday Book (the great tax census carried out by William the Conqueror's Exchequer in the 1080s) has the odd-looking *Brigealtier*, but otherwise the earliest document to contain the name, dated 1194, writes it as *Brigewaltier*, which is 'Bridge-Walter'. In other words, there is no water in the name at all, but only a man named Walter. The sense of the name was '[place at a] bridge [held by a man named] Walter' – or, in modern English, 'Walter's bridge'.

This outcome is not really surprising, because the sound /l/ was lost from the pronunciation of the name *Walter* centuries ago, even though we continue to write the name with the letter L, just as we write *walk*, *talk*, *folk* and *yolk* today where the /l/ was lost centuries ago. The surnames *Waters* and *Waterson* both mean 'son of Walter', just as *Jones* and *Johnson* both mean 'son of John'. A certain Walter Tyler, who led the Peasants' Rebellion in fourteenth-century England, is known to history as *Wat Tyler*. The famous Elizabethan courtier Sir Walter Raleigh almost certainly pronounced his name 'Water' – indeed, the title of one of his most accomplished poems, *The Ocean's Love to Cynthia*, dedicated to Queen Elizabeth I of England, only makes sense if it is interpreted as Wa(l)ter's love for the Virgin Goddess (in other words, Elizabeth). Only in modern times have we generally put that long-lost /l/ back into the pronunciation of *Walter*, under the influence of the spelling.

Slightly more complicated is the name of *Shrewsbury* in Shropshire in the west of England. This name is pronounced SHROZE-b'ry in Britain, except curiously in Shropshire itself, where the local pronunciation is SHROOZE-b'ry. The spelling suggests a connection with shrews, the tiny animals, while the majority pronunciation hints instead at a possible connection with Shrove Tuesday, the day before the beginning of Lent in February each year. But, as always, staring at the modern form of a name and making guesses is a waste of time. When we consult the documents, we find that the earliest recorded form of the name is *Scrobbesbyrig*. This name plainly contains the dative form of the very common Old English element *burg* 'fortified place', which still occurs today in dozens of place names, variously rendered as *-burg*, *-burgh*, *-bury*, *-borough*, *-brough* or *-boro*. But the first element is less obvious.

Some scholars prefer to interpret the name as 'Scrobb's fortified place', and thus as preserving a record of a now-forgotten local magnate who rejoiced in the name *Scrobb*, even though no such personal name is otherwise recorded. Most specialists, however, see the first element as nothing more than Old English *scrybb* 'scrubland', the ancestor of modern English *shrub* and of its variant *scrub*. This yields the etymology 'fortified place of the scrubland' – not very romantic, perhaps, but then most names have wholly unromantic origins. The name *Mississippi* may conjure up romantic visions of riverboat gamblers and Huck Finn, but it just means 'big river' in a local language. And the name of *Prague* may evoke elegant medieval architecture garnished with a whiff of Cold War espionage, but it appears to derive from a Slavonic word meaning 'woodland cleared by burning'.

The fascinating story of *Pimlico*

Let's take a look at the uncovering of the origin of a difficult name. The name I have chosen is *Pimlico*, whose story was worked out only a few years ago by my colleague Richard Coates. Although it is fairly typical of onomastic work, the story of *Pimlico* is particularly interesting.

Pimlico is today the name of a well-known district in southwest London, located within the borough of Westminster, most famous, perhaps, as the setting for the post-war Ealing Comedy *Passport to Pimlico*. The name is also found elsewhere in Britain and in Ireland, but these other occurrences are all first recorded considerably later than that of the Westminster Pimlico, and are presumably derived from it. The name *Pimlico* is first recorded for the place in Westminster in 1626, but this is not the earliest occurrence of the name.

Quite a few years earlier, we find the name *Pimlico* attached to a small district in a northern part of London called Hoxton. In particular, it was given to a celebrated and exceedingly popular ale-house located there. This ale-house was located close to a couple of theatres, and it is mentioned in a number of literary and theatrical works composed between 1609 and about 1658, including Ben Jonson's famous play *The Alchemist*, written in 1610. As long ago as 1849, an earlier investigator established that the earliest recorded reference to the name occurs in a tract published in 1598, called *Newes from Hogsdon* [i.e. Hoxton], which contains the line 'Have at thee, then, my merrie boyes, and hey for old Ben Pimlico's nut browne.' This allows scholars to conclude that *Ben Pimlico* was the name of the publican who owned the ale-house, and that his surname was transferred in turn to his ale, to his establishment, and to his house and a neighbouring alley. So far, so good, but now we run into a blank wall: no such surname as *Pimlico* is recorded anywhere else at all, and its formation is utterly opaque. There the matter rested for a century and a half, until Coates took up the chase.

Coates began by noting that the name is sometimes given in early sources as *Pemlico*, a fact which will be important. Then, finding no joy in Britain, he directed his inquiries to North America. His attention was immediately drawn to North Carolina, where the stretch of water lying between the Outer Banks and the coast proper is called *Pamlico Sound*. This sound takes its name from the river flowing into it, today called the *Tar-Pamlico*, but formerly, the records confirm, named simply the *Pamlico*. And the river in turn takes its name from that of a now vanished Native American people who once lived along its banks; their Algonquian name would more typically have been *Pamticough*, but either the local pronunciation was different or English-speaking settlers altered this to *Pamlico*. This *Pamlico* is very similar to the early variant *Pemlico* of the name we are interested in.

Did Coates immediately declare that he had found the origin of the name *Pimlico*? Certainly not, because that would be deeply unprofessional. For all anyone knows, there might be dozens of names resembling *Pimlico* in locations ranging from Montevideo through Mozambique to Mongolia. It is a constant error of linguistic amateurs and cranks to assume that, because they have uncovered a resemblance, they have identified the origin of the name they are playing with. The crucial part is to provide a *pathway*: to show, in our case, how the name could reasonably have travelled from North Carolina to London by 1598, especially since this was a time when no permanent English-speaking settlement had yet been founded in North America. (That first permanent settlement was Jamestown, in Virginia, founded in 1607.)

However, Pamlico Sound is by no means a totally insignificant locale in the English settlement of North America, for at its northern end there lies the island of Roanoke, the site of Sir Walter Raleigh's abortive first attempts at establishing an American colony, in 1585 and 1587. This is just early enough to pre-date that reference to Ben Pimlico in 1598, and so Coates turned his attention to the Roanoke settlers, noting first that a 1747 map of London records a street called *Virginia Row* not far from Pimlico's ale-house, which perhaps reinforces the suspicion that some of the returned Roanoke colonists might have settled in Hoxton.

Some of those colonists did indeed return from Roanoke to England; when Sir Francis Drake brought them back on his returning ship in 1586. The names of some of the returning colonists are recorded, and, fascinatingly, two of them were named *Bennet Chappell* and *Bennet Harrye*. Coates therefore wondered whether one of these men, as a result of some unrecorded incident while he was living at Roanoke, might have acquired the nickname 'Pemlico' or 'Pimlico', and whether he might have brought this nickname back to England with him and used it as a surname (until quite recently, what surname you used was fluid), perhaps out of pride (the incident reflected well on him) or out of whimsy (the incident was funny, and he had a sense of humour). Coates notes further that one of the reasons for the great popularity of Pimlico's ale-house seems to have been the availability there of a novel pleasure, that most famous product of Virginia and North Carolina, tobacco. Possibly Ben Pimlico, having become acquainted with the weed while at Roanoke, had taken steps to obtain a supply for his establishment.

That would seem to be that, but things are rarely so simple in this line of work. Just about to submit his account for publication, Coates stumbled across two more instances of *Pimlico*, instances which appeared to cast doubt on his conclusion. First, there is a *Pimlico Island* near Bermuda, a name for which we have no information at all about its earliest use. Second, there are several early references to a bird called the *pemblico*, found all along the Atlantic coast and, according to the 1624 account of Captain John Smith, leader of the Jamestown settlement, so called because that's what the bird's cry sounds like. (This bird is now known as Audubon's shearwater.) Could it be, then, that Coates's account is a hopeless fabrication, and that all the Pimlicos in fact take their names from nothing more than the imitative name given to this noisy bird?

Nothing for it, then, but to go back to the documents. This time Coates found an account of the history of the Bahamas, of uncertain authorship but dating from around 1630. And this account contains the following illuminating passage: 'Another smale Birde ther is, the which, by some Ale-banters of London sent ouer hether, hath bin tearmed pimplicoe, for so they Imagine (and a little resemblance putts them in mind of a place so dearly beloued) her note articulates.' In other words, the name was given to the bird by a group of Londoners arriving in the Bahamas merely because its cry reminded them of the name of their favourite ale-house, the celebrated and fashionable Ben Pimlico's of Hoxton.

Coates's story is therefore complete. Having originated in North America, the name *Pimlico* was carried to London, where it became a famous name, later to be transferred to a district of Westminster and elsewhere, and, scarcely two decades after its successful establishment in London, back to North America, where some of Ben Pimlico's homesick former customers gave the name to a noisy bird.

Coates therefore concludes that *Pimlico* is probably the first American name to be carried to Britain, and certainly the first name derived from a native

American language to take root in Britain. The origin of the Algonquian name *Pamticough* is unknown, though it may be a derivative of an earlier name of the river.

This vignette well illustrates the central requirements of good onomastic work: the importance

- of locating and consulting all available documentation, especially the earliest documentation;
- of taking into account *all* the information, and not just the bits that please you;
- of ensuring the linguistic forms are sensible and appropriate at the time at which the names were conferred;
- of ensuring that dates tally, so that names are not obliged to travel backward in time;
- of providing a plausible pathway by which the name could have got to where it is attested by the time it is attested;
- of being prepared to consider alternative accounts to the one you have already settled on as the likeliest.

To these I might add one more which did not happen to feature prominently in our case: the importance of evaluating the reliability of your sources. Just as you can't believe everything you read in the newspaper, you can't believe everything you read in even the most impressively dusty piece of parchment or vellum. Four hundred years ago, people were making just as many mistakes as we make today, and they were telling just as many lies.

Names and prehistory

North of the Black Sea lies a vast area of grassland, the *Pontic steppe*. In historical times these steppes have been occupied by speakers of Slavonic languages, Russians and Ukrainians, and we think of the steppes as the roaming ground of the famous Cossack horsemen. But the origins of the river names are interesting.

One of the great rivers of the steppes is the *Don*, made famous by the Russian writer Mikhail Sholokhov in his Cossack novels like *And Quiet Flows the Don*. To the west of the Don are three more great rivers, the *Donets*, the *Dniester* and the *Dnieper*. Specialists established long ago that all four of these names are built on a word *dānu*, meaning 'river'. There is nothing surprising about this, except that this *dānu* is not a Slavonic word: it is an Iranian word.

Today the Iranian languages extend from the Caucasus and eastern Turkey across Iran and Afghanistan into Pakistan – all entirely outside the Pontic steppe. Among the best-known Iranian languages are Kurdish, Persian and Pashto, although many others are spoken. But these river names tell us that

Iranian languages were once spoken across the Pontic steppes, long enough for the Iranian river names to become established and to be taken over by the Slavs when these people later settled in the area.

This is an example of how linguistic information from place names can often shed light on the prehistory of a region. In this case, we are lucky enough to know something about the identity of those ancient Iranian speakers: they were, in fact, the celebrated Scythians, Parthians and Sarmatians, who inhabited the steppe in the days of the ancient Greeks and Romans. But, even if we knew nothing about the Scythians and their relatives, we could still safely infer the former presence of Iranian-speakers in the steppes, through their linguistic legacy, the river names they left behind.

In fact, of all geographical features, rivers are perhaps the most likely to preserve ancient names from long-gone languages. In Britain, English speakers have taken over dozens of river names from the Celtic speakers who were there long ago: the *Thames*, the *Clyde*, the *Dee*, the *Humber*, the *Tyne*, the *Tees*, the *Tay*, the *Severn*, the *Tweed*, the *Trent*, the *Medway*, and most of the rivers called *Ouse*, among many others. Some of these names have transparent Celtic origins, while others are opaque in Celtic and may have been taken over by the Celts from speakers of still earlier languages. Indeed, it is almost unusual to find a river name of English origin, although one such is the *Mersey*, from an Old English name meaning 'boundary river': this river formed the boundaries between the Anglo-Saxon kingdoms of Mercia and Northumbria, and later between the counties of Cheshire and Lancashire. The creation of the new county of Merseyside in 1974 brought to an end more than a thousand years during which the river formed an important boundary.

We find much the same in the eastern United States, where most of the rivers have names taken from the local indigenous languages. Here and there we find a *Hudson* or a *Delaware* taken from a European language, but mostly we find names like *Connecticut*, *Potomac*, *Rappahannock*, *Allegheny*, *Monongahela*, *Ohio*, *Susquehanna*, *Tennessee*, and that most beautiful of American river names, *Shenandoah*. These river names preserve the now mostly vanished Iroquoian and Algonquian languages which were once spoken from the Atlantic coast westward to the Mississippi and the Great Lakes and beyond.

All over the globe, place names provide us with valuable information about ancient languages. In the Pyrenees, we find place names of Basque origin as far east as the valley of Arán, near Andorra; this territory has not been Basque-speaking for well over a thousand years, but clearly it once was. Even the valley name *Arán* itself appears to derive from Basque *(h)aran* 'valley', and so the local name *Val d'Arán* is literally 'valley valley' – a common kind of outcome when names pass from one language into another.

At the same time, deep in the heart of the Basque-speaking region we find a river named *Deva*, with a town of the same name at its mouth; this Celtic river name, frequent in formerly Celtic-speaking areas all over Europe, and representing a Celtic word for 'goddess', demonstrates that there were once Celtic speakers in the Basque Country, although that must have been a very long time ago indeed.

From *Kirkwall* in Orkney to *Derby* in the midlands of England and to *Wicklow* in Ireland, the frequency of Scandinavian place names bears quiet testimony to the former presence of Viking settlers in much of Scotland, England and Ireland. (These names are *Kirkju-vágr* 'church-bay', *Djúr-bý* 'deer-village' and (probably) *Víkinga-ló* 'Vikings' meadow' in Old Norse.) We find Greek names in Turkey, Etruscan names in Italy, Arabic names in Spain, Phoenician names in north Africa and Spain, Persian names in India, and French names in England, all bearing evidence of languages once present in these locations. An example of a French name in England is the towering cliff-face of *Beachy Head*, not far from Brighton; this derives from Old French *Beau Chef* 'beautiful head(land)', with the uncomprehending addition of English *head*, producing another tautologous name.

We find a particularly fascinating case in Greece. In classical times, both mainland Greece and the Greek island of Crete possessed a sizeable number of place names ending either in *-nthos* or in *-(s)sos*. Examples: *Amárynthos*, *Erýmanthos*, *Zakýnthos*, *Kórinthos*, *Périnthos*, *Ólynthos*, *Dírphōssos*, *Ilisós*, *Kēphis(s)os*, *Kerēssós*, *Parnassós*, *Pēdasos*, *Amnis(s)ós*, *Knōs(s)ós*, *Tylis(s)ós*. Some of these names, such as *Kórinthos* (English *Corinth*: source, via French, for the word *currant*) and *Knōssós* (English *Knossos*), are familiar to anyone who knows a little about ancient Greece.

When we come to analyse these, the first point to spring to mind is that each of these endings recurs so frequently in place names that it simply *must* have a single unified explanation, a single origin. Compare, for example, the ending *-burg(h)*, which occurs in so many town names in Britain. This too must have a single origin, and it does – with just the odd exception – in Old English *burh* 'fortified place'.

Secondly, these two endings are definitely not Greek, nor even Indo-European. So, the names containing them must have entered Greek from some other language in which these endings were commonplace. Linguistic amateurs have excitedly suggested Egyptian or Semitic, but neither of these contains suitable elements. The source must be another language, very likely one which is long extinct and unknown.

The interpretation is obvious, and it has been accepted by linguists for a long time. When Greek speakers entered what is now Greece, perhaps around 2000 BC or a little earlier, they found the territory already occupied by a people speaking a quite different language, one which is unknown to us.

These people had already constructed a large number of place names. Some of these names were simply retained by the Greeks – just as the English speaking settlers in North America and Australia retained many place names from the languages of the earlier inhabitants. In other words, the Greeks took these names over from a *substrate* language.

Apart from names, there are also some ordinary Greek words exhibiting these same endings. Again, these words are neither Greek nor Indo-European, and they must have been borrowed. Most of these words denote Mediterranean plants and animals which the early Greek-speakers would probably not have known before they entered Greece: *erébinthos* 'chickpea', *ólynthos* 'wild fig', *términthos* or *terébinthos* 'terebinth', *hyákinthos* 'blue-bell', *kypárissos* 'cypress', *kérasos* 'cornel cherry', *písos* 'pea', *bólinthos* 'European bison', and so on. A few of these words have other meanings, but all are words that might readily have been taken over by the Greeks from the earlier inhabitants of Greece. The most famous of these words is the celebrated Cretan word *labýrinthos* 'labyrinth'. It appears that the Greeks probably took their myth of the Minotaur and his labyrinth from the earlier pre-Greek inhabitants of the region. It is useful to compare the adoption by English-speakers of indigenous animal and plant names outside England like *skunk, woodchuck, kangaroo, wallaby, wombat, kiwi* and *squash*.

So, thousands of years ago, before the Greeks arrived, Greece was inhabited by an unknown people speaking an unknown language. Very frequent in that language, whatever it was, were the two endings *-nthos* and *-(s)sos*, or at least endings that were later taken into Greek in these forms. Speakers of that language used many everyday words containing those endings, and they constructed many place names involving the same endings. When the speakers of what would become Greek finally arrived in Greece, they took quite a few of these words and names into their own language. But then the earlier language died out, probably because its speakers abandoned it in favour of the now more prestigious Greek. Sadly, the speakers of this extinct language never acquired writing, meaning that their language was not recorded. Barring an amazing discovery one day, we will never know anything about this lost language apart from the few fragments of it acciden-tally preserved for us by the Greeks. But we know it was there, once.

The fading of names

When a name is first conferred, it is normally full of meaning, and it is regarded by the name-givers as eminently suitable for what it designates. Once the name has been given, however, in most cases it rapidly begins to lose its independent meaning and to be reduced to a mere label, an arbitrary sequence of sounds attached to the place or thing bearing it. The existence of the original meaning does not prevent speakers from altering the form of the name in any way they fancy, either in line with regular changes in the pronunciation of the language or in irregular and capricious ways. Before many generations have passed, the original meaning of the name may become obscure and difficult, recoverable only by specialists, and a few more centuries may render the origin of the name so opaque as to be beyond recovery.

The city name *New York* was coined less than four centuries ago, and its origin is still transparent to anyone who cares to think about it: the American city is named after the English city of York (via a dedication to James, Duke of York, brother of Charles II and commander of the English navy at the time of the transfer from Dutch hands), and the intended sense is 'the new city of York'. But, in practice, no one does think about this, and *New York* is for most of us, most of the time, no more than an arbitrary sequence of noises, on a par with *Chicago*, a name whose origin really is wholly opaque to anyone but a specialist.

The Taj Mahal was built only in the seventeenth century, between about 1631 and 1648, but already its name is so obscure that even specialists are not quite sure what the original sense was meant to be. The building was erected by the Mogul emperor Shah Jehan as a tomb for his beloved wife Mumtaz, and the name was conferred in Persian, the language of the Mogul court. *Mahal* is straightforward: this is Persian for 'abode' or 'palace'. But no such word as *taj* exists in Persian or in any other language of the area. Most specialists are agreed that the name *Taj Mahal* must represent an irregular alteration of an earlier *Mumtaz Mahal*, but there is disagreement on the significance of this name: some see it as meaning 'the abode (resting place) of Mumtaz', while others note that Mumtaz's full title seems to have been *Mumtaz Mahal* 'the exalted one of the palace', and they prefer to see the name of the tomb as deriving directly from this title. In less than four centuries, the name has become obscure.

Very few of the place names conferred by the English-speaking settlers of Britain are now intelligible without scholarly scrutiny, and quite a few are no longer intelligible at all. The Lincolnshire town of *Boston* is recorded in 1130 as *Botuluestan*, showing that its original sense was the unexpected 'Botwulf's stone' – that is, 'stone (marking a boundary or a meeting place) belonging to a man called Botwulf'. The settlers who carried this name to the city in Massachusetts had no inkling of this origin, nor were they interested.

The famous English port city of *Bristol*, earlier *Bristow*, derives its name, the scholars have determined, from Old English *brycg-stow* – that is, 'assembly point by the bridge'. Changes in pronunciation have obscured the identity of both of the Old English words, and the word *stow* 'assembly point' has disappeared from the language anyway, so the name would still be unintelligible even if it were pronounced 'Bridge-stow' today.

This fading into unintelligibility is generally the fate of names everywhere, even without the assistance of a shift of language, like the replacement of Celtic by English in most of Britain. All across Europe, names of rivers, mountains, towns and even countries are obscure, opaque and often mysterious. River names like *Rhine*, *Vistula*, *Elbe*, *Liffey* and *Danube* are difficult or impossible to unravel, though the last may perhaps be another of those Iranian river names from *dānu* (scholars are not sure about this one, because there are technical difficulties). The names of the *Alps*, the *Pyrenees* and the *Carpathians* have origins that can only be guessed at. Such famous cities as *Paris*, *Rome*, *Berlin* and *Moscow* bear names about whose remote origins little or nothing is known. And names of whole countries, like *Spain*, *Italy*, *Latvia*, *Lithuania* and *Albania*, are seemingly beyond interpretation.

Some of these names, we know, are derived from the names of peoples who once lived in or near the areas in question, but this realisation is of limited help. Knowing that Paris takes its name from the Parisii who used to live there is scarcely more illuminating than knowing that Estonia takes its name from the Estonians who live there now.

Names sink into obscurity fast. Even though Europe has been inhabited by fully modern human beings for something like 35,000 years, it is unlikely that many European place names are much more than about 3,000–4,000 years old. Yet even so a very high number of these names are already too opaque to be deciphered. This is pretty much what we find with place names in most parts of the world.

But perhaps not everywhere. Australia has been inhabited by our species for over 40,000 years, and perhaps for something like 50,000–60,000 years. Accordingly, we might expect the Australian landscape to be littered with thousands of opaque place names which are wholly unintelligible to even the most knowledgeable tribal elders.

But that is not what we find. In great contrast to Europe, most indigenous Australian place names have meanings which are largely or completely transparent – that is, they still mean something in the local language.

Take for example the survey of place names conducted by the linguist Bob Dixon in the area of Queensland occupied by the speakers of Yidiny. Out of 87 place names surveyed in the area, Dixon found that only one was unintelligible. This was *Murubay*, the name of a grassy mound. Uniquely in Dixon's list, this name means nothing at all in Yidiny and cannot be interpreted.

But the other 86 names were different. Of these, about half are identical to ordinary Yidiny words. Examples include the location name *Dyulugunu*, identical to *dyulugunu* 'black myrtle tree', the name of a tree which grows in abundance at this location, and *Ngawuyu*, the name of a rock, identical to *ngawuyu* 'salt-water turtle', apparently so named because a mythical hero saw such a turtle at this place. A number of others involve ordinary words with suffixes. For example, the location name *Dyirgardyi* is literally 'with grass', from *dyirgar* 'grass' and *-dyi* 'with', because that same mythical hero found grass growing here. In most of the remaining cases, the name is based upon an ordinary word with some kind of modification of the ending. For example, the hillside *Ngiyaman* takes its name from *ngiya* 'edge of mountain', with an unexplained addition, and the location name *Garbara* is merely an archaic form of *garba:r* 'mangrove tree'; the place name has failed to undergo the otherwise regular change in pronunciation which has altered the form of the ordinary word.

The Yidiny pattern appears to be typical of native Australia: place names are usually transparent in formation, with meanings that every speaker can easily recover. Why is Australia so different from Europe in this respect? After all, we know that words have changed their pronunciations in Australian languages about as fast as in European languages, and we also know that Australian languages, because of taboo restrictions, replace their words with completely different words *much* more frequently than do European languages. So why have most native Australian place names, after tens of thousands of years, not descended into unintelligibility, as has happened in Europe in a vastly shorter time?

There is no simple answer to this, but it appears that native Australians are far more interested than Europeans in retaining the *meanings* of place names. As I explained above, once we confer a name, however suitable, it promptly loses its independent meaning and is reduced to a mere label. It appears that the same thing does not happen in native Australia. In Australia, if the ordinary processes of language change threaten to make a name opaque, the name must be updated in some way to maintain its intelligibility. Native Australians can tolerate a certain degree of obscurity in a name, so long as the overall meaning of the name remains clear, but they will not usually allow a name to descend into unintelligibility.

Suppose the same policy were adopted in the English-speaking world. Then we would have to update the place names rather often, in order to keep their meanings fresh and transparent.

For example, the original sense of *Eborakon*, the ancestral form of *York*, is thought by some scholars to have been 'yew-tree estate'. So, it appears, we should replace the opaque name *York* by the transparent *Yew-Tree Estate*, and the name of the American city should likewise be altered to *New Yew-Tree Estate*. This decision would yield further fallout: the Queen's son would be the *Duke of Yew-Tree Estate*, and the consequences for the song *New York, New York* hardly bear thinking about. We would also need to make a decision about *Yorkshire*: though *shire* scarcely exists any longer in its earlier sense of 'administrative division', the word still maintains at least a marginal presence in the language, and the recent films of Tolkien's *Lord of the Rings* have made the word prominent again, so perhaps we can make do with a cricket team called *Yew-Tree-Estateshire*. The disappearance of Old English *lifer* 'mud' means that *Liverpool* must be updated to *Muddypool*. And, since the obscure first element in *Manchester* appears to be a Celtic word **mamm-* 'breast', apparently applied to a breast-shaped hill, we are in some danger of winding up with a football team called *Breast-Fort United*, an outcome which will please few fans of the Red Devils. Likewise, *Chicago*, which derives from an Algonquian word *shikaakwa*, meaning both 'skunk' and '(smelly kind of) wild leek', will apparently have to be updated to something like 'Skunk-Leek' (my kind of town).

Finally, before we leave the Australians, there is one more aspect of native Australian naming practices which is worthy of some attention. Australian names show a high frequency of what are called *incidental names*, names which record incidents that once occurred at the named locations. Above we saw some examples of Yidiny place names derived from incidents in the life of a mythical hero. In Europe, such incidental names are rare to non-existent, but they are curiously frequent in the United States.

The name of Massacre Rocks, Idaho, commemorates the killing of some settlers which took place there in 1862. The ferocious-sounding Hatchet Lake, Arkansas, is in fact so named because a surveyor cut his knee on a hatchet there. Kettle Creek, Colorado, and Kettle Creek, Oregon, are both named because somebody lost a kettle at each place. Most absurdly of all, a town in California received its name as follows: the settlers asked the local postmaster, who was eating a bag of peanuts at the time, to suggest a name. The town is now called *Peanut*. American place names seldom feature the deeds of mythical heroes, but they appear to be a symphony to forerunners who were clumsy, careless, absent-minded, violent, or just a little hungry.

Names and politics

Names can be changed for all sorts of reasons, but political reasons are especially prominent and interesting. To take a simple case, it is hardly surprising that the German names of the cities *Stettin* and *Danzig* were officially replaced by the Polish forms *Szczecin* and *Gdańsk* when these cities were annexed by Poland in 1945. Nor is it surprising that the former British colonies of *Northern Rhodesia*, *Southern Rhodesia* and *The Gold Coast* quickly underwent name changes to *Zambia*, *Zimbabwe* and *Ghana* upon independence.

The nationalist movements of our day have produced many such cases. For example, with the end of Franco's brutal dictatorship in Spain and the establishment of democracy in the 1970s, speakers of the several minority languages of Spain have been demanding and getting official status for their own forms of place names. The Basque provinces formerly known by their

Spanish forms *Vizcaya* and *Guipúzcoa* are now officially known by their Basque forms, *Bizkaia* and *Gipuzkoa*, and the Basque town of *San Sebastián* is now *Donostia*. Likewise, the Catalan city of *Lérida* is now officially *Lleida*, and similar changes have been carried out elsewhere in Spain.

Some especially vexing cases have arisen from the disintegration of the former Soviet Union. Take the new republic of Ukraine. The long domination of Ukraine by Russia had the effect that Ukrainian names became known to the rest of the world in their Russian forms. Now, of course, the Ukrainians would prefer to see the world using the authentic Ukrainian forms. To fall into line with this desire, however, we would have to replace our familiar forms *Kiev*, *Odessa* and *Chernobyl* by the Ukrainian forms *Kiyiv*, *Odesa* and *Chornobil* – and most of us just don't want to do that. The problem is that a name like *Kiev* is as well established in English as, say, *Rome* and *Naples*, and we are hardly likely to replace these traditional forms by their Italian equivalents, *Roma* and *Napoli*. (On the other hand, the traditional English forms *Lyons*, *Marseilles* and *Tangiers* have now been largely supplanted by the more accurate versions *Lyon*, *Marseille* and *Tangier*.)

Very recently, the name of the world's highest mountain, situated on the frontier between Nepal and Tibet (currently ruled by China), has been producing a small political storm. Its Nepali name is *Sagarmatha*, while the Tibetan name is *Chomolungma* (in Chinese, *Qomolangma*), both names reportedly meaning something like 'mother goddess of the world'. Both of these names have their champions as the sole 'true' name for the mountain. But most of the world knows the mountain as *Mount Everest*, the name conferred by the British administrators of India in honour of Sir George Everest, the British surveyor general of India. Interestingly, we *all* pronounce this wrong. Everest apparently pronounced his name as if it were the word *eve* followed by *rest*.

Dealt with more peacefully is the case of that famous rock formation in the middle of Australia, which happens to occupy a central place in indigenous Australian culture. That rock was given the English name *Ayers Rock* in 1873, after Sir Henry Ayers, then the prime minister of South Australia, but after complaints from the Aboriginal inhabitants the official name is now the indigenous *Uluru*.

Bilingual societies can suffer from complicated problems of naming. An outstanding example is Belgium, divided between speakers of Dutch and of French. The Belgians have been obliged to draw up elaborate laws determining which language(s) can or must be used in every region of the country. These laws can make life interesting for a foreign visitor.

Suppose you are driving from the Dutch-speaking region to the French-speaking region. When you start your trip, the road signs will be given *only* in Dutch, even for places in the French-speaking region. If you cross the officially bilingual region around the capital city, you will suddenly see the names of cities given in both languages. Then, in the French-speaking region, *only* French names will be displayed, even for places in the Dutch-speaking region.

So, if you start in Antwerp, and head for *Liège*, you must know that you should be following the signs for *Luik*. After a while, the signs will change to *Luik/Liège*, and then they will change to *Liège* exclusively. But then, if you want to return, you must watch for signs pointing to *Anvers*, since only when you reach the bilingual area will you start to see signs for *Antwerpen*. The locals are used to this, but outsiders can find it bewildering. For the country which is home to so many European institutions, this practice doesn't seem very European, but so heated are the divisions in Belgium that each linguistic group refuses to allow the use of the other group's language on its territory.

In our politically sensitive era, quite a few names have recently been changed for a reason which is easy to understand: the names were insulting. People habitually give names to other people in ways which are largely haphazard. For example, in English, the Welsh, the Basques, the Dutch, the Germans, the Hungarians, the Albanians, the Greeks and the Finns – among many others – are called by names that these peoples have never applied to themselves. These idiosyncratic names are the result of a variety of historical accidents, and we retain them, odd as they may be, because they are not perceived as insulting in origin.

But other traditional English names really are insulting. For example, we have historically called the people of northern Scandinavia the *Lapps*, but this name is suspected of being offensive in origin, and today careful writers prefer to use the name *Sámi* (or *Saami*), the name these people give themselves. Likewise, our familiar name *Eskimo* was originally an insult, reportedly meaning 'eaters of raw meat' in an indigenous language of Canada, and today we avoid this name in favour of the self-designations *Inuit* (for the eastern group) and *Yupik* (for the western group). There are many such cases.

As these examples suggest, people are passionate about names. That passion can run to small details.

The Hawaiian language has an exceptionally small number of consonant sounds: only eight. But one of those eight consonants is a sound which does not occur as a separate consonant in European languages and for which the Roman alphabet provides no letter: the glottal stop [ʔ]. For lack of a better idea, in the romanised spelling system devised by Europeans for the Hawaiian language, the glottal stop is spelled with an apostrophe. However, when Hawaiian words and names are taken into English, the apostrophe is silently dropped. For example, that celebrated Scrabble™ word *aa* (a kind of lava) is properly written *'a'a* in Hawaiian, with two vowels, and *luau*, the name of a Hawaiian feast, is properly *lu'au*.

The problem is that the glottal stop occurs in the name of Hawaii itself: the Hawaiian form is *Hawai'i*. The official American form of the state name is

Hawaii, but native Hawaiians resent this, and they would like to see the official form changed to *Hawai'i*. The last time I checked, the state authorities were still using the apostrophe-free spelling; interestingly, the county of Hawai'i (in other words, the largest island in the Hawaiian chain) is now using the native spelling, however.

Organised naming: Maxwell and the love goddesses

In most cases, place names are assigned over a long period, with each name reflecting some local circumstances at the time of its assignment. Nobody is in charge of assigning names, and names just happen. The result may be a crazy-quilt of different kinds of names. My home state of New York provides a good example. There are native American names: *Canandaigua, Chatauqua, Irondequoit, Cheektowaga, Adirondack, Manhattan*. There are names imported from Britain and Ireland: *New York, Albany, Rochester, Norwich, Ulster, Kingston, Bath, Newark*, even *Brighton*. There are names formed in conventional ways from English elements: *Watertown, Queens, Oyster Bay, Ogdensburg, Orchard Park, Little Valley, Westons Mills*. There are Dutch names conferred by the early Dutch settlers: *Schenectady, Hudson, Yonkers, Brooklyn, Cohoes, Rensselaer*. There is a scattering of names taken from all over Europe: *Barcelona, Dunkirk, Geneva, Waterloo, Hamburg, Salamanca*. We find the odd biblical name (*Jericho*) and the odd French name bestowed by French explorers (*Champlain*). We have the usual collection of formations in that favourite American element *-ville*: *Portville, Manorville, Terryville, Youngsville, Schuylerville, Niverville*. There is a startling collection of names from classical antiquity: *Rome, Syracuse, Ithaca, Troy, Utica, Athens, Macedon, Corinth, Carthage, Ilion*. There are odd invented names: *Fluvanna, Katonah, Mineola, Unadilla* and the almost inevitable *Fredonia*. There are also a few names of unknown origin, the best-known being *Buffalo*.

The New York pattern is typical of the USA, and not so different from the rest of the world. Once in a while, however, we encounter a different state of affairs: a large set of names must be assigned to a region which is virtually devoid of them, and this enterprise is undertaken by a committee which resolves to proceed according to certain rules. The recent mapping of the previously invisible sea-bed provides a possible example, but the best examples lie off the earth altogether.

Human beings have always been able to see the face of the moon turned towards the earth. But the other planets in our solar system long remained little more than dots of light. In recent years, however, advances in telescopes, in spacecraft, in radar, and in other kinds of technology have finally allowed astronomers to explore the surfaces of Mercury, Venus and Mars, as well as the other side of the moon, the one we never see from earth. The result has been a flurry of naming perhaps unparalleled in human history, as thousands of suddenly visible features have been granted the dignity of names.

Astronomers, rather like biologists, have long operated with one big rule of naming: the first scientist or group to discover an object or a feature is entitled to name it. But there have to be guidelines as to what counts as an acceptable name. For example, it has been the custom since ancient times to name the planets after characters in Roman and Greek mythology: Mercury, Venus, Mars, Jupiter, Saturn … But when the Prussian-born English astronomer William Herschel discovered a new planet in 1781, he proposed calling it *George*, in honour of his patron, King George III. Fortunately, this eccentric suggestion was not accepted, and astronomers finally settled on the more suitably mythological name *Uranus*. When the next two planets were discovered, in 1846 and in 1930: the dignified labels *Neptune* and *Pluto* were briskly conferred. There is some evidence that this classical tradition may now be in decline, however. The 'near-moon' recently discovered (almost) orbiting Earth was named *Cruithne*, after a Celtic moon goddess.

The guidelines used by astronomers are seldom stringent. The more prominent features of the near side of the moon were long ago given romantic Latin names. A few examples are *Mare Imbrium* (the Sea of Rains), *Mare Frigoris* (the Sea of Cold), *Mare Serenitatis* (the Sea of Serenity), *Oceanus Procellarum* (the Ocean of Storms), *Palus Nebularum* (the Marsh of Mists), *Sinus Roris* (the Bay of Dew), *Lacus Somniorum* (the Lake of Dreams), *Mare Humorum* (the Sea of Moisture), the unnecessarily alarming *Mare Crisium* (the Sea of Crises), and of course the famous *Mare Tranquillitatis*, the Sea of Tranquillity, where the Apollo 11 spacecraft landed in July 1969.

These mostly watery names were conferred in hope, not in knowledge, and we now know that the surface of the moon is so dry that it makes the Sahara look soggy by comparison. The names conferred in recent years exhibit a startling diversity of origins. Among the many hundreds of new names are *Plato*, *Seneca*, *Plutarch*, *Franklin*, *Atlas*, *Chevallier*, *Alexander*, *Tenerife*, *Agassiz*, *Mt Blanc*, *Daguerre*, *Horrocks*, *Schroter*, *Fourier*, *Doppelmayer*, *Walter*, *Leibniz*, *Milne*, the slightly jarring *Straightwall Mountains*, and the positively ridiculous *Mare Smithii*, 'the Sea of Smith'. The result is not so very different from New York State, except for the overwhelmingly frequent use of the surnames of people to coin names of features.

In one case, however, the astronomers have put their collective scientific foot down and insisted on accepting only names conforming to a rigid rule. This has occurred in the case of the planet Venus.

Venus is something of a special case among the planets, because it is wrapped constantly in thick white clouds: the surface is forever closed to us. The only way to examine it is with radar, since radar waves can penetrate those clouds. But the first attempts, with earth-based radar, succeeded in revealing hardly any features, and only three names were conferred.

Then it became possible to put radar-carrying spacecraft into orbit around Venus, and to send high-quality radar pictures back to earth. This was done first with the Pioneer Orbiter and the Venera missions, and more recently with the technologically much superior Magellan probe. As a result, the surface of Venus has now been mapped out in great detail, and dozens of new names have been assigned to the previously invisible features of the surface.

As this mapping began, the astronomers made a decision: since Venus is the only planet named after a female, all of the names conferred upon the planet's features must be female names. Unfortunately, this ruling was made only after the earlier earth-based mapping had produced three named features. Two highland areas were given the utterly bland names *Alpha* and *Beta*. But the third feature was a towering mountain range, the highest on the planet and higher than Mount Everest, and this was dubbed the *Maxwell Mountains*, after the Scottish physicist James Clerk Maxwell, one of the founders of the science of electromagnetism so useful for mapping the planet. Having already been properly conferred, this name could not be erased, and so it has remained: the only male name on a planet with otherwise exclusively female names, such as two vast upland areas, or *terrae*, named *Ishtar* and *Aphrodite*. These names, like that of the planet itself, represent ancient goddesses of beauty, love and sex.

The smaller highland areas, or *regiones*, include the *Alpha* and *Beta* just mentioned, as well as *Asteria, Metis, Phoebe, Tellus, Eistla, Atla, Ovda, Tethus, Themis* and *Thetis*, most of these being the names of nymphs in classical mythology. The lowland areas, or *planitiae*, include *Atalanta, Lakshmi, Lavinia, Leda, Niobe, Helen, Guinevere, Aino* and *Sedna* – again a mythical bunch, although a strikingly eclectic one.

The deep canyons, or *chasmae*, include *Artemis, Devana, Diana, Heng-O, Dali* and *Juno*, also mythical. But the craters are named after real people, among them *Colette, Lise Meitner, Cleopatra, Mead, Pavlova, Sacajawea, Golubkina* and *Sappho*. Among the large rock formations, or *rupes*, are *Ut* and *Vesta*. Finally, the mountains include *Akna, Freyja, Hathor, Rhea, Danu, Gula, Maat* and *Theia*, as well as the isolated and doubtless embarrassed *Maxwell*. And there are oddities, such as the curious circular feature called *Eve*.

I am not sure how the sober and all-business Swedish physicist Lise Meitner would feel about being surrounded by a group of love goddesses and nymphs not best known for having their clothes on. Perhaps the writers Sappho and Colette are a little more at home, but we might wonder why the erotic writer Anaïs Nin has not so far been granted a place in the topography of Venus. Also still denied a place is Marlene Dietrich, and the same goes for other modern goddesses like Rita Hayworth, Marilyn Monroe, Greta Garbo or even Madonna, so far refused the honour already granted on other heavenly bodies to countless obscure male scientists, to the creator of Winnie-the-Pooh, and to that enigmatic Mr Smith.

Finally, we can only wonder at the emotions of that unbending Presbyterian, James Clerk Maxwell, on finding his name apparently trapped for all time in what looks like a largely heathen ladies' powder room.

Conclusion

In some ways, onomastics acts as a microcosm for the study of language change. We can observe how originally meaningful words and phrases gradually become commonplace and eventually meaningless. We are also lucky because we can sometimes observe the act of creation of names – something normally denied us for other kinds of words. Finally, onomastics reinforces one of the abiding truths of the study of language change: without evidence, all we are left with are guesses. With sufficient experience, these can become *informed* guesses, but they are nonetheless to be treated cautiously. When no or little experience is involved in this work, the results can be deeply misleading, however.

In the next chapter, we will be considering the history of the English language, employing many of the skills we have acquired in the preceding chapters.

5   Where does English come from?

English today and yesterday

Today English is the mother tongue of hundreds of millions of people. It is also spoken as an everyday second language by many millions more, and it is by far the language most learned as a foreign language. In almost every global domain, English is the language of first choice for dealings between people. When an Egyptian plane flies into Moscow airport, the pilot talks to the air-traffic controllers in English. When a Swede negotiates a deal in Thailand, the negotiations are conducted in English. When Brazilian biochemists publish their latest research, they publish it in English. When a public statement is issued by the Secretary General of the United Nations, or by the President of the International Olympic Committee, or by the Secretary General of NATO, that statement is almost always issued in the first instance in English.

English is the first language of the Internet, of popular music, of almost every branch of science, of maritime navigation. Indeed it would be difficult to think of a context where English is not used, even by non-native speakers. In the nineteenth century, the language of diplomacy and of fine arts was French: today it is English. In the nineteenth century, the language of such scientific and scholarly fields as chemistry and linguistics was German: today it is English. English has taken over the world on a scale never before seen. Greek, Latin, Chinese, French and Arabic have all been immensely important languages at certain times and in certain places, but not one of them has ever approached the awesome dominance now achieved by English. English has become the first truly global language.

How and why has this come about? In 1600, English was spoken nowhere but the British Isles, and it was far from universal even there. It was the first language in most of England, but in the southwestern county of Cornwall the Celtic language Cornish was the mother tongue of many people. Almost the whole of Wales was still solidly Welsh-speaking, and in fact Welsh speech spilled across the border into adjoining areas of England. In Scotland, English had established itself in the Lowlands, although in a highly distinctive and divergent form, but the inhabitants of the Highlands and the Western Isles spoke yet another Celtic language, Scottish Gaelic, while Shetlanders and the people of Orkney were still speaking the Norn language introduced centuries earlier by

Scandinavian settlers. Almost the whole of Ireland was Irish-speaking, save only for often beleaguered groups of English speakers in Dublin, Wexford and Waterford in particular. The people of the Isle of Man spoke another Celtic language, Manx.

And that was it. No other English-speaking location existed. Sir Walter Raleigh's first attempts at establishing an English colony in North Carolina had recently collapsed in disaster, and there was no English-speaking settlement anywhere in the Americas. There was as yet no English presence in Africa or Asia, while Australia and New Zealand had not even been discovered by Europeans.

In Europe, France and Spain had for some time been the most powerful countries. Italy was still politically fragmented, but the brilliance of Italian civilisation allowed Italian to co-exist with French as one of the two premier languages of high culture. The wealth and political clout of imperial Spain had helped to give Spanish a role as a leading European language, but English was insignificant. A few European traders and diplomats learned English for professional reasons, but, for most people of the day, learning English was a priority the way learning Norwegian is a priority for English speakers today. Indeed, it had not been many years since the first official attempts since Anglo-Saxon times at translating the Bible into English had led Henry VIII's Chancellor, Sir Thomas More, to snort derisively that the words of the Lord were being rendered into 'the language of plough-boys'.

We must recognise, therefore, that it was not the particular excellence of English which made it the world language. Instead, colonialism and economic, political and cultural power spread the language. In 1607, the first permanent English-speaking settlement outside the British Isles was established at Jamestown in Virginia. Before long, almost the entire east coast of North America was occupied by English speakers, and there were also English-speaking settlements in the Caribbean. Although Britain would eventually lose the thirteen colonies which formed the United States, it retained Canada while keeping an eye out for imperial prospects elsewhere, including India, Australia and New Zealand, many parts of Africa, Malaya and Singapore, Hong Kong, the Pacific, a number of strategic possessions in the south Atlantic, the Mediterranean and the Middle East.

The Industrial Revolution of the late eighteenth century onwards was largely carried out in Britain, which became the world's first industrial superpower. By the end of the nineteenth century, the wealth and power of the British Empire had helped to make English a language of some importance in Europe and in the world. Even so, the language of European diplomacy was still French, and French, in most people's ears, still had more cachet than the upstart island language.

Meanwhile, the young United States had been occupied in expanding across the continent to the Pacific Ocean. By 1850, the territory had been successfully annexed, at the expense of the Mexicans and of the Native Americans, and the next fifty years were devoted to occupying and exploiting it. The Spanish-American War of 1898 made the USA a major imperial power (although it never called itself such). In the Philippines and other islands which came under American administration as a result of the war, English quickly replaced Spanish as the language of government, education and prestige.

While the First World War ultimately ensured the downfall of the European empires, including the British, the late but significant intervention of American forces on the Allied side led to a growth in prestige and political power for the United States which was magnified greatly by victory for the United Nations in the Second World War, a victory which left the USA as the only combatant whose industrial plant was left intact.

But it was not just the military and industrial muscle of the USA which led to the success of English. As the world recovered from the devastation of the war and grew more prosperous, American culture began to exert an almost hypnotic effect. Hollywood movies, blue jeans, rock music, soap operas, Coca-Cola, hamburgers, TV sitcoms, baseball caps – all these American staples caught the imagination of young people everywhere, and the transformation that has been dubbed 'Coca-colonisation' was underway. It was not so much British or American gunboats and commerce that won the world: it was Elvis Presley, trainers, *The Godfather* and *Friends* that made a knowledge of English indispensable for fashion-conscious youngsters everywhere.

This is quite a success story for something that started out as the not especially significant language of an island off the west coast of Europe. But how did English get to that island in the first place? How did it develop there?

The Indo-Europeans

The human species, *Homo sapiens*, has existed for perhaps 150,000 or 200,000 years; for a large part of this time humans have had language. But because writing was not invented until comparatively recently and there was no way of keeping records, we have little or no idea about what languages people spoke. However, towards the end of the eighteenth century, European linguists began to figure out how to recover some of our unrecorded linguistic past.

A little more than 6,000 years ago – just before 4000 BC – a smallish community of people lived somewhere in eastern Europe or in western Asia (probably the steppes of southern Ukraine and Russia): the *Indo-Europeans*, speakers of *Proto-Indo European*, or *PIE*. PIE was never written down, but we know a good deal about the language from its descendants, and also about the culture of the people who spoke it.

Painstaking work by linguists over two centuries has given us an enormous amount of information about this wholly unrecorded language. This information does not result from speculation: instead, it derives from the application of rigorous methods to the data available to us in the living and recorded languages which, as we will see, are directly descended from PIE – including English.

From these linguistic conclusions, we can draw conclusions about Indo-European culture. For example, we can reconstruct a PIE word for 'bride-price', *wedmo-, and so it seems safe to conclude that a man who wanted to marry was obliged to pay a bride-price to the family of his intended.

PIE was a grammatically complex language in comparison to Modern English. It had three grammatical genders, and several different classes of nouns and verbs requiring different sets of endings according to this function. It had a very large amount of the meaningful alternation of the type we see in English *sing*, *sang*, *sung*, and *write*, *wrote*, *written*, and also a considerable number of the alternations we see in *sing* and *song*, or in *gold* and *gild*. In pronunciation, PIE was fairly simple, with only a small number of consonants and vowels, but the language did permit combinations which would look unusual in most modern European languages, such as *$pnk^w tós$ 'fifth' (from *$penk^w e$ 'five'), *wnatks 'leader, lord' and *$h_3 régs$ 'ruler, king'. (The asterisks here indicate that these words are nowhere recorded but have been reconstructed by linguists; k^w is a kind of [k] sound pronounced with rounded lips; and h_3 – along with h_1 and h_2 – is a conventional symbol for consonants pronounced towards the back of the mouth which we know existed but without being able to say exactly how they were pronounced.)

We know that the speakers of PIE could count up to ten, because we can reconstruct their words for the numerals from 'one' to 'ten'. But it seems likely that they could not count any higher. They did have at least one bigger counting word, *kmtóm, which is the direct ancestor of the first part of English *hundred*, but there is reason to believe that this word simply meant 'lots' in PIE. We can still see this in a number of later IE languages, where the word for 'hundred' can also stand for 120 and 144.

The Indo-Europeans had one generic term for 'metal', which we reconstruct as *$h_2 eyes$-, using another of those phonetically obscure consonants, but it seems likely that copper was the only metal they did anything with, while iron and bronze were unknown. From this form derives Latin *aes*, which could mean any base metal or alloy, but primarily, in early texts, copper, as well as English *ore*.

They recognised at least two levels of social organisation: a smaller one *$dómh_2 os$, roughly 'household', and a larger one *wik-, roughly 'clan'. In addition, they recognised a unit called the *$génh_1 es$-, or 'family', the group of people related by blood and marriage within which genealogical descent was reckoned. The first of these is the remote source of *domestic*, and the third is the source of *generation*, both of these being taken by English from Latin (*kin* is the native word derived from *$génh_1 es$-). It is much less obvious that the second is the source of *economics*, whose ancient sense was something like 'household management'.

The Indo-Europeans practised a polytheistic religion with a large number of divinities each of whom had specific responsibilities assigned. Few of the Indo-European divine names can be reconstructed, as with **dyéus ph₂tér*, literally 'sky father', which is the direct ancestor of Ancient Greek *Zeus* (the first part only) and of Latin *Jupiter* (the whole thing). The first element is also the ancestor of the *Tues* in English *Tuesday*.

The Indo-Europeans practised pastoralism. They probably kept both cows and pigs, but the animals on which they principally depended were sheep and goats. We can reconstruct quite a few PIE words pertaining to these animals, including **h₂owis* 'sheep', the remote ancestor of the native English word *ewe*, and **bʰugos* 'he-goat', the ancestor of English *buck*, formerly a he-goat but now usually a male deer.

They also practised agriculture, though agricultural terms are harder to reconstruct with confidence. We have the words **yéwos* and **gʰrh₁nóm*, both 'grain' in general (the former is reflected in Modern English *yeast*; the latter has *corn* as its native reflex; *grain* and *granary* are borrowings from French with the same ultimate source). Several words for 'barley' have survived, but none for 'wheat', which was perhaps unknown to the Indo-Europeans. Reconstructible words for 'plough', 'harrow', 'sow', 'sickle', 'thresh' and 'grind' confirm the existence of cereal-based agriculture among the speakers of PIE, however.

These people also had horse-drawn chariots. We know this because we can reconstruct a number of words pertaining to these artefacts, including **h₁ékwos* 'horse', **kʷekʷlóm* 'wheel' and **h₂aks-* 'axle'. This conclusion is important, because archaeologists suggest that horse-drawn chariots were used by no one before about 4000 BC; we can be confident, therefore, that PIE must still have been spoken as a more-or-less unified language at this time.

The Indo-European dispersal

Around 6,000 years ago, the speakers of PIE began to spread out from the smallish area they had previously occupied. Some moved westward, further into Europe, while others went eastward, further into Asia. While they dispersed, of course, the ordinary processes of linguistic change were continuing to operate. Everybody's speech was therefore diverging from the speech that was in use when PIE was still a fairly homogeneous language occupying a small area, but naturally the same changes did not occur everywhere. Every local speech variety was undergoing its own individual changes, in grammar, in pronunciation, and in vocabulary. After several centuries, the now well-dispersed local varieties were already very different from the unified PIE speech of the original group, and also very different from one another. For a time, these local varieties could still plausibly be regarded as no more than regional dialects of a single language, but eventually the accumulated differences became so great that this was no longer possible. PIE had split up into several entirely different *daughter languages*.

Thanks to the accidents of history, we know quite a bit about some of these diverging groups, while about others we know little or nothing.

Two large groups can be at least dimly discerned as early as perhaps 2000 BC. In Anatolia (modern Turkey), speakers of a branch of Indo-European (from now on, IE) settled: the branch we call *Anatolian*. (In fact, one or two specialists think that PIE actually originated in Anatolia, but this is a minority view.) Several Anatolian languages are recorded in writing from the second millennium BC, the most important being *Hittite*, the language of a powerful ancient empire.

Around the same time, speakers of another branch of IE moved through the Balkans and down into the area now known as Greece. This branch was the direct ancestor of Greek, though at this early date the language would still have been very different from the Classical Greek of Plato or Herodotus.

It was probably around the same time that a third branch began what would be a long journey to the east. This branch, known as *Indo-Iranian*, consists of two main sub-branches, *Indic* and *Iranian*. We have written evidence that Indic had reached modern Syria no later than 1400 BC, and probably much earlier. But the speakers of Indic kept moving eastward, until they finally settled in northern India, probably in the first millennium BC. For Iranian, we have less information, but we know that Iranian speakers occupied the steppes north and east of the Black Sea for many centuries before eventually moving into the areas they occupy today, chiefly Iran and Afghanistan and some neighbouring regions.

Other IE speakers settled in the Balkans, but our information here is so sparse that we have little more than a few language names to work with, like *Illyrian*, *Dacian*, *Macedonian* and *Thracian*. By about 1000 BC, the *Italic* group had occupied a large part of Italy. And at some stage the speakers of the *Baltic* group moved into the area along the coast of the Baltic Sea, the speakers of *Armenian* and of *Albanian* arrived in their historical homelands (the Armenians probably via southeast Europe and Anatolia), the speakers of the *Tocharian* group settled around oases in what is now western China, and the speakers of the *Slavonic* branch found themselves occupying a gradually expanding region of eastern Europe.

There may well have been other groups of Indo-Europeans in various parts of Europe, but information is lacking. There is a limited amount of evidence in place names for what scholars term *Old European*. But much evidence has been obscured by the fact that in the last millennium BC another branch of IE began to expand almost explosively: Celtic.

Starting, it is generally agreed, from a homeland in east-central Europe, almost certainly around 1200 BC, Celtic speech began spreading with astonishing speed and effectiveness across Europe. Within only a few centuries, Celtic languages were established from Ireland and Britain in the west across France, the Low Countries, much of Spain, Switzerland, northern Italy, southern Germany, Austria, Bohemia, much of the Balkans, and even part of Anatolia (the Galatians, to whom St Paul wrote an epistle in the first century AD, were Celts, settled around modern Ankara). It appears that Celtic speakers were the first people in Europe to master the use of iron, and it may simply be that their iron tools and iron weapons gave them an unbeatable advantage.

But Celtic domination of Europe would prove to be short-lived, for a couple of reasons. One of those reasons was taking shape in the north, where we must now turn our attention.

Proto-Germanic

One of the latest branches of IE to emerge clearly from obscurity is the one we are most interested in here. In the first millennium BC, a group of IE speakers were settled in southern Scandinavia, Jutland and the north German plain. For some reason, the changes which their speech variety had undergone had been unusually dramatic – in pronunciation, in grammar and in vocabulary. We call their branch of the family the *Germanic* branch, and by about 500 BC these people were speaking a language which was greatly changed from its PIE ancestor: *Proto-Germanic*.

There are no records of Proto-Germanic, because its speakers had no writing. But we know a great deal about it from its daughter languages.

Proto-Germanic had lost a great deal of the grammatical complexity inherited from PIE. But it was grammatically complicated in comparison with Modern English. For example, it retained the three grammatical genders of PIE, and it still had many grammatical endings, with a considerable number of classes of words requiring different sets of endings. It had also managed to acquire some new grammatical constructions which had not been present in the ancestral language. For example, Proto-Germanic had greatly simplified the PIE verbal system, but in the process it had invented a new way of constructing past-tense forms of verbs, one not previously found anywhere in the IE languages. This new past tense was made by suffixing a /d/ or a /t/ sound to the verb. English still has this system today, as in *love/loved* and *walk/walked*.

Proto-Germanic had also acquired a great deal of vocabulary not found in other IE subfamilies. Some of these words were perhaps built on inherited IE stems, but others were very likely taken from some unknown and now long-dead language or languages which were already spoken where the early Germanic peoples subsequently settled. Among the new words were the ancestors of English *rain*, *finger*, *hand*, *blood* and *boar* 'male pig', all of which are found in every Germanic language, but nowhere else.

Table 5.1 *Some Grimm's Law changes*
(a) PIE (and Latin) /p t k/ > Germanic /f θ h/
(/θ/ is the sound of English *th* in *think*)

Latin	English
pater	*father*
piscis	*fish*
ped-	*foot*
tres	*three*
tenuis	*thin*
turdus	*thrush*
cornu	*horn*
cord-	*heart*
collis	*hill*

(b) PIE (and Latin) /b d g/ > Germanic /p t k/
(but PIE /b/ was extremely rare)

decem	*ten*
dent-	*tooth*
duo	*two*
granum	*corn*
genu	*knee* (whose /k/ used to be pronounced)
gelidus	*cold*

The pronunciation of Proto-Germanic had undergone a series of startling but highly regular changes. One of the most famous of these is the *First Germanic Consonant Shift*, otherwise known as *Grimm's Law*, named after Jacob Grimm, the pioneer historical linguist and, along with his brother Wilhelm, collector of folklore and stories; some Grimm's Law changes are presented in Table 5.1.

After around 500 BC, the speakers of Proto-Germanic began spreading into a larger area, and their speech slowly split up into a number of distinct daughter languages, one of which was destined to become English. Linguistically, the languages descended from Proto-Germanic are usually classified into three groups. The northern group stayed in Scandinavia. The eastern group moved first into Poland but then continued moving restlessly across southwest Russia, Ukraine, the Balkans, Italy, France, Spain and, for some, north Africa. The western group established itself in north-central and northwestern Europe.

Eventually the Greeks and more especially the Romans became aware of these Germanic neighbours to the north. After one disastrous attempt at incorporating a large stretch of Germanic territory into their empire, the Romans settled in the first century AD for placing their northern frontier along the rivers Rhine and Danube, with the Germanic tribes on the other side and outside direct Roman control. This state of affairs remained relatively stable for several centuries.

The period of stability was ended by invasion. The Huns, a group of nomadic peoples originating in central Asia, began moving into Europe from the east and exerting pressure on the settled Germanic speakers. The Germanic speakers reacted to the threat by pressing in turn against the Roman Empire. Avoiding the Roman garrisons, Germanic war parties slipped across the frontier into the empire and began raiding the Roman farms and cities; more organised raids and invasions followed. In 476, the last Western Roman Emperor abdicated. Any centralised power remaining in Italy was seized by a succession of Germanic strongmen. Although a considerable number of Germanic speakers settled in the Western Empire during this period, their descendants eventually switched over to the language of the majority which, with the exception of north Africa (where the Vandals settled), was a form of Latin. A few Germanic words survived in some of these languages, however, such as French *bleu* 'blue', Italian *albergo* 'inn' and Spanish *blanco* 'white'.

On the European continent, Germanic dialects brought by the immigrants were only successful in surviving (and 'defeating' Latin) for the first 100km or so over the Rhine or Danube. Thus the previously Latin- (or Celtic-)speaking regions of northern Belgium, the southern Netherlands, the German Rhineland, Luxembourg, Lorraine and Alsace in France, German-speaking Switzerland, southern Germany and Austria are now Germanic in language (although some of the local dialects demonstrate considerable influence from Romance languages). Small groups of Germanic speakers survive in northern Italy today, even though their contact with the Germanic north has been very limited. Most impressive of all in terms of survival was Crimean Gothic: in the early seventeenth century the Spanish ambassador to the Khanate of the Golden Horde (a Tatar group based in the Crimea), who happened to be a native Dutch speaker, was shocked to hear some locals speaking a language whose words he recognised as similar to his own. These were, we think, descendants of the Goths who stayed in the Crimea rather than entering the Roman Empire in the fourth and fifth centuries.

But despite these small-scale survivals, it has to be recognised that the linguistic effects of the Germanic 'take-over' of the Western Roman Empire were not great.

Germanic varieties in Britain

There is one exception to this tendency, however – the Roman province of Britannia – essentially modern England and Wales. Left to defend itself around 410, Britannia entered what is probably the only true 'dark age' of the Dark Ages. We know very little about what happened in what was to be England for most of the fifth and sixth centuries. By the time Britannia was reconnected with the post-Roman world around 600, the south and east of the former province was dominated by Germanic – English – speakers. It should be stressed, however, that, with the exception of a few slaves and mercenaries, Germanic varieties had been previously unknown in Britannia, where Latin was the dominant language, but rural people would have mainly spoken British, the ancestor of Modern Welsh, Cornish and Breton. The ancestor of English came from elsewhere.

During the period of Roman power in Britain, the ancestor of English at this time was a collection of local Germanic dialects spoken along the North Sea coast of the continent, in parts of what are now the Netherlands, Germany and Denmark. This collection of dialects we call *North Sea Germanic*.

The speakers of North Sea Germanic made little use of writing, and we have no written texts of any length in their language. But the Germanic speakers did have the *runic futhark* (named for the first six letters), an alphabet whose forms derive largely from Roman models. What little writing we have from this time amounts to brief inscriptions on swords and stone, normally commemorating someone or expressing ownership.

Living along the North Sea, these people were less disturbed than their cousins by the Hunnish invasions. But in the fourth century AD, the removal of Roman troops from Britannia left a power vacuum in an island whose riches, good soils and temperate climate the Germanic peoples across the North Sea obviously coveted.

Exactly what happened next is obscure. According to one story, the suddenly independent British, who had not had to defend themselves for centuries, now found themselves under attack by the Irish and other neighbours. They appealed to the Germanic speakers for help, something the Roman authorities themselves had earlier done. In any event the Germanic speakers certainly began moving into Britain in some numbers. Within a couple of generations, there were so many Germanic speakers in Britain that their Germanic speech had entirely displaced the earlier Celtic speech from large tracts of Britain.

The Germanic tribes that provided most of the new settlers were the Angles (from Schleswig-Holstein in northern Germany), the Saxons (from the area around the mouths of the Weser and the Elbe in Germany), the Jutes (from Jutland in Denmark) and perhaps also the Frisians (living in the islands off the North Sea coasts of the Netherlands and Germany). Since the first two groups were the largest, the settlers came to be known collectively as the Anglo-Saxons by Latin writers. The southern part of Britain acquired the new name Angle-land, or England, and the intrusive Germanic speech of the settlers was dubbed Anglish, or English. English therefore originated as the local Germanic dialects of those dwellers along the North Sea who happened to cross over to Britain.

The several Germanic tribes occupied different parts of Britannia. The Jutes (and, perhaps, the Frisians) settled in the southeastern corner, modern Kent and on the Isle of Wight. The Saxons established themselves along all the rest of the south coast, and also on the north side of the Thames estuary. The rest of England, the midlands and the north (including some of southeast Scotland), was settled by the Angles.

Where the Saxons settled, some transparent local names were conferred, and these names have endured: the territory of the East Saxons (Essex), of the Middle Saxons (Middlesex), of the South Saxons (Sussex), and of the West Saxons (Wessex). There are still counties of England named Essex and Sussex today, and Middlesex survived as a county until local government reforms in the late 1960s. On the other hand, Wessex had dropped out of use until it was partly revived by the writer Thomas Hardy and again by Queen Elizabeth II when she made one of her sons Earl of Wessex.

By the eighth century, the Anglo-Saxons were beginning to write their English language quite regularly. For this purpose, they largely abandoned the runic futhark, using instead a version of the Roman alphabet, supplemented with a few runic letters and other special characters to represent English sounds for which the Roman alphabet provided no letters. This early form of English, known as Old English, was very different from the modern language. It was still a very typical Germanic language, with several different classes of words requiring different sets of endings. Here is a sample:

Her…Ælfred cyning…gefeaht wið ealne here, and hine geflymde, and him æfter rad oð þet geweorc, and þær sæt XIIII niht, and þa sealde se here him gislas and myccle aðas, þet hi of his rice woldon, and him eac geheton þet heora cyng fulwihte onfon wolde, and hi þæt gelaston…

Unless a Modern English speaker has studied Old English, this would seem like a foreign language. Here is a word-for-word gloss:

Here…Alfred king…fought against whole army, and it put-to-flight, and it after rode to the fortress, and there camped fourteen nights, and then gave the army him hostages and great oaths, that they from his kingdom would [go], and him also promised that their king baptism receive would, and they that did…

The structure of the language still being obscure to Modern English speakers, a full Modern English translation is necessary:

Here [in this year] King Alfred fought against the whole army, and put it to flight, and rode after it to the fortress, and there he camped for fourteen nights. And then the army gave him hostages and great oaths that they would depart from his kingdom, and they also promised that their king would receive baptism. And they did these things.

The first passage *is* English, but so much has happened to the language in the last 1,100 years that we would be pushed to recognise it as such. Much has changed since then – in pronunciation, structure and vocabulary. In the following sections we will be concentrating mainly on this final category, primarily because the results are normally more clear-cut. If anything, however, structural changes to English have been more significant than changes in vocabulary over the last 1,000 years.

The Scandinavian contribution

From the late eighth century on, the prosperity and cohesion of the English kingdoms was jeopardised by contact on English soil with speakers of North Germanic varieties, whom we conventionally term the Vikings. Some of these Scandinavians were indeed the pirates and brigands of popular legend. Most, however, were farmers and traders whose lives were not at all different from those of the indigenous English. Although the effect of these migrations was felt throughout England, it was the north of the country, especially the land south of the River Tees and north of the River Humber, which was affected for longest. Former political entities – most notably the kingdom of Northumbria – were discarded in favour of a new kingdom of York, a major 'player' in the Viking world, whose *þriðingar* (Old Norse for 'thirds') are still visible in the three *Ridings* of Yorkshire. Scandinavian dialects probably continued to be spoken in isolated parts of the north until the twelfth century.

In the northern and eastern midlands of England, lying north and east of a line running from the River Dee at Chester to the River Thames at Westminster, Scandinavian rule was more short-lived, but considerable numbers of Norse-speaking settlers, we believe, moved there. This settlement was probably at its strongest in the north of the region, around boroughs such as Derby, Leicester and in Lincolnshire. This area, along with the north, became known as the *Danelaw*, due to a treaty of 878 which defined where the writ of English and Danish law would run in England. This somewhat separate status continued to be recognised linguistically until the local government reforms of 1975. In southern England, for instance, counties were divided into *hundreds*, based originally upon the number of able-bodied men who could be called up to form a mass defence force. In the Danelaw, the same unit was called a *wapentake*, the Viking Norse word for the stash of arms kept for these events.

To the west and south of this line, Scandinavian rule was temporary. Indeed, it was from the kingdom of Wessex, previously something of a backwater, that resistance turned to reconquest, in the first instance in the person of King Alfred, called the Great (reigned 871–99). Simplifying somewhat, Wessex became 'England' and, indeed, the written dialect of its royal chancery, late West Saxon, became the first standardised form of English.

Inevitably, these differences in settlement history had linguistic repercussions. Northern English dialects have many more Scandinavian words than do midlands dialects (including the London dialect that is the source of present-day Standard English). Southern dialects, where they still exist, have even less Norse influence exerted upon them.

The North Germanic dialects brought to England were obviously related to English. There is a long-standing debate among historical linguists over whether the two were mutually intelligible. My own feeling is that it depends on what is meant by *intelligibility*. It is very likely that Scandinavians and native English would have had considerable problems understanding each other, but would still recognise the many words they had in common. Over time, people in these situations make *accommodations* to each other – they avoid words they know the other people don't know but emphasise common vocabulary, use simplified grammatical structures, and so on. Many of the structural developments through which English has passed may be attributed to these contacts in northern England.

One result of this close contact was that hundreds of Old Norse words and forms found their way into English. Some of those Scandinavian words have remained confined to the English of the north of England and, often, of southern Scotland, such as *lug* 'ear', *bairn* 'child' and *kirk* 'church'. But many others spread more widely, until they finally became universal in English.

For example, the native English word for 'take' was *niman*, which would have become *nim* if it had survived. But it didn't, except in the word *nimble*: Old Norse *taka* prevailed, leading to Modern English *take*. Similarly, Old English *giefan* 'give' became Middle English *yive* (just as Old English *geolu* became *yellow*), but the Old Norse form *give* eventually drove the native version out of the language.

In very early Old English, the consonant sequence /sk/ changed into the single sound /ʃ/ we spell <sh> today. So, for example, Old English *fisc* had once been pronounced /fisk/ but by the time of King Alfred it was pronounced in a similar manner to the modern pronunciation. As a result of this change, no native English word ever contains the sequence /sk/ – with a couple of exceptions like *ask* and *tusk*, which have complicated histories. But Old Norse retained /sk/: most everyday words in English beginning with this sequence come from Old Norse, including *sky*, *skin*, *skid*, *scales* (for weighing), *skip*, *skittish*, *scant*, *skittle*, *skulk*, *skull*, *scare*, *scathe*, *scoff*, *scold*, *scorch*, *score*, *scrap*, *scream* and *scrape*. Interestingly, native English *shirt* and Scandinavian *skirt* are the same word in origin. We can assume, I think, that the word meant 'large garment worn close to the skin'; over time – and perhaps through developments in fashion (and greater affluence) – the English form came to be associated with a garment covering the torso, while the Norse word now refers to a garment covering the upper legs.

An interesting case is that of *window*. The Old English words for this object were *eagthyrl* 'eye-hole' and *eagduru* 'eye-door'. But these were driven out of the language by Old Norse *vindauga*, literally 'wind-eye'. Later, Old French *fenester* became a competitor, and this was used side by side with *window* until the mid 1500s, after which the Scandinavian word triumphed. Oddly enough, in

Table 5.2 *Old Norse words in English*

Nouns	Adjectives	Verbs
husband	*big*	*hit*
law	*awkward*	*die*
fellow	*flat*	*get*
outlaw	*happy*	*raise*
knife	*ill*	*cut*
root	*loose*	*call*
anger	*wrong*	*crave*
bark (of a tree)	*low*	*droop*
wing	*meek*	*drown*
awe	*odd*	*gape*
band	*rotten*	*gasp*
bank	*rugged*	*glitter*
brink	*same*	*guess*
bull	*tight*	*kindle*
crook	*ugly*	*lift*
girth		*ransack*
haven		*thrive*
keel		*thrust*
loft		*want*
mire		
race		
slaughter		
stack		
steak		

the modern Scandinavian languages, while Danish and Norwegian use a descendant of the Old Norse form, Swedish uses a form descended from Old French, probably via German.

Also from Old Norse is *leg*. The Old English word was *sceanca*, which has become our word *shank*, remembered now largely in the nickname of Edward I of England, called *Langshanks* because of his long legs. But *shank* has now become specialised to denoting the lower part of the leg and to certain metaphorical uses, and the Old Norse word has taken over as the ordinary anatomical term.

Other words of Old Norse origin are listed in Table 5.2.

In some cases, as with *give*, the Old Norse word replaced a related English word. We have Old Norse *sister* in place of native *suster* (or *swoster*), *weak* in place of *woak*, *birth* in place of *birde* and *loan* in place of *lean*.

There were more complicated developments. Old English *dream* meant 'joy', but the word changed its meaning under the influence of Old Norse *draumr*, which meant 'dream'. Similarly, Old English *gift* meant 'bride-price', but it acquired the meaning of Old Norse *gipt* 'gift' – and it also acquired the initial consonant of the Scandinavian word, since the native form should have developed into *yift*.

The contact with Norse went well beyond the borrowing of random words. The Old English third-person pronouns were *he* 'he', *heo* 'she', *hit* 'it' and *hi* 'they'. But it appears that plural *hi* became rather uncomfortably similar in sound to the singular forms, because English speakers adopted the Scandinavian pronoun *they*, which eventually more or less displaced the native form. Old English *hi* had a dative form *hem*, and this inflected form still survives in Modern English as the form we write *'em*, as in *Give 'em my regards*. Indeed, some scholars have suggested that central elements of the structure of English – possibly word-order patterns and the presence of a discrete definite article – are the result, at least in part, of the influence of Norse.

What are we to make of the Scandinavian influence on English? Although there are only a few hundred Norse words in Standard English, they are generally homely and used on a day-to-day basis. In fact, it would be very difficult to say more than one or two sentences without using a Norse borrowing. In the areas where the main contact between English and Norse speakers took place – northern England – many more words were borrowed. But the nature of the contact remains the same: essentially between equals intimately interacting in a domestic setting. The structural changes we touched on briefly would support this view – lengthy and intense contact would be necessary for these outcomes.

The next major external influence upon English was of a very different kind.

Norman French

In 1066, Duke William of Normandy led an army across the English Channel into England, defeating the defending English army at Hastings, and assumed the throne of England. Until 1400, when Henry IV usurped the throne, all the kings of England from the Conquest on were born outside the kingdom; normally in France. While many of them spoke English, French was their mother tongue. For the new aristocracy, on the other hand, English became within three or four generations the language of everyday communication in most families. Until the fourteenth century, however, French, and French alone, had prestige. Indeed, a number of the most prominent examples of early French literature, such as the *Song of Roland*, were actually composed in England. As a result, the blossoming English literary tradition was largely forgotten, as almost all writing was carried out in French or Latin.

Old English was most certainly not an undeveloped vernacular, lacking in the vocabulary required for a sophisticated and complex society. In fact, Old English had developed quite a large vocabulary of abstract and technical terms, using the ordinary Germanic word-forming processes of compounding,

Table 5.3 *Some Old English vocabulary*

lustfullic	'pleasure-full'	joyful
with-sprecan	'against-speak'	contradict
to-cuman	'to-come'	arrive
god-spellere	'good-message-er'	evangelist
boc-cræftig	'book-crafty'	learned, erudite
tungol-witega	'star-knower'	astrologer
heah-fæder	'high-father'	patriarch
leornung-cniht	'learning-boy'	disciple, apprentice
ingethanc	'in-thought'	conscience
oferlufu	'over-love'	adulation
hat-heort	'hot-hearted'	passionate
ath-bryce	'oath-breaking'	perjury
emn-niht	'even-night'	equinox
treowyrhta	'wood-wright'	carpenter
cypmann	'purchase-man'	merchant

prefixation and suffixation. Table 5.3 presents just a small sample of that rich Old English vocabulary. The first column gives the Old English form; the second column is a literal piece-by-piece translation; and the third column is its Modern English equivalent.

But these words are unfamiliar to us. After the Conquest, French became the language of prestige and status in England, while English enjoyed little standing. A knowledge of English was useful only in dealing with the common people, but advancement required French.

For English speakers with ambition, French words came to seem far more elegant and graceful than their crude English equivalents. As a result, upwardly mobile English men and women began to pepper their English speech with French words, the same French words which were in constant use by the Norman overlords. It is understandable that native English *here* and *að-bryce* should have been displaced by French *army* and *perjury*, since the French words were the only ones in use in the army and in the law courts. But English speakers went much further. For instance, they abandoned *to-cuman* for French *arrive*, *leornung-cniht* for *apprentice*, *ingethanc* for *conscience*, *hat-heort* for *passionate* and *treowyrhta* for *carpenter*. Moreover, as often happens when speakers move from one language to another, as Norman French ceased to be anyone's native language in England in the course of the thirteenth and fourteenth centuries, originally French speakers couldn't always 'find' the right English word and used the French equivalent instead. Because most of these final French speakers were politically or economically powerful, their language, even when technically 'wrong', was inevitably influential. After three centuries practically the entire native English abstract and technical vocabulary had been obliterated in favour of words taken from Norman French or from Latin. It is estimated that between 60 and 80 per cent of the native English vocabulary disappeared during this bloodletting.

The Norman flood brought us *picture, question, treasure, mercy, suspense, reception, immediate, pure, crime, subtle, exempt, suffice, mirror, music, defend, control, journal, multiply, journey, region, country, office* and countless others.

Practically all of English words beginning with /v/ are of Norman French origin: *virtue, vanity, vowel, virgin, vassal, vault, vary, value, vacant, vanquish, vermin* and even *very*.

Native English words never contain the digraph <oi>, and almost all words containing it come from Norman French: *oil, coin, boil, join, point, poison, soil, cloy, toil, loyal, royal, joy, poise, foil, destroy, alloy, ointment* and others.

Norman French contributed practically the entire traditional vocabulary of linguistics: *language, sentence, question, noun, verb, adjective, pronoun, tense, case, participle, infinitive, subject, object* and many more.

In fact, even such everyday Old English words as *andwlita, ea, weald* and *berg* disappeared from the language, replaced by their French equivalents *face, river, forest* and *mountain*. Old English *dal* was reduced to a regionalism, *dale*, and the normal word became *valley*.

But despite this overwhelming influx of French words, the backbone of English vocabulary has remained resolutely Germanic. Personal pronouns, grammatical words, number names, most body-part names, most kinship terms, names of basic materials, most names of natural phenomena and of geographical features, everyday verbs and adjectives – all are native English. They include the following words: *me, you, and, the, with, to, in, not, two, seven, head, heart, arm, foot, man, woman, child, father, mother, daughter, stone, wood, iron, gold, sun, moon, star, wind, rain, snow, tree, road, path, stream, ford, bridge, come, go, think, believe, speak, wonder, live, laugh, stink, red, black, old, young, new, little* and *short*.

In spite of the vast – indeed, overwhelming – effect of Norman French on English vocabulary, English is still undeniably a Germanic language. English sentences may contain French and Latin words, but those sentences are put together in native English. Moreover, unlike the Norse influence just discussed, the French influence on English is largely concentrated in high prestige and abstract semantic fields. French words are much less well represented in the everyday fields where Norse is strong. Nevertheless, even if we didn't know the history behind the Norman Conquest and its aftermath, we would still be able to see this difference.

The resurgence of English

By the fifteenth century, English had become the most prestigious language variety used within England, with the exception of Latin. Poets like Chaucer, Gower and

Langland, active in the second half of the fourteenth century, had helped establish this primacy; the fact that Gower and Chaucer – by far the most influential of this grouping – came from the southeast of England and wrote in dialects from that area could only help to increase a prestige which was already considerable because of the presence of the royal court and administration at Westminster.

In the early 1400s, young men who had been educated first in English rather than French began to take their places within the royal administration. By 1420–30, these men were now in positions of considerable authority. In using a written English derived from the practices of a limited number of London schools, a new, highly influential, 'house style' began to spread in the administration. This house style – dubbed *Chancery Standard* after the Royal Chancery by scholars – was quickly exported outside government. People wishing favours would naturally write in a way intended to be ingratiating to the centre; the fact that the new style was inevitably seen as the 'voice of the king' could not have hindered its spread. By 1500, the Chancery Standard had become the primary, and soon after the only, acceptable form of written English.

In the course of the fifteenth century, a new technology – possibly at least partly inspired by prior Chinese innovations – which allowed the mass production of the same version of the same text began to spread in Europe: movable-type printing. This technology had profound effects upon all European languages: as printing spread, the varieties of a given language which each printer chose came to be seen as having a particular authority within that community. Since print shops tended to congregate in centres of economic and political power – such as royal capitals – where the local language variety was already prestigious, (near) uniformity and prestige often worked hand in hand.

In the case of English, printing was first introduced in the 1480s by William Caxton. Some histories of the English language tend to exaggerate Caxton's importance to its development; largely, I think, because he is the first writer who was able to broadcast his work in considerable quantity with a relatively small amount of effort in comparison with the laborious copying by hand which preceded it. It was Caxton's ability to familiarise and popularise the already existing Chancery Standard which guaranteed its position as the ancestor of modern Standard English. It is certainly true that Caxton's work, although over 500 years old now, is much easier for a contemporary English speaker to read than that of Langland, writing essentially in a dialect deriving from the south-west midlands of England only some hundred years before that.

But this newly prestigious English was not considered by many users to be entirely appropriate to the domains in which it was intended to be used. After centuries of being subordinate to French and Latin, it was difficult to see English as being their equal. This was particularly the case with Latin, which was central to the experience of literacy in western Europe at the time and was also – through the Vulgate translation of the Bible – seen as the language of God.

At the same time, the English monarchy came very close to becoming the rulers of France. Now, however, there was no organic connection with a particular region of that country; there was no Normandy with which the rulers of England shared a common dialect. Indeed, the English power base throughout these years was in southwestern France, where the locals spoke a Romance variety which had more in common with Catalan or Italian than with the French of Paris.

Despite the considerable enmity that existed between England and France during this period (and, in one form or another, festered until the nineteenth century), French remained an influence of some importance upon the English language. Now, however, it was the prestigious speech of Paris which became the primary source of new vocabulary. Indeed, so prestigious was this new source that words which had already been borrowed from Norman French were reborrowed; we can trace these separate origins through the divergent sound patterns of the two dialects. Thus English has both Norman French *warranty* and Parisian French *guarantee*, for instance. While the difference in meaning between these two words is technical, that is not the case with *cattle* (Norman French) and *chattel* (Parisian French). Both originally meant 'possession'; the former has become increasingly specialised in relation to bovine mammals (although elements of its original meaning remain). This kind of distinguishing process is, of course, quite natural: there are very few occasions where a language actually needs two words which mean exactly the same thing. This process has continued. *Cavalier*, originally merely a Norman word for a horseman, has been joined in English by Parisian *chevalier*. On this occasion, however, the /ʃ/ in the latter tells us that this was a borrowing from the seventeenth or eighteenth centuries, rather than earlier, since it was during this period that Parisian <ch> ceased to be pronounced with the same sound as found in English *church*.

There had always been borrowings from Latin into English. Latin was the language of the Church, of learning and of high prestige. The meanings associated with *grammar* discussed in Chapter 2 demonstrate this importance: possession of Latin had magical connections for many people. But the level of borrowing from Latin which occurred in the fifteenth and sixteenth centuries was unprecedented.

Not all of the Latin words used in the language during this time were eventually accepted into the language: while *modern* was borrowed, *sempitern* 'always eternal', first used in the same poem, was not. Often this was due to the perception of redundancy: *sempitern*, for instance, isn't really necessary when we have *eternal* already. Some of the (attempted) borrowings were also considered pretentious by some and termed 'inkhorn words', words which passed from the writer's inkhorn to the page without ever being used in anyone's speech. But the perception that Latin rather than French origins were somehow preferable encouraged changes in the spelling of certain words, such as *doubt* for *dout* or *plumber* for *plummer*, which we'll discuss further in Chapter 7.

By the end of the sixteenth century, English had become a supple vehicle of expression across a wide range of domains. It was the language of law, government, the (Protestant) churches and a considerable and developing literature. Although something like a standard variety existed, it was not fully focussed and codified. Spellings were still highly variable (within a set of options). Creative artists could still experiment in vocabulary and structure in ways which would be considered deeply avant-garde today. Let's take a look at a famous speech by Shakespeare:

> Will all great Neptune's ocean wash this blood
> Clean from my hand? No; this my hand will rather
> The multitudinous seas incarnadine,
> Making the green one red.

Observe how effectively Macbeth jumps from plain English into baroque Latin polysyllables and then back again: this is unlike anything which had come before and, in reality, unlike anything which would follow in a fully codified English.

With the publication of the 1611 Authorised Version of the Bible, however, which itself was the product of over a century of experimentation, the greatest of authority was vested in the rather conservative London English it represented. Written in a relatively plain style which did not encourage experimentation and the borrowing of too many Latin or Greek words when native English ones sufficed (if you want to see what I mean by this, compare the language of the dedication of the Authorised Version to that of the translation itself), its authority gradually encouraged uniformity of use and discouraged experimentation.

Speakers of English were at something of a crossroads in 1611. New worlds were opening – both in space and in thought – which would inevitably affect the language profoundly. Many of these changes will be dealt with in Chapters 6 and 7. But before we leave the subject, an interesting question needs to be asked: to what extent could we turn the clock back and retrieve a 'native' English?

English vocabulary and 'purity'

Probably because of its contacts with Norse and, in particular, French, English is, in fact, unusually receptive to non-native words. While speakers of the language have never borrowed French vocabulary at the speed they did in the Middle Ages in the modern era, there are always a few words, such as *quiche* or *baguette*, which infiltrate due either to need or prestige. This borrowing impulse has been extended to any other language with which English has come into contact. In the last hundred years, *karaoke* has been borrowed from Japanese, *yoghurt* from Turkish, *kayak* from an Eskimo language, and so on. Very few people ever complain vociferously about this process (although someone might object to a particular word or set of words). This, even more than the borrowing, is unusual when compared with practically all other standardised European languages. In practice, speakers of these languages regularly borrow from external sources; this is often perceived as in some way 'diluting' the language, however. Vocabulary purism is practically unknown for English: indeed, English speakers often find purist outbursts pointless and faintly eccentric. They are also linguistically interesting.

In 1340, the Kentish monk Dan Michel wrote a book which he called *The Ayenbite of Inwyt* – in modern spelling, 'The Again-bite of Inwit'. This strange-looking title corresponds to Modern English 'The Remorse of Conscience'. The Latin word *remorsum* really does mean 'biting again', and the metaphor here is the notion that feelings of guilt keep biting (gnawing) at the sufferer. Latin *conscientia* is really 'with-knowing' rather than 'in knowing', but the monk preferred the second interpretation, using the native English word *wit*, which in his day meant 'knowledge', though it has since changed its meaning rather dramatically.

Michel's book enjoyed a certain notoriety, but his suggestions did not catch on. French and Latin continued to prevail in the English abstract vocabulary, and there was little interest in coining or using native English equivalents.

In the nineteenth century, the Dorset poet William Barnes raised a lonely protest against the mass of foreign words in English. He suggested, for example, that *omnibus* (modern *bus*) might be replaced by the native English creation *folkwain* 'people wagon' – a word which is curiously almost identical in formation to German *Volkswagen* 'people's car'.

In 1966, however, the humorist Paul Jennings provided us, in the pages of *Punch* magazine, with an example of what English might have been like if the Norman Conquest had never happened, and if William Barnes's dreams had come true. Here is an extract, in which the author adopts the conceit that William of Normandy was defeated at Hastings:

In a foregoing piece (a week ago in this same mirthboke) I wrote anent the ninehundredth yearday of the Clash of Hastings; of how in that mighty tussle, which othered our lore for coming hundredyears, indeed for all following aftertide till Domesday, the would-be ingangers from France were smitten hip and thigh; and of how, not least, our tongue remained selfthrough and strong, unbecluttered and unbedizened with outlandish Latin-born roots of French outshoot...Our Anglish tongue, grown from many birth-ages of yeomen, working in field or threshing-floor, ringing-loft or shearing-house, mead and thicket and ditch, under the thousand hues and scudding clouds of our ever-othering weather, has been enmulched over the hundredyears with many sayings born from everyday life. It has a unbettered muchness of samenoiselike and againclanger wordgroups, such as *wind and water, horse and hound, block and tackle, sweet seventeen*...The craft and insight of our Anglish tongue for the more cunning switchmeangroups, for unthingsome and overthingsome withtakings, gives a matchless tool to bards, deepthinkers and trypiecemen.

Some of Jennings's coinages may be difficult: *samenoiselike* means 'onomato-poeic', *againclanger* means 'alliterative', *switchmeangroup* means 'metaphor', *unthingsome* means 'abstract', *overthingsome* means 'metaphysical', *withtak-ing* means 'concept' (Latin *conceptus* is literally 'with-taking'), and *trypiece* means 'essay'.

How does this strike you? Would English be better off without its tens of thousands of borrowed words? Would the language be richer and more expres-sive if we said *foregoing* instead of 'preceding', *yearday* instead of 'anniver-sary', *othering* instead of 'changing', *hundredyear* instead of 'century', *inganger* instead of 'invader', *outshoot* instead of 'derivation', *enmulch* instead of 'enrich', *unbettered* instead of 'unsurpassed', and *deepthinker* instead of 'philosopher'?

Before leaving Jennings, I might point out that he slipped up slightly. The words *remained, noise, age* and *piece*, which occur in the passage, are in fact loans from French, if perhaps rather well-disguised ones, and *bard* is taken from Irish or Welsh. (And *loft* comes from Old Norse, although this is at least Germanic.) Even with scrupulous attention, it is not easy to get through a sentence of English without using any words of foreign origin.

The extensive foreign contributions to English vocabulary have produced an extraordinarily rich and expressive language. We can choose native English words for a blunt and direct style, or we can prefer French and Latin words for an elevated and subtle effect.

Conclusion

There is nothing *providential* about the present status of English. Its peculiar position as world language has been achieved through non-linguistic means. What *is* interesting about the history of English is the remarkable time-depth we can achieve when discussing a language which, until relatively recently, was rather obscure. During that period, we have seen how internal change can be affected by external contacts, a point to which we will return with other languages in Chapter 8. Most of all, the vocabulary of English has been changed and formed by external contacts.

Modern English is not monolithic, of course. It exists in a range of different dialects, primarily unwritten, which are often strikingly different from each other. More visibly, it also exists in a range of national standard versions, not normally *that* different from each other, but sufficiently so (and sufficiently associated with notions of national pride) to be remarked upon. The next chapter will deal with the most striking of these distinctions: between the 'mother' variety, British English, and that used by the most economically and politically powerful English-speaking country, American English.

6   Why is American English different from British English?

In the early seventeenth century, the first English-speaking colonists settled in North America, first in Virginia, then in Massachusetts, and before long along the entire east coast. Reinforced by a steady flow of English speakers from all parts of England and Wales and later also of Scotland and Ireland, these settlements guaranteed that English would be the principal language of the little colonies which would eventually grow into the United States of America, the largest English-speaking nation in the world. Today more than half of all native speakers of English are American citizens.

Those early settlers of North America took with them the same English they had spoken at home. Yet today the differences between British and American English are numerous and prominent. There are differences in pronunciation. To an American, *fertile* rhymes perfectly with *turtle*, while to a Briton these words do not sound even vaguely similar. And, to an Englishman, a *klahk* is a person who performs routine paperwork in an office, while to an American a *klahk* is a machine that tells you what time it is. There are differences in spelling: British *colour* and American *color*; British *civilise* and American *civilize*; British *theatre* and American *theater*; and many others. There are differences in vocabulary. The season after summer is *autumn* in Britain but *fall* in the States, and the thing you turn to get water is a *tap* in Britain but a *faucet* in the States. There are differences in word meaning. The *first floor* is located above the ground floor in Britain, while in the USA it *is* the ground floor. And there are even differences in grammar. Where an American says *I've just gotten a letter*, a Briton must say *I've just got a letter*, which is possible for the American but means something completely different – something along the lines of 'I have only got one letter'.

Where have these differences come from? And why are there so many of them? In this chapter, I'll try to provide some answers to these questions, illustrating them with examples, often those which confuse British people most.

As a taster, however, I will concentrate on one word which sums up the comment of George Bernard Shaw (neither British nor American, it should be noted) that Britain and the United States are 'divided by the same language'.

Aluminum

The name of the light, silvery metallic element with the atomic number 13 and the chemical symbol Al differs on the two sides of the Atlantic in a unique way: the British form is *aluminium*, with five syllables, while the American form is *aluminum*, with four. No other English word exhibits this peculiar kind of variation. *Magnesium*, for instance, has exactly this form everywhere in the English-speaking world, while the word *platinum* likewise shows no regional variation in form at all. So why the transatlantic difference in *alumin(i)um*?

In my experience, almost every person in Britain believes that the explanation is simple: the Americans have messed up the language *again*. But is this the case?

The metal itself was not known in ancient times, but one of its compounds was. This compound, called *alumen* by the Romans, is an astringent which is useful in stopping the bleeding from small cuts. In English, this compound is called *alum*; it is still used to make the styptic pencils used in boxing.

Another compound, which we now know to be the oxide of the metal, was isolated much later and named *alumina*; alumina is an important constituent of clays and of certain minerals, such as sapphire. And it was from alumina that the pure metal was finally isolated in the early nineteenth century.

The distinguished English chemist Sir Humphry Davy gave himself the task of naming the new metal. His first proposal (in 1809) was to take the existing name *alum* and simply add the Latinate suffix *-ium* to the end, producing *alumium*, but his friends disliked this name and persuaded him to think again. So, observing that the metal was derived from alumina, Davy simply changed the ending of this name to the metallic *-um* and thus came up with *aluminum* (in 1812). This new name spread rapidly throughout the English-speaking world, including of course the United States.

But then, some years later, another (anonymous) British chemist decided that names of metals 'ought' to end in – *ium* (as with *magnesium* and *potassium*; how he would reconcile this categorisation with the form of the gas *helium* is unrecorded, sadly), and so he proposed a change from *aluminum* to *aluminium*, with a slightly different spelling and a very different pronunciation. Within a few years the altered form *aluminium* had established itself in Britain.

In the USA, the American Chemical Society noted that the British had changed the name to *aluminium*, and, because most scholars in the young United States still looked to Britain as the main source of cultural and intellectual developments at this time, the Society changed its official form of the name to match the new British one. However, already used to Davy's original choice, *aluminum*, Americans continued to use this form, and they ignored the Society's official decision. This state of affairs continued for decades, with the Society officially recognising the newer British form, and everybody else in the States clinging to the older. Finally, in 1925, realising that no one was paying any attention to its earlier decision, the American Chemical Society bowed to reality and changed its official form back to *aluminum*.

Oddly, the curious British campaign in favour of *-ium* never reached *platinum*, with nobody arguing instead for **platinium*. Nevertheless, the Britons have never hesitated to play fast and loose with the language when it suited them, as we will see below. Tinkering with English is by no means an exclusively American hobby.

Why are the words different

The greatest differences between British and American English are in vocabulary. Entire books have been published consisting of nothing but lists of such differences. Some of these differences are obscure, while others are famous. Table 6.1 presents a small sample.

Because of a few cases like UK *lift* versus US *elevator*, there is a perception in Britain that American words are generally longer than the corresponding British words, when these differ. This is often taken by Britons as proof of American prolixity or pompousness. But this is not so, and there are just as many examples in which it is the British word which is longer. A book of recipes is a *cookbook* in the US, but conventionally a *cookery book* in the UK. The grassy strip between the two sides of a US *divided highway* or a UK *dual carriageway* is the *median* in the US but the *central reservation* in the UK. The British have no monopoly on brevity.

There are many reasons why the British and the Americans so often have different words for things. One is geography.

There is a plant whose fragrant leaves are often used as seasoning in cooking. These leaves are called *coriander* in Britain but *cilantro* in the USA. France has for centuries been regarded in Europe as the country with the most sophisticated high culture, not least in cuisine. French cultural influence on British English has been enormous – nowhere more than in matters of cuisine – and British *coriander* is taken from French *coriandre*. But faraway France has had almost no direct influence on the USA, and none at all on American cuisine, apart from the – only vaguely French – Creole and Cajun cuisines of Louisiana. But the US shares a long border with Mexico. Mexican cuisine, popular in many parts of the USA, uses the herb in question. Its Spanish name is *cilantro*, and that is what was borrowed into American English.

A similar discrepancy can be found in the names of the fleshy vegetable called *courgettes* in Britain but *zucchini* in the USA: the British name is taken from French again, while the American name this time comes from the language of the Italian immigrants who introduced it to American cooking.

Table 6.1 *Some British–American vocabulary differences*

UK	US	UK	US
lift	*elevator*	*pavement*	*sidewalk*
boot (of a car)	*trunk*	*waistcoat*	*vest*
leader	*editorial*	*vest*	*undershirt*
laundrette	*laundromat*	*aubergine*	*eggplant*
bowler (hat)	*derby*	*handbag*	*purse*
off-licence	*liquor store*	*pram*	*baby buggy*
beetroot	*beets*	*fringe* (hairdo)	*bangs*
head teacher	*principal*	*banknote*	*bill*
biscuit	*cookie*	*queue*	*line*
scone	*biscuit*	*flat*	*apartment*
fancy-dress party	*costume party*	*pensioner*	*retiree*
sleeping partner	*silent partner*	*lorry*	*truck*
football	*soccer*	*trousers*	*pants*
crisps	*potato chips*	*slowcoach*	*slowpoke*
fish slice	*pancake turner*	*rocket* (herb)	*arugula*

Another reason for transatlantic differences in vocabulary is merely different selection. Four or five centuries ago, the season after summer could be called either *fall* (a native English word) or *autumn* (a word taken from French). Both words were in use in Britain, and both were carried across the Atlantic to the American colonies. But the Americans gradually began to prefer the native word until it was finally the only word left in everyday speech, while *autumn* became confined to formal or poetic styles only. In Britain, precisely the opposite development occurred, as speakers increasingly preferred *autumn* for everyday use. The word *fall* became rarer. By the late nineteenth century, it was virtually gone in Britain except in the fossilised expression *spring and fall*; this phrase was used by the English poet Gerard Manley Hopkins as the title of one of his most famous poems, but today *fall* is completely foreign to most British people. Some elderly speakers of the traditional dialects of the English southwest may still use the word occasionally, but they are probably few in number now.

Much the same happened with the words *tap* and *faucet*, except that this time it was the British who finally settled on native English *tap* and the Americans who came to prefer the French word *faucet*.

For the most part, however, the lexical differences between British and American English are merely the inevitable result of two or three centuries of separation and independent development. Until well into the twentieth century, it took weeks of sailing to get from Liverpool or Bristol to New York, while any part of the vast interior of the USA required months of

Table 6.2 *British and American automobile vocabulary*

British	American
windscreen	*windshield*
bonnet	*hood*
wing	*fender*
quarterlight	*wing*
boot	*trunk*
carburettor	*carburetor* (with a different pronunciation)
indicator	*turn signal*
hazard lights	*flashers*
running lights	*parking lights*
tyre	*tire*

laborious travel from anywhere in Britain. Even if Americans and Britons had been eager to use the same words – and most of them were not – there were huge practical obstacles. When people on one side of the Atlantic needed a new word, they invented one, and they didn't bother whether other speakers in other countries thousands of miles away might be using a different word for the same thing.

Trains and cars provide good examples of this. As these new technologies spread on both sides of the Atlantic, they produced a large number of new, but often different, words. Just to start with, the new train systems were dubbed *railways* in Britain but *railroads* in the USA. Each of the individual units within a train came to be called a *carriage* in Britain but a *car* in the States. The person driving the train became a *train driver* in Britain but an *engineer* in the USA. The place where passengers got on and off was generally a *station* on both sides, but the American practice of attaching a storage building to a small local station led Americans to use *depot* (pronounced 'DEE-po') for a small station. A train stopping at every local station along a route became a *stopping train* for Britons but a *local* for Americans. And, as is well known, a ticket good for a complete trip is a *return ticket* in Britain but a *round-trip ticket* in the States.

Cars, invented decades later than trains, provide more dramatic differences, as demonstrated in Table 6.2.

A curious difference here is British *tyre* versus American *tire* for a rubber wheel covering. English speakers had for centuries been applying the name *tires* to the iron rims of wagon wheels. When the newfangled air-filled rubber rims were invented for motor cars, the Americans simply transferred the name to the new invention. But the British became so excited by the new gadgets that they decided a new name was called for, and so they capriciously changed the spelling to the more exotic-looking *tyre*.

Utterly mysterious to Americans are the British terms *off side* (for the side of the car where the driver sits) and *near side* (for the other side). The American terms are the altogether more transparent *driver's side* and *passenger side*, and probably no American has yet understood why the side farther away from the driver should be the 'near' side. Equally unfathomable to Americans is the British custom of applying *inside lane* to the lane next to the edge of the road and *outside lane* to the lane next to the middle of the road.

More recent still is the technology of films. Here, probably because of the enormous predominance of the Hollywood film industry, transatlantic differences are few. But the product itself has multiple names. The term *moving picture* has been used in English for centuries to label the output of all kinds of quaint mechanical gadgets, but the first record of its use in connection with films dates from 1896 – provided by Queen Victoria, no less! The slightly different version *motion picture* is recorded from 1891, in the USA.

The Americans soon settled on *moving picture* as their preferred word, but it wasn't long before this was clipped to *movie*, first recorded in 1912, which quickly went on to establish itself as the everyday American name. While the longer form *moving picture* gradually dropped out of use, the other form, *motion picture*, remained in American use, but as a much more formal term. Today this formal version is heard only in the name of the Academy of Motion Picture Arts and Sciences – the body that awards the Oscars – and in all those irritating trailers announcing 'Now a major motion picture!' (apparently Hollywood does not admit to any minor motion pictures).

British English went a different route. The word *film* had come to be applied to the strip of material on which the pictures were recorded, and in Britain this name was soon transferred to the movie itself – a use recorded in Britain from 1905. For many years, then, *movie* and *film* were a prominent transatlantic pair.

In recent years, however, the American *movie* has come to be heard frequently in Britain, probably because this word sounds cooler or zippier or more streetwise than *film*. At the same time, the British *film* has crept into use among Americans, many of whom have apparently decided that this word is more dignified and hence more appropriate for serious discussions than *movie*.

Another early name for the technology was *the flickers*, possibly derived from the jumpy experience for the viewer when film was shown too slowly and the separate still pictures which make up the moving image were perceptible. Shortened to *the flicks*, this has remained a very informal American word, as in *We're going to the flicks*, and it has also caught on in Britain. Furthermore, it has given rise to a new singular form *flick*, meaning '(an individual) film', as in *Spielberg's new flick*.

The place in which movies are shown also has different names. The first American name was *nickelodeon*, from *nickel* – the price of admission was five cents – and *Melodeon* 'music hall'. But the name didn't last long, perhaps because the price went up – although the word was later revived for a juke box costing five cents. Americans then seized upon the existing word *theater*, the usual name for a place providing public performances, and coined *movie theater*. In Britain, the situation was a little more complicated. The machine which showed the film had been dubbed a *cinematograph*, and the French version of this word was promptly shortened in French to *cinéma*. The shortened version was taken into British English as *cinema*, and the theatre accordingly came to be known as a *cinema hall* or *house*. This was itself shortened to *cinema*, which became the ordinary British word for a hall where a film is viewed communally.

The level of influence American English has had over British English vocabulary related to an industry dominated by America can be repeated in a wide range of fields. While the flow is not entirely one-way, the American contribution to the vocabulary of world English has been enormous. Among the countless American coinages are these: *radio, disc jockey, waterfront, right away, get along with, fall for, make the grade, break even, get around to, babysitter, boyfriend* and *girlfriend, scrape the bottom of the barrel, know-how, grapevine, in the red, bandwagon, hitchhike, show business, merger, publicity, executive, hindsight, gimmick, commuter* and *rare* (of a steak). No English speaker can open her mouth without taking advantage of this vast and often colourful American contribution.

American spellings

For a number of historical reasons, the English spelling system is complex, irregular and often downright eccentric. We pronounce the words *rite, write, right* and *wright* all the same. The past tenses of the verbs *lead* and *read* are *led* and *read*, which rhyme, but only the first gets a spelling change – while the name of the metal *lead* is pronounced like *led* but spelled like the verb *lead*. The words *through, bough, dough, cough* and *rough* look as if they should rhyme, but no two of them do. The vowel of *day* is spelled in a dozen or more different ways: *day, weigh, rain, lake, gauge, mania, prey, suede, veil, eh, great*, and the now old-fashioned *gaol*. And we have all sorts of mysteries like *debt, phlegm, autumn, knot, quay, sign, people, buoy* and *thyme*. Some of this eccentricity will be discussed in the next chapter.

Indeed, so eccentric is our spelling that you might think a few regional differences would hardly cause any comment. But not so. Even though Britons and Americans agree on the spellings of more than 99 per cent of English words, the transatlantic differences in the spelling of the small number of remaining words are conspicuous to everybody, and they attract a great deal of comment.

Why don't all English speakers spell all English words in the same way? To begin with, the fixing of English spelling was a long, slow, gradual process extending over centuries. In the Middle Ages, there was no agreed spelling system, and everyone used whatever spellings were normal in their region and appealed to them on that occasion. Here is a small sample from the year 1476, extracted from a letter by John Paston, a tiny part of the voluminous correspondence of the Paston family of Norfolk:

Mastresse, thow so be that I, vnaqweyntyd wyth yow as yet, tak vp on me to be thus bold as to wryght on to yow wyth ought your knowlage and leve, yet, mastress, for syche pore seruyse as I now in my mind owe yow, purposyng, ye not dyspleasyd, duryng my lyff to contenue the same, I beseche yow to pardon my boldness, and not to dysdeyn, but to accepte thys sympyll bylle to recomand me to yow in syche wyse as I best can or may jmagyn to your most plesure.

Observe that the word *mistress* is spelled in two different ways in this one sentence. At this time, and for centuries afterwards, such fluctuation in spelling within a single document was commonplace.

With the introduction of printing into England in the 1470s, English spelling began to grow more consistent, since the printers found it convenient to choose particular spellings and to stick to these as far as possible. But standardisation was a slow process. William Shakespeare, for instance, spelled his own name in several different ways – and fluctuation in spelling was still common in the seventeenth century, and far from rare in the eighteenth.

From the seventeenth century on, dictionaries of English began to be written, and the decisions of the lexicographers (dictionary-writers) helped to provide some further stabilisation. Even so, by the time of American independence in 1783, English spelling was still not fully fixed: there were still a number of words with multiple spellings.

In Britain, these variable spellings were addressed by the formidable figure of Dr Samuel Johnson, who compiled his own dictionary of English, published in 1755. In the cases of doubtful spelling, Johnson chose the forms he preferred, and his choices – many of which had already been selected in earlier dictionaries – have largely become the standard spellings in Britain. Let's look at some of his decisions.

English has a verb-forming suffix *-ize*, of Greek origin. This suffix occurs in very many verbs of some age in the language, like *realize*, *civilize* and *satirize*, and it is often used to coin new verbs, like *demonize*, *finalize* and *hospitalize*. Traditionally, this suffix was spelled *-ize* in English, and it still is in American English, where nothing has happened. In French, however, the spelling *-izer* gave way centuries ago to the changed spelling *-iser*, as in French *civiliser* 'civilise'. As so often, what the French were doing induced the British to do the same, and so many British writers began to write *realise* and *civilise* in place of the traditional forms. By Johnson's day, these new spellings had become common, and Johnson gave them his seal of approval.

As a result, the altered spellings with *-ise* are now preferred by most Britons. But not by all: some conservative quarters in Britain still insist on the old spellings in *-ize*. The august Oxford University Press prefers *-ize* in all its publications, including its dictionaries. The same was true of the *Times* newspapers before Rupert Murdoch bought them. Today, the traditional spellings in *-ize* are still universal in American English, but they are confined to a small and shrinking minority of conservative writers in Britain. Complaints about the change in spelling are now rare, but fans of the TV detective Inspector Morse – an Oxford man, of course – may recall that the eponymous sleuth, in dismissing a supposed suicide note as a forgery, shouted angrily at Sergeant Lewis 'You can't spell *realize* with an S, Lewis – it's illiterate!'

Much the same thing has happened with another familiar group of words spelled differently on the two sides of the Atlantic: the group represented by the words *theatre* and *centre*. The traditional English spellings of these are *theater*, *center*, and so on, and these spellings were well established by the seventeenth century. But, of course, the French spellings of these words are *théatre*, *centre*, and so on. Eager to claim some of the prestige of French for their own language, British writers began using the French spellings in English, and again Dr Johnson approved the new spellings. This time no conservatives held out in Britain, and *theatre* and *centre* are now the only possibilities in British English. But the older spellings remain undisturbed in American English, where they are likewise the only possibilities.

Why did these French-inspired changes in spelling find no lasting foothold in American English? The breadth of the Atlantic Ocean was no doubt one factor. But there was another one, much more important: Noah Webster (1758–1843).

Webster was an American writer with clear ideas. In an age when Americans were still inclined to look to the mother country for guidance on the language, Webster saw no reason to tolerate such an attitude. In his sturdy opinion, American English was every bit as good as the English of Britain, and perhaps even superior in vigour and inventiveness. Webster resolved to turn his back on Britain. American English should go its own way, and Webster was there to help it.

Webster's 1828 dictionary was as influential in the young United States as Johnson's had been in Britain three-quarters of a century earlier. The American had no time for the Frenchified pretensions of the British: he insisted on the traditional spellings *civilize* and *theater*, and his influence was great enough to see off any hesitant American inclination to follow the British lead here. Webster saw himself as a reformer who would free the language from many of the encumbrances it had accumulated during its long centuries of written history. To this end, he proposed a number of 'simplified' spellings. Not all his proposals won acceptance in the United States, but a few of them did.

One that did was the group of words containing *colour* and *humour*. Though the spellings of these words had earlier been as variable as those of any other words, by the seventeenth century all these words were largely spelled with -*our*. The spellings like *colour* were almost universal in Britain, and these were the spellings carried to the New World.

But Webster saw a chance to improve English spelling. He proposed removing the apparently useless letter U from these words and writing instead *color* and *humor*, which was also the spelling in Latin and therefore prestigious. Unlike some of Webster's other 'improvements', this one was warmly received, and the new spellings rapidly displaced the old ones in American English. Today *color* and *humor* are the only possibilities in American English, while *colour* and *humour* are likewise the only possibilities in Britain.

In fact, it is not difficult to see the attraction of Webster's simplification in this case. With all these words, the established spelling in Britain presents some fiendish complexities. The problem is that the U in these words disappears when certain suffixes are added – but not when other suffixes are added. So, for example, British spelling has *humour* but *humorous* and *humorist*. It has *vapour* but *vaporise* and *evaporate*. Worst of all is *colour*. British spelling requires *colourful* and *colouring*. Mysteriously, it also requires *colourist*, in spite of the spelling of *humorist*. With the suffix -*ation*, the preferred spelling is *coloration*, but this time the variant *colour-ation* is recognised by British dictionaries – if only because many people have no idea how to spell it.

These British spellings demand agonies of indecision and much hasty checking of dictionaries. And that's without even mentioning the many words that lack the U even in Britain, such as *terror*, *stupor*, *motor* and *pallor*. Thanks to Webster, however, the Americans have no anxieties here at all: the American spelling is always with -*or*, in every case, regardless of what suffixes may be present. It should be noted, nonetheless, that Dr Johnson was more consistent than is modern British English practice, employing spellings like *authour* for *author*, for instance.

Another of Webster's simplifications which caught on in the United States concerns the words like *traveller*. In British spelling, it has long been usual to double the final L of a verb whenever a suffix is added. So, *travel* forms *travelled*, *travelling* and *traveller*, and the same doubling occurs with other such verbs – *revel*, *unravel*, *pencil*, *bedevil*, *channel* and so on.

Webster saw no point in this doubling, and he proposed removing it. Again his countrymen agreed with him, and the American spellings are *traveled*, *traveling*, *traveler*, and likewise with all the other verbs of this type.

These are the principal differences between British and American spelling. Most of the remaining cases are miscellaneous one-offs. For example, American English requires *sulfur*, the spelling used in classical Latin, while British English has opted for *sulphur*, a quaint medieval spelling arising from a confused idea that the word was of Greek origin and so should have PH in it. On the other hand, British English prefers *artefact*, following the classical Latin spelling, while American English has *artifact*, following the medieval Latin spelling.

Britain formerly preferred *connexion*, but this spelling has now given way almost entirely to *connection*, long preferred in the USA and more obviously parallel to cases like *direction* and *section*. In a similar way, British *millepede* has now yielded to the American style *millipede*, and the highly eccentric British *foetus* has now been supplanted by the etymologically correct *fetus*, which has always been the only possibility in American English. (The Latin form was *fetus*, and the spelling *foetus* was originally an outright blunder.)

Pronunciation differences

The larger part of Great Britain has been occupied by English speakers for something like 1,500 years. This has provided more than enough time for large regional differences to evolve, in grammar, in vocabulary, and most obviously in pronunciation. The differences in accent (and dialect) between people from Somerset, London, Birmingham, Liverpool, Yorkshire, Newcastle, Glasgow, the Welsh valleys and elsewhere are very great, sometimes great enough to prevent understanding. But English speakers first reached the east coast of America only about 400 years ago, and they began settling California only about 150 years ago. Regional differences in American English are therefore much smaller than in Britain, simply because there hasn't been so much time for these differences to develop. Even so, the east coast is already home to some very prominent regional accents: no one would confuse the accent of New York with that of Boston or of North Carolina. Much of the rest of the country, though, has been settled so recently and so fast that noticeable regional differences in pronunciation have begun to emerge only quite recently.

However, it is still obvious to everybody that American accents are collectively very different from all the accents of Britain. There is perhaps no American accent today that might be mistaken for any kind of British accent, though some of the accents of New England sound anglicising to other American ears – if probably not to British ears. What are the reasons for these conspicuous transatlantic differences in pronunciation?

There is, of course, only one possible explanation: since the English-speaking settlement of America, changes in pronunciation have occurred on one side of the Atlantic but failed to spread to the other side. In fact, there have been very many changes in English pronunciation during the last 400 years. Some of these have affected both sides of the Atlantic. Some have affected only one side. Some have affected one side and spread to a little bit of the other side. Many have affected only part of one side, but often a prominent part. There are even one or two cases in which identical changes have occurred independently on both sides of the water, but at different times. Here we have space to look at only a few of the more prominent changes.

Difference 1: /r/-dropping

This is the simple label for what is technically termed *non-prevocalic /r/ loss*. This is a change in pronunciation which gained prominence in the south of England in the late eighteenth and early nineteenth centuries: the consonant /r/ disappeared from speech everywhere except before a vowel. In other words, /r/ disappeared in cases like *far, dark, bird, beer, cork, farther* and *order*, but it remained in cases like *red, try, three, arrange, berry* and *far away*. In the new kind of pronunciation resulting from this change, which we call *non-rhotic* ('/r/-less'), *star* rhymes perfectly with *Shah*, and *farther* is pronounced just like *father*. Neither of these things is true for speakers who retain the older style of pronunciation, which we call *rhotic* ('/r/-ful').

This new non-rhotic pronunciation arose among speakers of no particular social distinction, and at first it was stigmatised as a vulgarism in England. Over time, however, the new pronunciation crept up the social scale, until finally it became accepted by the upper classes in England as the elegant way to speak. Today non-rhotic pronunciation is the educated norm in all of England, and it is also typical of vernacular speech in all of England and Wales apart from the southwest of England (the 'West Country') and Northumbria in the far north. Scottish and Irish speakers firmly retain their /r/s, however. The more conservative rhotic speech of the West Country now sounds quaint to most people in England, and West Country speakers who want to be regarded as educated hasten to get rid of their native /r/s. (If you're not acquainted with it, the West Country accent is the 'Aar, Jim lad' accent always given to the sailors in portrayals of Stevenson's *Treasure Island*, which is set in that part of England.)

The new non-rhotic pronunciation was carried to the east coast of the USA and established itself in cities like Boston, New York and Philadelphia, places which a couple of centuries ago were still inclined to look to the 'mother country' for standards in English. But the new pronunciation made little headway in Canada, and it never crossed the Appalachians at all: the American speech of most of the country retained the historical /r/s in all positions, just as in the West Country.

Today non-rhotic speech is beyond question the prestige norm in England, and also in all the English-speaking countries of the Southern Hemisphere, which were mainly settled by non-rhotic speakers from England in the nineteenth century. But those American accents without /r/ – particularly that of New York City – seem actually under threat from the return of conservative rhotic pronunciations.

Into the early decades of the twentieth century, eastern Americans still regarded /r/-less speech, the kind heard in England, as elegant. It is quite noticeable that a number of American actresses of the 1930s and 1940s had non-rhotic – and in fact strongly anglicising – accents. Among them were Bette Davis and Katharine Hepburn, both born in New England in the first decade of the twentieth century. But the steadily growing prominence of midwestern and western accents, with their conspicuous /r/s, on the radio, in Hollywood films, and eventually on television, finally made rhotic speech the prestige norm in the American media, and the old non-rhotic accents were no longer favoured by performers with claims to elegance. Grace Kelly, who was born in 1928 into a rich and well-connected family in Philadelphia, a traditionally non-rhotic area, but more than twenty years later than Davis and Hepburn, was perhaps the last American actress to cultivate an anglicising accent, but by the 1950s it was the mainstream, /r/-full, accents of Marilyn Monroe and Doris Day that were the norm in Hollywood.

So, /r/-dropping is an innovation of England which has spread to a substantial part of the English-speaking world, but which, after a long flirtation, has failed to be accepted in North America. Americans and Canadians, like the Scots and the Irish, cling resolutely to the older pronunciation here. Some scholars have suggested that rhotic pronunciations have become associated with 'heartland' values in the USA rather than the worrying speech (and even more worrying politics) of the immigrant populations of the eastern cities with its lack of /r/.

Difference 2: /t/-tapping

Perhaps the single most striking feature of American pronunciation to British ears is the phenomenon of */t/-tapping* (or, in American terminology, */t/-flapping*). In an accent with /t/-tapping, the consonant /t/, when it occurs in the middle of a word or a phrase, and certain other conditions are met, is pronounced as a *tap* – that is, as a very brief flick of the tongue against the gum-ridge. Most American accents have this tapping, though in fact tapping applies not only to /t/ but also to /d/. As a result, in a tapping accent, *atom* sounds just like *Adam*, *latter* sounds just like *ladder*, and *waiting* sounds remarkably similar to *wading* (though these last two often remain marginally different).

British speakers often say that Americans 'pronounce their /t/s as /d/s', though in fact this is not what happens, and almost all Americans will strenuously deny this charge: Americans are sure that their /t/s are still /t/s, in spite of the phonetic tapping which goes on.

There is no doubt at all that this tapping of /t/ and /d/ is an American innovation; surprisingly little is known about its origins. Descriptions of American pronunciation produced in the early years of the twentieth century do not mention tapping at all, suggesting that it was not prominent at the time, and in fact the few sound recordings of American English that survive from this time do not show much tapping either. It therefore appears that tapping is a very recent development in American English, at least as a widespread phenomenon, although it may perhaps have been present much longer in some local areas.

But, at least since the 1940s, tapping has been close to universal in American speech, so we appear to be looking at a change in pronunciation which has spread with almost blinding speed. Tapping is also now commonplace in Canada, though it is not so pervasive there as it is south of the border.

Very strikingly, though, tapping is no longer a strictly North American feature: it has begun to turn up in English speech all over the world. In recent years, /t/-tapping has been observed in various vernacular accents of Britain, Ireland, Australia and New Zealand. It appears to be gaining ground in these countries. It may be that /t/-tapping will be universal in English in another two or three generations, in which case what is now a prominent transatlantic difference will no longer be so.

Are these other examples of tapping independent developments, or are they the result of American influence? Nobody knows for certain, since we just haven't had enough linguists and phoneticians stationed in every corner of the world to monitor the change. But the distinguished British phonetician John Wells thinks that the rapid spread of tapping is most likely the result of American influence – in which case its spread makes it the first distinctively American contribution to the worldwide pronunciation of English.

Difference 3: bath-broadening

Most varieties of English make a difference in pronunciation between the vowel in *can* and the vowel in *can't*. But only a few make a distinction between *cat* (pronounced /æ/ or /a/) and *bath* (pronounced /ɑː/). This distinction affects the following words: *bath*, *grass*, *fast*, *raft*, *master*, *dance*, *chance*, *aunt*, *can't*, *laugh*, *pass*, *plaster*, *after* and a number of others.

On the whole, these words have the *cat* vowel in the north of England, in Scotland, in Ireland, in Canada, and in all of the USA except part of New England. They have the *bath* vowel in the south of England, in Wales, in much of New England, and in all the Southern Hemisphere countries (although there is some variation with some of the words – most notably *bath* and *France* – in Australia).

This distribution should be enough to tell you what has happened: in all these words, the *cat* vowel is original, but they have shifted to the *father* vowel in the south of England, a change in pronunciation carried to all of the late-settled Southern Hemisphere countries but so far to nowhere else except Wales and New England.

This *bath*-broadening is a peculiar change. It did not happen in a regular and predictable way: instead, it applied to some words but not to other, similar words. Generally, it applied to a word containing the *cat* vowel when this vowel was followed by one of the sounds /s/ (as in *pass*), /f/ (as in *laugh*) or /θ/ (as in *bath*), or by the sequence /ns/ (as in *dance*) or /nt/ (as in *aunt*). But there are a number of exceptions: *gas*, *bass* (the fish), *mass* (amount of material), *Afghan*, *ant*, and quite a few others. There are also variable words: *plastic* and (Roman Catholic) *mass* usually have the *cat* vowel in *bath*-broadening accents, but sometimes they have the *bath*-vowel (particularly with the latter in 'old' English Catholic families).

Difference 4: Spelling pronunciation

Another group of words which are pronounced very differently on the two sides of the Atlantic is the group containing *fertile*, *sterile*, *missile*, *mobile* and *docile*. In the USA, these words have weak second syllables, so that *missile* sounds just like *missal*, *fertile* rhymes perfectly with *turtle*, and *docile* rhymes perfectly with *fossil*. In Britain, all these words are pronounced with strong second syllables which sound like *mile*. Why the striking difference?

The first edition of the great *Oxford English Dictionary*, compiled in Britain in the late nineteenth and early twentieth centuries, recommends the American-style pronunciation in every case, though it recognises the current British pronunciation as a second possibility in some cases. Clearly, then, we are looking at another British innovation, and a very recent one. Pronunciations rhyming with *mile* were just beginning to become noticeable in Britain in the late nineteenth century but were not yet accepted as the educated norm. Since then, these new pronunciations have driven the older ones entirely out of the language in Britain, while at the same time they have had no effect at all on American speech, which retains the traditional pronunciation, with a weak final syllable, in every case.

Where did the British change come from? It is an example of what we call a *spelling pronunciation*. During the nineteenth century, the rate of literacy grew enormously in Britain. This rapid growth in literacy had an interesting consequence: very many people began learning words for the first time by seeing them in writing, rather than by hearing them in speech. As a result, they guessed at the likely pronunciations of these words by looking at their spellings. Since *fertile* and the other words are spelled like *mile*, many Britons jumped to the conclusion that they must also be pronounced like *mile*, and, as a result, the new spelling pronunciations became frequent in speech – so frequent that eventually nobody was using any other pronunciation. By some chance, this never happened in the USA, where the new pronunciations are still wholly unknown.

There are other cases of spelling pronunciations in English. Centuries ago, the consonant /t/ was lost in an English word whenever it was preceded by /f/ or /s/ and followed by /n/ or /l/: *soften, fasten, hasten, castle, whistle, rustle, bustle, mistletoe* and others. In all of these words, the archaic spelling system retains the letter <t> just for old times' sake, even though nobody has pronounced a /t/ in any of them for centuries.

The silent <h> which was inherited from French, as in *heir, hour* and *honest*, has also given rise to some spelling pronunciations. Everybody now pronounces an /h/ in *host*, and almost everybody now pronounces an /h/ in *hotel*. In Britain, everybody now puts an /h/ into *herb*, while in the USA nobody does, and Americans retain the traditional pronunciation with no /h/, producing another striking transatlantic difference. On the other hand, many Britons have no /h/ in *adhesive* and *adhere*.

One more spelling pronunciation is audible in the names of the days of the week. These were traditionally pronounced with a weak final syllable, as though they were *Sundy, Mondy, Tuesdy*, and so on; accordingly, *Sunday* and *Monday* were perfect rhymes for *Lundy* (the name of an island), and *Friday* rhymed with the female name *Bridey*. These pronunciations are still usual in the USA, but in Britain a spelling pronunciation has altered the final syllable of every one of these, and most Britons now say *Sun-day*, with the second syllable pronounced just like *day*.

Difference 5: Unrounding of the *pot* vowel

We saw in Chapter 1 that earlier English ran into a problem with the vowels of *cot* and *caught*, which became uncomfortably similar in pronunciation. The solution in England was to move the vowel of *caught* to a new position, away from the vowel of *cot*, which has remained essentially unchanged. American English opted for the other solution, and it moved the vowel of *cot* in the opposite direction. In fact, American pronunciation moved the *cot* vowel so dramatically that it became identical to the *cat* vowel. This change is termed *the unrounding of* /ɒ/, where /ɒ/ is the phonetic symbol for the traditional value of the *cot* vowel.

But the American solution is not unknown in England. Queen Elizabeth I, in her private letters, spelled *stop* as *stap*, *God* as *Gad*, and so on with other such words. This can only mean that she too spoke with an accent in which the American solution had been adopted: the *cot* vowel had been moved forward in the mouth and (very likely) merged with the *father* vowel. Naturally, the portrayers of Queen Elizabeth I on screen, from Bette Davis and Flora Robson to Cate Blanchett, have declined to reproduce this pronunciation, which today sounds undignified to British speakers.

Difference 6: Stress retraction

Native English words are stressed on the first syllable: *thunder*, *wonderful*, *carefully*. The only exceptions are words containing prefixes, like *overcome*, *unhappy*, *forget* and *befriend*. But words taken from other languages often have the stress on a later syllable, as in *information*, *kangaroo*, *linguistics*, *psychology*, *raccoon* and *specialisation*. However, the native English pattern has been pervasive, and English speakers, all over the globe, exhibit a powerful tendency to move the stresses in these foreign words back to the first syllable.

There are very many English words of foreign origin which used to be pronounced with stress on the last syllable but which are now often heard with stress on the first syllable. A few examples are *magazine*, *research* and *cigarette*. In probably every English-speaking country, you can hear some people pronouncing these with final stress while other people pronounce them with initial stress. So far, we have no transatlantic difference.

But a few of these at least come close to being British–American differences. For example, the word *detail* is *always* pronounced with initial stress in Britain, while in the USA final stress is at least as frequent as initial stress. In Britain, *translate* always has final stress but initial stress in the States. More spectacular is the case of *inquiry*, which is always stressed on the second syllable in Britain but always stressed on the first syllable in the USA.

However, there is one group of words which constitutes an unmistakable transatlantic difference. These are the two-syllable words borrowed from modern French, such as *ballet*, *garage*, *café*, *croquet*, *beret* and *pastel*. In American English, these words are *always* stressed on the last syllable, while in British English they are always stressed on the first syllable. Although one or two of these words, like *ballet*, have been present in English for several centuries, most of them did not enter English before the nineteenth century, or in some cases even the early twentieth century. The

British–American differences here, then, do not really result from any changes at all, but only from decisions about how to treat these words in different places.

One result of this has been that speakers on one side of the Atlantic are startled by the pronunciations on the other side. Partly responsible for this is the universal English habit of reducing a syllable lacking the main stress. Take the word *café*, for example. Here the careful American kaf-FAY easily turns into k'FAY, which sounds odd to British ears. At the same time, the careful British KAF-fay just as easily turns into KAFFy – a perfect rhyme for *taffy*. Likewise, British *garage* commonly rhymes perfectly with *marriage*; British *beret* commonly sounds just like *berry*; British *ballet* commonly rhymes perfectly with *rally*; and British *croquet* commonly rhymes perfectly with *poky* – all of these being pronunciations which are very strange indeed to American ears.

They can even lead to misunderstandings. In my first few days in Britain, I was dumbfounded to hear a British TV newsreader apparently refer to 'Dame Margot Fonteyn, the well-known belly dancer'.

These are some of the pronunciation differences affecting groups of words. Many other differences are confined to single words. For Americans *codify* rhymes with *modify*, while for Britons it has the vowel of *code*. On the other hand, for Britons *granary* rhymes with *tannery*, while for Americans it has the vowel of *grain*. For Americans, *tomato* rhymes with *potato*; for Britons it famously does not. Britons stress *miscellany* on the second syllable; Americans on the first. Americans stress *controversy* on the first syllable, while Britons are more and more often now stressing it on the second – a recent development, and one which still annoys conservative British speakers. The pronunciation of *ate* as *et* has long been considered elegant in Britain, but it is regarded as ignorant in the USA, and it is now declining in Britain. The usual educated British pronunciations of *suggest*, *figure*, *recognise*, *manufacture* and *liqueur* – 'sa-JEST', 'figga', 'rekanise', 'mannafacture' and 'li-CURE' – all sound extremely uneducated to Americans, while the American pronunciation of *moths* – ending like *scythes* – sounds hilarious to Britons.

Differences in grammar

Among regional varieties of vernacular English, differences in grammar are considerable: *Us is ready*; *I seen him yesterday*; *They comes here regular like*; *I might could do it*; *I ain't seen nobody*. But most of these distinctive vernacular forms are not accepted as standard on either side of the Atlantic, and the grammatical differences between educated varieties of British and American English are in fact rather few. Still, a few differences do exist. Let's look at some of the more prominent ones.

Difference 1: The subjunctive

One of the most striking and even jarring grammatical differences between American and British English arises with certain verb-forms. American English makes a sharp and consistent difference in meaning between pairs of sentences like the following:

    (1) Susie insists that they be locked up.
    (2) Susie insists that they are locked up.

The first of these means 'Susie is demanding that they should be put behind bars', while the second means 'Susie is asserting strongly that they are already in jail.' This is a big difference, and it would not occur to an American to tangle these up.

Not so in British English, however. Structure 1 is practically non-existent in Britain, where it can be found only in the formal English of a few conservative speakers. In practice, British speakers say *Susie insists that they are locked up* in order to express 'Susie is demanding that they should be put behind bars.' Americans typically find this British construction bewildering.

The same difference is found after a large number of verbs with meanings like 'suggest', 'recommend', 'insist', 'demand' and 'require', and with structures like 'be important'. Here are some American/British pairs:

    AmEng: I suggest that Susie take the job.
    BrEng: I suggest that Susie takes the job.
    AmEng: The report recommends that he be promoted.
    BrEng: The report recommends that he is promoted.

This difference carries over to the past tense:

    AmEng: Susie insisted that they be locked up.
    BrEng: Susie insisted that they were locked up.
    AmEng: I suggested that Susie take the job.
    BrEng: I suggested that Susie took the job.
    AmEng: The report recommended that he be promoted.
    BrEng: The report recommended that he was promoted.

In all of these examples, the verb-form which appears in the American construction but not in the British construction is the simplest possible form of the verb, the form which is entered in a dictionary, and which is variously called the *base form* or the *bare infinitive*. For historical reasons, however, when one of these forms occurs in the constructions we are talking about here, it is called a *subjunctive*.

This so-called subjunctive is in fact a much-reduced remnant of what was a thousand years ago a whole array of subjunctive verb-forms in English. We may therefore conclude that American English has to some extent retained the ancient subjunctive, while British English has lost it almost entirely. And this conclusion is largely true, but with a rider. It does not seem to be the case that Americans have faithfully preserved the subjunctive through thick and thin, century after century, while the British were carelessly losing track of it. Instead, it appears that the subjunctive construction largely died out in American English during the nineteenth century, just as in Britain, but that it then made a dramatic comeback in America in the twentieth century, almost from the grave. Some scholars would suggest that this is due to the greater concentration on *prescriptive grammar* ('grammar' as found in grammar books rather than in everyday speech) in American education than in mainstream British education.

Difference 2: The present perfect

British speakers will probably find the following exchange wholly unremarkable:

> Susie: Have you eaten yet?
> Mike: Yes; we've just finished.

The verb-forms displayed here, with the auxiliary *have*, are instances of what is called the *present perfect*.

In American English, there is a high probability that this exchange will take a slightly different form:

> Susie: Did you eat yet?
> Mike: Yes; we just finished.

This time there are no present-perfect forms, and both speakers are using the *simple past* tense.

The present perfect is by no means absent from American English. But Americans seem to use the present perfect less frequently than do British speakers, and this failure to use the present perfect when it is possible is perhaps the feature of American grammar that strikes Britons most emphatically.

How did this difference come about? One popular suggestion is that the perfect was once usual in America, but that its use has declined over time, possibly because of the effect of the millions of European immigrants, few of whose languages contain a distinction comparable to English *I ate* and *I have eaten*. Obvious though such a view might appear, there is little direct evidence to support it. Another possibility is that the perfect has always been rather uncommon in English, and that the modern British taste for it is a rather recent development. There isn't much evidence for this view either, however.

Arguing against the first proposal is the observation that the American reluctance to use the perfect applies only to certain functions of the perfect, but not to all of them. For example, every American unhesitatingly says *Have you ever been to Europe?*, and nobody would try to express this as *Were you ever in Europe?*, which is possible but has a quite different meaning.

Interestingly, a recent study by Geoffrey Sampson has revealed that – contrary to expectation – the present perfect is in fact virtually extinct in the vernacular speech of southern England – though the perfect remains vigorous in northern England and in Scotland, and it remains a necessity in educated speech even in the south. Nobody knows how this has happened, but Sampson is inclined to suspect American influence. It seems that the difference is no longer quite so transatlantic after all.

Difference 3: Collective nouns

A third prominent difference of grammar between British and American English involves what we call *collective nouns*. Collective nouns are nouns naming groups of people, such as *committee, government, cabinet, working party, council*, and the official name of most sports teams. When one of these nouns occurs in its singular form, then American English requires singular agreement, while British English permits plural agreement and sometimes requires it.

American English requires *The government has announced a tax cut*. British English allows, and often prefers, *The government have announced a tax cut*, which is simply ungrammatical for Americans. Some British commentators suggest that plural agreement is especially to be expected in British English when the collective noun is used in a way that emphasises the presence of several people in the group, as in *The Cabinet are divided on this issue*. Quite possibly, but American English still demands *The Cabinet is divided*.

This difference shows up most clearly with the names of sports clubs. Britons almost unfailingly say *Liverpool have signed a new midfielder*; though *has* is technically possible here, no one ever seems to use it. In great contrast, Americans allow only *Buffalo has signed a new tight end*, and *have* in this sentence would be instantly ungrammatical.

How did this difference arise? I have seen very little work on this topic, and I don't feel confident about making assertions. My impression, however, is that earlier English was not particularly consistent about this kind of agreement, and that the two observable patterns have simply developed independently on the two sides of the water.

Difference 4: Compound nouns

We are already beginning to run a little short of significant grammatical differences, but here is one which is at least interesting. It involves compound nouns constructed by combining two simple nouns. English regularly forms compound nouns constructed by combining two simple nouns: *girlfriend, card game, chessman, ice cube, tennis racquet, footrace* and countless others. It used to be the case that the first element must always appear in what we might call its *singular form*, though a better label would be its *stem form*. So, a person who steals cars is a *car thief*, and not a **cars thief* (the asterisk here marks an impossible form). A football player who scores lots of goals is a *goal-scorer*, and not a **goals-scorer*. A man who runs endlessly after women is a *skirt-chaser*, not a **skirts-chaser*. Paul Simon or Paul McCartney is a *songwriter*, and never a **songswriter*, even though each has written many songs.

So powerful is this rule that it even applies to nouns that have no singular. For example, *oats* has only a plural form, and it has no singular at all: **an oat* is impossible. But it forms compounds like *oatmeal* and *oatcake*, and never like **oatsmeal* or **oatscake*. Likewise, we have *trouser pocket*, and not **trousers pocket*, even though no such word as **trouser* exists: **I need a new trouser*. (Exception: this last is normal for workers in the garment trade, but not for anyone else.)

This is the tradition. Naturally, English being English, a handful of exceptions have been long tolerated, such as *newspaper* and *sportswriter*. In recent years, though, things have changed.

When I first came to Britain, in 1970, I was soon struck by the frequency of exceptional forms. Everywhere I saw, and still see, forms like *trades union*, *greetings card*, *drugs pusher*, *expenses claim*, *examinations board* and *crafts teacher*. All of these are ill-formed in my American English, which allows only the forms without that <s> in the middle. Clearly British English has innovated here, I thought to myself: it has begun departing radically from the traditional patterns of English word formation.

But now I find that something similar is beginning to happen in American English. American English has not yet gone nearly so far as British English, and all the examples above are still unacceptable for most Americans. Change is taking place in baseball terminology, however.

The New York Yankees are a baseball team, and for as long as the team has existed its fans have been called *Yankee fans*, and its current manager has been *the Yankee manager*. Suddenly I find that the younger baseball writers are consistently describing Rudolph Giuliani as *a Yankees fan*, and Joe Torre (the incumbent) as *the Yankees manager*. This started happening perhaps only around ten years ago, but now it is pervasive. It's too early to say what the outcome will be, but it may be that the prominent transatlantic difference I found in 1970 will no longer be one.

Difference 5: Shall

British English (or at least England and Wales: Scotland is much closer to America on this occasion) still retains the auxiliary *shall* for use in cases like *I shall do it* – though this form is now decidedly formal and confined to educated speakers. American English has completely lost *shall* in this function, and it permits only *I will do it* or *I'll do it*. In American English, *shall* survives only when something like a binding offer is being given in the function illustrated by this example: *Shall I open the window?* Otherwise, *shall* is dead in the USA – and its future is uncertain even in Britain.

Difference 6: Other differences

The remaining grammatical differences are mostly rather trivial. Both varieties retain the traditional form *I've forgotten her name*, but only American English still has *I've just gotten a letter* – the form found in Britain in the sixteenth century – while standard British English has replaced this with *I've just got a letter* – or, increasingly now, with the alternative *I just got a letter*, possibly under American influence.

British English permits questions like *Have you any children?*, while American English prefers *Do you have any children?* To the question *Have you got rye bread?*, Britain prefers the answer *Yes; we have*, while the USA typically uses *Yes; we do*.

Britons say *He drove right past me – he can't have seen me*. Americans say *... he must not have seen me*. There are a few differences with prepositions. Britons *cater for* something, while Americans *cater to* the same thing. While the 'official' standard form is *different from* in both countries, the vernacular version is *different to* in Britain but *different than* in the States.

British English permits sentences like *Immediately she had arrived, we sat down to work*. This does not work for Americans, who require *Immediately after...* or *As soon as...* British English uses *in case* in a way that strikes Americans as odd: *There is a plastic screen around an ice-hockey rink, in case spectators are hit by the puck*. Americans require *... to keep spectators from being hit by the puck*.

Finally, Britons commonly use the phrase *your one*, as in *Which is your one?* Americans require *Which is yours?*, which is also the form preferred in formal written British English.

Summary

The many and prominent differences between British and American English have mostly arisen because of changes in English that have occurred on one side of the Atlantic but not on the other since the settlement of North America by English speakers several centuries ago – though some of the differences result from differing choices between competing forms that were already in the language at the time of the settlement. Changes have occurred equally on both sides of the pond, and it is not possible to say that one of the two varieties has changed more dramatically than the other during the last 400 years – except perhaps in pronunciation, where there is a good case that Britain, or at least the south of England, has changed more substantially than has America.

In the next chapter we will consider a further ramification of the history of English: its spelling system.

The mess that is English spelling

English has probably the most eccentric, irregular and infuriating spelling system in the world. While other languages, like Spanish, Italian and Finnish, have largely regular spelling systems with only a few exceptions here and there, English spelling is so densely buried in exceptions that the regularities can be hard to find.

On the one hand, a single sound gets multiple spellings. For example, all of the following words are perfect rhymes for most speakers of English (though not for Scots): *herd, bird, word, curd, heard, inferred, stirred, purred*. One rhyme, at least eight spellings. On the other hand, a single spelling often represents several different sounds: *through, dough, bough, cough* and *rough* look as if they should all rhyme, but in fact no two of them do.

So messy is English spelling that it becomes an entertaining exercise to find all the ways of spelling any single sound. Take the sound /ai/, as in the word *eye*. In how many different ways do we spell this sound in English? Here's a list, not guaranteed to be complete. Four or five of these are 'regular' spellings, found in a large number of words, while others are idiosyncratic spellings confined to a handful of words or even to a single word.

<i>	*I, pi, ivory, cacti*
<i…e>	*ride, wine, mile*
<ie>	*pie, die*
<ig>	*malign, sign*
<igh>	*sigh, high, tight*
<is>	*island*
<ic>	*indict*
<y>	*by, fly, why*
<ye>	*dye, lye, rye, bye*
<eye>	*eye*
<uy>	*buy, guy*
<ei>	*seismic*
<ais>	*aisle*

This is already thirteen different spellings for one sound, with very little in the way of rules for choosing one spelling or another (note *by*, *bye* and *buy*, for example, not to mention the colloquial *bi*, meaning 'bisexual'). And this number is in no way unusual. Try the sound /ei/, as in *day*. Here the first four are 'regular' spellings.

<a>	*atoll, acorn, potato*
<a...e>	*pane, hate, rake, fate*
<ai>	*pain, hail, vain*
<ay>	*pay, day, ray*
<au>	*gauge*
<e>	*elan, sauté*
<e...e>	*fete* (for most speakers)
<ei>	*vein, veil*
<ey>	*whey, they, grey*
<eig>	*deign, reign*
<eigh>	*eight, weigh, sleigh*
<ea>	*great, steak*
<eh>	*eh*
<es...e>	*demesne* (for some speakers)
<ao>	*gaol*

This time we have at least fifteen spellings. Let's try the sound /iː/, as in *see*. About four of these are regular.

<i>	*machine, libido, ski*
<ie>	*field, piece*
<e>	*we, be, he, edict*
<ee>	*see, bee, free, tree, week*
<ea>	*weak, bean, bead, sea*
<ei>	*seize, ceiling*
<ey>	*key, geyser* (for some speakers)
<eo>	*people*
<es...e>	*demesne* (for some speakers)
<ay>	*quay*
<ae>	*algae, Caesar*

English spellings for vowel sounds are, shall we say, uninhibited. But it is not only vowel sounds which exhibit such varied spelling. Look at the consonant sound /k/, which occurs at each end of the words *cook* and *kick*.

<k>	*king, key, cook, work, ankle, sky*
<c>	*cat, clam, sac, tic, music, acorn, scar*
<ck>	*sick, tack, beckon*
<q>	*quite, queen, banquet*
<qu>	*quiche, queue*
<que>	*torque, pique*
<cq>	*acquire, acquaint*
<cqu>	*lacquer, racquet*
<cc>	*accurate, soccer, tobacco*
<ch>	*chorus, chlorine, chemist, ache, ochre, lichen, tech*
<kh>	*khaki, khazi, khat, ankh*

And, on top of this, the consonant sequence /ks/ is often spelled with the single letter <x>, as in *six* and *sex*.

Given any speech sound of English, there are usually a number of ways of rendering it in our peculiar spelling system. But we don't only have many spellings for one sound. We also have many sounds for one spelling. Consider the sounds that can be spelled <ch>. There are at least three:

/tʃ/	*child, chase, rich, much*
/ʃ/	*chef, champagne, creche, sachet*
/k/	*chorus, chemist* (as above)

And Scottish varieties add a fourth, the distinctive Scottish consonant /x/, as in *loch* and in many names, such as *Auchtermuchty*.

In fact, there is no English letter which infallibly spells the same sound, and there is no English sound which is infallibly spelled in the same way. Even such generally reliable letters as <m>, <z> and <f> fail us in the words *mnemonic*, *zeitgeist* and *of*, and less obviously also in such words as *summer*, *puzzle* and *offer*, each of which contains two instances of the letter but only one instance of the sound.

Quite a few English words appear to be spelled in such eccentric ways that they seem to have been designed as a kind of torture for weak spellers. There is no principle of English spelling, however feeble and inconsistent, which can predict such crazies as *buoy, debt, one, have, people, autumn, two, eye, gauge, doubt, come, sieve, ghost, yacht* and *who*. And, for most of us, there is likewise no rhyme or reason to cases like *phlegm, knife, quay, buy, island, gym, aisle, mortgage, listen, caught, brooch, cough, height, only, foreign, indict, pneumatic, sign, yolk* and *mnemonic*.

It is dispiriting to discover that *lemon* does not rhyme with *demon*, that *fever* does not rhyme with *never*, that *geese* does not rhyme with *cheese*, or that *golf* does not rhyme with *wolf* (for most speakers, anyway). A capital letter makes all the difference in *polish* and *Polish*. And we have the bizarre case of *unionised*, which to most people suggests 'organised into unions', with one pronunciation, but which to a chemist suggests 'not ionised', with a quite different pronunciation.

And I haven't even said much yet about our unpredictable stress. Quite often, a single spelling must stand for two quite different words differing in the placement of the stress. Typical examples are *object* and *record*:

> *I object to this proposal.*
> *This is an interesting object.*
> *I'd like to record this interview.*
> *I'd like to keep a record of this interview.*

Our spelling system gives us no help at all in keeping track of these unpredictable stresses, and we just have to work on context.

In some cases, these variable pronunciations drive us into the arms of the hyphen, in a desperate attempt to avoid bewildering our readers:

> *She recovered the sofa.* ('She got the sofa back.')
> *She re-covered the sofa.* ('She put a new cover on the sofa.')

How did all this begin?

To begin with, our alphabet does not contain nearly enough letters. The English version of the Roman alphabet has only 26 letters, but practically every accent of English has 24 consonant sounds and somewhere between 14 and 20 vowel sounds, for a total of between 38 and 44 distinctive sounds which in principle ought to be spelled differently. A mere 26 letters is not nearly enough to do this straightforwardly.

This shortage of letters can be explained as follows. The first consonant letters were invented by speakers of the Semitic languages in the Near East, and then the first complete alphabet – with vowel letters – was invented by the ancient Greeks; even the Greek version was not quite good enough to write Greek unambiguously. The Greeks passed a version of their alphabet to the Etruscans, a non-Indo-European people of considerable cultural sophistication who lived in Tuscany and the area around in the first millennium BC, who passed it in turn to the Romans, who then found themselves looking at an alphabet with just 19 letters: A B C D E F H I K L M N O P Q R S T U.

The Latin language of the Romans had only 15 consonant sounds, plus five short vowels, five long vowels, and a few diphthongs, like the /au/ in *laus* 'praise', which sounded very much like our word *louse*. The letter Q, which had been invented by Semitic speakers to spell a consonant pronounced at the back of the mouth found in their languages, was of no real use to the Greeks, who simply dropped it, or to the Romans, who, out of respect for tradition, kept it anyway and invented a job for it. The Romans decided that the sound sequence /kw/ would be spelled QU in their language. This decision has been so carefully maintained by Europeans for 2,000 years that nobody in Europe ever uses the letter Q except before a U (except when transcribing languages like Arabic into Roman script). This is an illustration of how conservative writing systems can be.

In the alphabet the Romans inherited, the letter C stood for the sound /g/, while K stood for /k/. But the Romans, probably under the influence of the language of their Etruscan teachers, avoided K and began using C for *both* /g/ and /k/, leaving K unemployed apart from one or two special words. This is why Gaius Julius Caesar wrote his name *C. IULIUS CAESAR* (although the Caius in Caius College Cambridge is pronounced the same as *keys*!). Eventually, however, the inconvenience of this ridiculous decision struck home. Instead of reviving the exiled letter K, however, the Romans chose in the second century BC to invent a new letter by adding a stroke to the C, thus producing G.

During the same period, the Romans began to take over words and names from the then more prestigious Greek. Since Greek had a few sounds absent from Latin, the Romans borrowed three additional letters from the Greek alphabet, X Y Z, and tacked these on to the end of their own alphabet, where they were used mainly for spelling Greek words. With the newly invented G, these borrowings brought the Roman alphabet to 23 letters.

The Latin consonants included one pronounced like English <w>, as in *wet*, and another pronounced like English <y>, as in *yes*, represented in phonetic script as /j/. Since their alphabet had no special letters for these sounds, the Romans adopted a harmless-looking device, associating these consonants with similar vowel sounds. They were already using the letter U to spell one of their short vowels, the one similar to the vowel in English *put*, and the corresponding long vowel, much as in English *moon*. But they adopted U to spell their consonant /w/ as well. In the same way, they were using I to spell another short vowel, roughly as in English *bit*, and the corresponding long vowel, as in English *beat*, but they used the same letter as well to spell their consonant /j/.

As a result of these decisions, the chief Roman god, Jove, had a name which was pronounced 'yowis' but written *IOUIS*; the Latin word for 'wine' was pronounced 'weenum' but written *UINUM*; and the Latin word for 'young', pronounced 'yoo-weh-nis' was written *IUUENIS*. (The Romans used only capital letters; small letters did not achieve a fully independent status until centuries after the fall of the Roman Empire.) But we have changed the original Roman spelling of Latin for our own convenience, taking advantage of one more feature of the Roman alphabet which I haven't yet mentioned.

The letters I and U had two written forms apiece. The first could be written either I or J, while the second could be written either U or V. The choice was purely a matter of taste and convenience, and U was no more a different letter from V than B is a different letter from b among us. This lack of distinction remained the norm in Europe for many centuries after the Romans had disappeared, even after the sounds /j/ and /w/ had changed into quite different consonant sounds in spoken Latin (roughly the initial sounds in English *judge* and *vine*). In English, even up to the time of Shakespeare and beyond, we find spellings like *couer* for modern *cover* and *jt* for modern *it*. Eventually, however, in England and elsewhere, the custom grew up of writing the letters I and U for the vowel sounds but J and V for the consonant sounds. This overdue distinction gave our alphabet two extra letters, and we are now only one short of the modern total of 26.

In fact, that 26th letter had been invented some centuries earlier; and this time English played a large part in its creation.

Classical Latin had a consonant /w/, as we have just seen. Early on, however, the pronunciation of this consonant changed substantially in popular speech, from [w] to [v]. So, for example, the word *vinum* 'wine' changed its pronunciation from 'weenum' to 'veenum', and likewise for every other word in the language which had contained a [w] sound. But then the speakers of English adopted the Roman alphabet in order to write their language. And English has and had a consonant /w/. Since the Latin letter V, or U, now stood for [v], the English speakers had a problem: how should they spell their /w/?

The solution which the English finally settled on was a digraph: a sequence of two letters to represent one sound. The digraph they picked was UU, or VV (these two were the same, of course). So, for example, the word for 'wine' came to be written 'uuin' or, equivalently, 'vvin'. So familiar did this digraph become that eventually readers, writers and finally printers began to think of it as a single letter, different from all the other letters. And this is why the new letter bears the name 'double-U', and why nobody was troubled that a double-U looks on the page much more like a double-V.

With the creation of W, and with the separation of J and V from I and U, the Roman alphabet reached its modern total of 26 letters. Or at least it did for English speakers. Even though it would be decidedly useful to have an extra ten or fifteen letters at their disposal, English speakers have resolutely refused to extend the alphabet. In this determination English speakers are alone.

Every other European language which is written in the Roman alphabet copes with the shortage of letters by using diacritics (marks which are added to letters or symbols to show their distinctive pronunciation), resulting in symbols like *é*, *ç*, *ñ*, *ü*, *ø*, *å*, *ź*, *č* and many others. Since this is still not enough, very many languages further resort to digraphs (sequences of two letters) like *ch*, *ai*, *nh*, *ll*, *cz*, *tx*, or even trigraphs and tetragraphs, like French *oeu* (as in *coeur* 'heart' and *oeuvre* 'work') and German *tsch* (as in *tschüss* 'see ya!' and *deutsch* 'German'). English speakers refuse to make any systematic use of diacritics, and their use of digraphs is decidedly half-hearted and inconsistent: *child* but *chorus*, *bread* but *bead*, *thing* but *thyme*, and so on.

This willingness to modify the alphabet, often combined with a degree of enthusiasm for modernising the spelling system, has left most European languages with a far more orderly spelling than English has. But there is a down side: every written language has its own conventions, and these are often unpredictably different from other people's conventions.

Several years ago, a British friend of mine had to travel to the city of Århus in Denmark. She caught a flight to Copenhagen, made her way to the bus station, and looked for a bus to Århus. At the station she discovered that the bus stops were arranged alphabetically by destination. So she joined the queue at the A stop, and waited. And waited. After four hours, she finally asked someone for help, only to discover that, in Danish, the letter Å is considered a distinct letter from A, and it has its own place in the alphabet – right after Z. By the time she learned this, she had missed the last bus to Århus.

Historical spelling

The single most important reason for peculiar spellings in English is a simple one: we use historical spellings. Words aren't spelled the way they are pronounced today, but instead are spelled the way they were pronounced hundreds of years ago.

For example, until at least the sixteenth century (and much later in Scotland), words like *knife*, *knot* and *know* really were pronounced with a /k/ sound before the /n/. But for the last four to five centuries, most speakers have dropped the /k/ in every case. Nevertheless, the <kn> spelling was already conventional, and has never been modernised to reflect the new pronunciation.

The same is true of words like *write*, *wrong* and *wrestle*. These words were once pronounced with an initial /w/ sound, and again archaic spelling insists on retaining the letter <w>, even though the /w/ in these words disappeared from speech much earlier than the /k/ we have just been looking at, and long before the time of Shakespeare, except in northern Scotland, where a naughty child is often a *vratch* (wretch) and a carpenter a *vricht* (wright).

Words like *night*, *light* and *fight* were formerly pronounced with a consonant just before the /t/, a consonant like the Scottish sound in *loch*, for which we use the symbol /x/. Medieval English spelling used the letter sequence <gh> to represent this sound. But then this consonant disappeared from English (except in parts of Scotland, where it can still be heard with these words; all Scots maintain the sound in place and personal names). Nevertheless, English spelling has simply continued with the spellings that made sense eight hundred years ago.

In a few cases, though, the sound spelled <gh> did not disappear. In a few words like *cough*, *rough* and *enough*, something different happened. For lack of evidence, we have had to reconstruct the events surrounding these words, but here is what some scholars think happened. As the sound /x/ gradually disappeared from English speech, there remained, as always, a handful of conservative speakers who were still pronouncing it. When other speakers heard the conservative speakers pronouncing *cough* and *rough* with the traditional consonant on the end, they didn't recognise the noise, which was absent from their own speech, and so they assumed that they must be hearing the sound /f/ – the nearest sound they possessed to the vanishing consonant. As a result, many people began pronouncing *cough* and *rough* with an /f/ sound at the end, and for a few words this pronunciation gradually became established as the norm.

Our determination not to meddle with centuries-old spellings is also the reason for paradoxical spellings like *mood*, *good* and *blood*. Four hundred years ago, all these words rhymed, and so they all acquired similar spellings. But very complicated developments in the pronunciation of the English vowels between 1600 and 1700 meant that – in most accents, anyway – these words all wound up with different vowels. But we still use the archaic spellings.

Our devotion to archaic historical spellings has left us with spellings like *rite*, *write*, *right* and *wright*, all of which are now pronounced identically by most English speakers, but spelled differently. Perhaps the outcome is an unnecessary complication, but then again perhaps it is genuinely useful to have different spellings for these words of very different meanings. The same has happened with pairs like *see* and *sea*, and *meat* and *meet*, which are spelled differently because they were formerly pronounced differently, and the English language has simply kept their medieval spellings, as though as a reminder that a difference was once made that is now lost.

Dictionaries are littered with miscellaneous examples of the failure to keep English spellings in step with our pronunciations. The word that used to be spelled *pratty* has changed over the centuries; in this case the pronunciation has moved all the way to *pritty*, but the spelling went only as far as *pretty* and then became 'fossilised'. Something similar has happened with the word *English* itself, which used to be pronounced by English speakers the way the word still is in German, with the initial vowel being the vowel in *get*.

But changes in pronunciation are not the only reason for eccentric spellings.

Norman French, Latin and Greek

In 1066 the French-speaking Normans conquered England, and their Norman French became the prestige language of England for the next two or three centuries. Thousands of Norman French words poured into English, where they often displaced established native words.

When English speakers took French words into their language, they usually tried at first to reproduce the French pronunciation as best they could. Over time, however, as these French words became English words, their pronunciations were usually adjusted to some degree towards the norms of English pronunciation, so that the words lost their obviously 'foreign' patina.

But the spellings were another matter. English speakers, in taking words from Norman French, were strongly influenced by the conventional French spellings, and they retained those spellings, at least in part, though not as a rule entirely. This was true regardless of how they were pronouncing the words in English. And this policy had consequences. One such was the extended use of single letters to spell multiple sounds. For example, the Normans used the letter <c>, in some but not all circumstances, to spell both the sound /k/ and the sound /s/. We see these two functions in our words *calendar* and *cellar*, both of which were taken from Norman French. The Normans likewise used the letter <g> to spell two quite different sounds, and we faithfully adopted this practice too: both values can be seen and heard in the word *gauge*, taken from Norman French.

The English devotion to Norman French spellings is also the reason for much of the familiar confusion with <ie> and <ei>. Generations of English-speaking schoolchildren have struggled to master the rules and the exceptions here, and to remember to write *seize* but *siege* – both of these words coming, of course, from Norman French, in which there really was a difference in pronunciation which has not survived in English.

The pre-eminence of Norman French showed itself in other ways. Some of the traditional spelling conventions of English were lost and replaced by new ones based on French spelling or devised by Norman scribes. A splendid example is the introduction into English of the letter sequence <qu>. English had not previously used the letter <q> at all, and the sound sequence /kw/ had always been spelled <cw>, as in *cwic* 'quick, alive' and *cwen* 'queen'. (Strictly, of course, it was the early versions of <w> which were used.) But the Normans had faithfully preserved a version of the ancient Latin rule about writing <qu> for /kw/, and English speakers retained it in the words taken from Norman French, like *question*. Moreover, this new convention was extended to native words, and so the above-mentioned English words were re-spelled *quick* and *queen*, and likewise for all the other words in /kw/. As a result, English spelling acquired the use of the letter <q>, and also the familiar spelling rule that <q> can only occur before <u>.

This habit of retaining French spellings in English contributed to another prominent feature of modern English spelling. This feature is called *morphemic spelling*, and the label means that an element is spelled in essentially the same way even when its pronunciation changes greatly as a result of the addition of suffixes. For example, we took from Norman French such pairs as *nature* and *natural*, *medicine* and *medicinal*, *physic* (an archaic word for 'medicine') and *physician*, *oblige* and *obligation*, and our decisions about how to spell these pairs have made morphemic spelling the norm in the elevated and technical part of English vocabulary. Compare the quite different policy followed in the native English part of the vocabulary, where the words are typically so short that morphemic spelling would be hard to maintain: *deep/depth*; *gold/gild*; *bake/batch*; *long/length*; and so on.

In fact, the impact of Norman French on English spelling was really quite profound, though not all of the consequences involved complications. For example, English had lacked the consonant /v/ as a completely separate sound (a *phoneme)* until it was acquired in dozens of French words like *virtue*, *vowel*, *virgin*, *value* and *very*, and the choice of a suitable spelling was in this case eminently reasonable. But we also acquired another consonant sound from Norman French, this time somewhat indirectly, and this one causes problems. The rarest consonant sound in English is the one that linguists represent as /ʒ/, called 'long z' or simply 'ezh'. This sound occurs only in words taken from other languages, and mostly in words taken from Norman French. It occurs in the middle of *measure, pleasure, leisure, seizure, azure, illusion, vision, closure*, among others (although these words don't actually have /ʒ/ in French: original /zj/ changed to /ʒ/). We have never managed to come up with a consistent way of spelling this sound, and the more recent addition of further words from modern French, like *rouge* and *genre*, and words from Russian, such as *Zhivago*, has not helped.

But Norman French is not the only language which has contributed to our generally complicated spelling. Around the fifteenth century, English speakers began taking large numbers of words into the language directly from Classical Latin. They did this largely in order to provide the elevated and technical terms in which they judged English to be deficient. Such now-familiar words as *malleable*, *permanent*, *potent*, *investigation*, *globe*, *intermission*, *compulsion*, *introduction*, *universal* and hundreds more were self-consciously extracted from the pages of the Latin authors and inserted into texts written in English. Whatever pronunciation was settled on, these words were adopted with the closest approximation to the Latin spelling that could be accommodated. Usually the Latin ending had to be suppressed, since English no longer had a comparable set of endings, but otherwise the Latin spellings were preserved intact.

In large measure, these Latin words reinforced the spelling conventions already introduced from French. In some respects, though, the Latin words brought further conventions with them. For example, because of their differing Latin sources, English formerly used the spellings *direction* for one word but *connexion* for another. American English abandoned the distinction as pointless long ago, and has for generations written *-ection* uniformly for both words; in Britain, the same change has occurred only in the last few years.

However, given the earlier impact of French words and practice, the impact of Latin words on English spelling was much less dramatic than that of another classical language.

English-speaking writers had earlier added to English a number of words of Classical Greek origin, mostly words which had been taken from Greek into Latin and hence were borrowed as Latin words (or in a Latin form). But eventually it came to seem reasonable to begin taking over words directly from Classical Greek. This was particularly done in order to fulfil a need for new technical terms in a variety of disciplines, a practice still active today. But we seldom bother to import entire words from Classical Greek, since the ancient Greeks had little of the technology we now take for granted. Instead we assemble a set of building blocks, in the form of stems extracted from Greek, and use these to construct new technical terms as we need them.

Among those building blocks are such items as *electro-* 'electricity', *zo-* 'animal', *biblio-* 'book', *bio-* 'life', *astro-* 'star', and *thermo-* 'heat' (as prefixes) and *-logy* 'study', *-phile* 'lover', *-mania* 'excessive desire', *-graphy* 'writing' and *-pathy* 'disorder' (as suffixes). From this large set of building blocks, technical terms of any required meanings can be manufactured on the spot, such as *biology* 'life-study'. Where necessary, additional Greek elements can be added, as in *hyperthermophile* 'high-heat-lover', a recently coined term for an organism that flourishes at temperatures near the boiling point of water.

The Greek forms had somehow to be converted into our Roman letters. For this purpose, we have long used a conventional system. Each Greek letter is represented consistently by one or two of our letters. So, for example, Greek mu (µ) and nu (v) are simply rendered as <m> and <n>, while Greek phi (φ) and chi (χ) are rendered as <ph> and <ch>, and Greek upsilon (υ) is rendered as <y> (except, of course, with many of these letters in scientific contexts). This set of equivalents is followed religiously.

It is this system which produces the rather distinctive appearance of words of Greek origin, generally spelled with otherwise unusual combinations like <ph>, <ch>, <ps>, <y> and <rh>. Typical examples are *psychology*, *thermodynamics*, *astrophysics*, *nymphomania* and *tracheostomy*. The spelling of these items is something of a law unto itself, and it pays no particular attention to any other spelling conventions. Only in these Greek-derived words do we normally use <ph> to spell the sound /f/, and only in these words do we write <ps-> or <pn-> at the beginning of a word just to spell what we pronounce as /s/ or as /n/, as in *psychopath* and *pneumonia*. And, for the most part, it is only in these words that we find the sound /m/ spelled <gm>, as in *phlegm* and *paradigm*.

An unusual example of this process is *ptarmigan*, the name given to the high mountain grouse found in Scotland. This word is actually derived from Gaelic *tarmachan* 'grouse'. But sometime in the eighteenth century someone with a classical education connected the word to the Greek root *ptero-* (as in *pterodactyl* – 'wing finger'), meaning 'wing', probably because he felt that Greek was much more impressive than Gaelic (or because he believed, as some Romantics did at the time, that Gaelic was actually a form of Greek: something you could only think if you didn't know both).

These Greek words are now overwhelmingly dominant in our technical vocabulary, including medical terminology, and every moderately literate user of English is acquainted with the highly distinctive appearance of words like *synaesthesia*, *photosynthesis*, *hyperkinetic* and *chromatography*.

Between them, Latin and Greek have contributed one very prominent set of variable and often confused spellings to English. Latin had a pair of diphthongs /ae/ and /oe/, and Greek had a similar pair, /ai/ and /oi/, which are conventionally rendered in Latin and in English as <ae> and <oe>. These diphthongs are always retained in English in the spelling of proper names, such as Latin *Caesar* and Greek *Oedipus*. But, in words which are not names, their treatment is positively chaotic: we are not consistent in our decisions; the British and the Americans often make different decisions; and we sometimes change our minds.

The study of fossils is *palaeontology* in Britain but *paleontology* in the USA. Child medicine is *paediatrics* in Britain but *pediatrics* in the States. But the former British *encyclopaedia*, from the same Greek stem (*paidos* 'child'), has now mostly given way to *encyclopedia*, the form always preferred in American English. Probably nobody writes *oecumenical* for *ecumenical*, and absolutely nobody writes *oeconomics* for *economics*, even though the Greek source has the diphthong (it is *oikos* 'household').

Latin *foetidus* gives US *fetid*; the British form used to be *foetid*, but *fetid* is now generally preferred in Britain. Apparently by some outright confusion, Latin *fetus*, which gives American *fetus*, produced the bizarre form *foetus* in Britain for many years, though this erroneous form is now strongly disfavoured, and it is rejected in British technical use.

Words from the rest of the world

English speakers have never tired of borrowing words from other people's languages, and they have never changed their policy for writing them. When a word is taken from a language written in the Roman alphabet, English speakers practically always keep the original spelling, regardless of how they pronounce the word.

This policy is the reason for the unusual spellings in many borrowed words; some examples are presented in Table 7.1. At least, this is what happens when we borrow the word from the written language. Sometimes we take words instead from the spoken language, in which case the original spelling is ignored. For example, the American English word *hoosegow* 'jail', made famous by any number of Hollywood westerns, was taken from Mexican Spanish *juzgado*

Table 7.1 *Some 'foreign' words in English*

Italian	German	Polish
cello	*sauerkraut*	*zloty*
linguini	*blitzkrieg*	**Afrikaans**
pizza	*angst*	*trek*
Icelandic	*flak*	**Dutch (although the Dutch**
geyser	**Spanish**	**originals are spelled differently)**
French	*paella*	*gherkin*
champagne	*chorizo*	*yacht*
coup	*sangria*	*gherkin*
beret	**Portuguese**	*yacht*
soupçon	*auto-da-fé*	
bivouac	**Welsh**	
Basque (via Spanish)	*corgi*	
jai alai	**Finnish**	
Norwegian	*sauna*	
ski		

'courthouse'; since it was borrowed by ear, the Spanish spelling was ignored, and English speakers simply spelled the word the way it sounded. (In small western towns, the courthouse and the jail were usually in the same building.) And the American slang term *capeesh?* 'understand?' was taken orally from an unwritten local dialect of Italian, probably Sicilian; the written Italian form is *capisce*.

Most of our borrowings from Irish have been taken over orally, often via bilingual speakers. Only a handful of Irish words have come into English through writing, and these retain their Irish spellings, like *Dáil* (the Irish lower house of parliament) and *Taoiseach* (the Irish prime minister). More typical borrowings, though, are words like *banshee*, from Irish *bean sídhe*, *leprechaun*, from Irish *leipreachán*, and *shamrock*, from Irish *seamróg*. The same is true for Scottish Gaelic words.

When words are borrowed from languages that are written in something other than the Roman alphabet, more work is required. In principle, we have a system for converting other important scripts into our Roman letters, but in practice we do not always stick to our systems, and anyway those systems sometimes change.

For example, we have a system for converting words and names from the Russian Cyrillic alphabet. This system is based on the Russian spelling, and not on the Russian pronunciation, which is why we usually spell Russian names the way we spell *Gorbachev*, even though something like *Gorbachof* would represent the pronunciation more directly. But, of course, we are not consistent. The author of *The Cherry Orchard* and the composer of the *Nutcracker* both pronounced their surnames with the same initial consonant, and they both spelled their surnames with the same initial letter in Cyrillic, and yet we write *Chekhov* for the first but *Tchaikovsky* for the second, so regularly that now the alternative spellings *Tchekhov* and *Chaikovsky* look wrong to many of us. It is likely that the composer's name was affected by the French spelling conventions of the musical culture of the time; why this has persisted is a mystery, however. In any event, continuing indecision about how to write *borshch*, or *borsht*, or *borsch*, or whatever, shows that we are far from having a consistent policy for converting Russian words.

For Japanese, there are several systems available for spelling words and names taken from the language, but in practice we almost always prefer the Hepburn system (a romanisation system in use in Japan from the 1870s on), which gives us such now-familiar spellings as *sushi*, *tsunami* and *Fuji*, even though professional linguists generally prefer the linguistically more sophisticated Yale system (a romanisation system worked out in the 1940s), in which the same words come out as *susi*, *tunami* and *Huzi*. Hepburn has the advantage for English speakers of representing the Japanese pronunciation more directly from the point of view of English phonology, though in practice we usually don't bother with the Japanese long vowels, and we write, for example, *sumo* where strict Hepburn would have *suumo*.

For Mandarin Chinese, there are at least half a dozen systems on the market for converting Chinese words and names into our alphabet. Until the 1960s, the Wade-Giles system was almost universal in the English-speaking world, but then, partly at the request of the Chinese government, we switched abruptly to a quite different system, Pinyin, preferred by the Chinese authorities. It was this shift that suddenly altered the familiar forms of so many Chinese names, as *Mao Tse-Tung* became *Mao Zedong* and *Peking* became *Beijing*.

But the great complication with Chinese words in English is that most of them are not taken from Mandarin, the principal and official language of China, but rather from one or another of the several southern Chinese languages. (The label 'Chinese' covers at least seven quite distinct languages, all of them mutually incomprehensible; for historical reasons, these are referred to as 'dialects'.) The people who run Chinese restaurants are practically always speakers of these southern languages, and thus familiar Chinese words like *dim sum* and *wok* are not in fact taken from Mandarin Chinese at all, and the Pinyin system is of no use in representing them. We just have to do the best we can in putting them into English (or, indeed, any language).

Another language for which a consistent system of transcription does not seem to have been achieved is Modern Greek. Names of Greek items of food and drink are put into English in a way that is somewhat hit-or-miss. While we mostly seem to agree on *ouzo* and *moussaka*, some of us write *tzatziki* while others prefer *tsatsiki*, and other words exhibit similar fluctuation.

With Arabic, the regional varieties of that language differ so greatly from one another that sometimes they are not even mutually comprehensible, and indeed by some standards Arabic is really several distinct languages. The pronunciation of words and names varies enormously from place to place, and the traditional standard variety of Arabic, called 'Classical Arabic', does not correspond at all well to anybody's speech. This is why the Libyan leader's surname appears variously in English as *Gaddafy* or as *Qadhafy*, or something else, while his given name likewise turns up as *Muammar* or as *Moamer*, or something else.

With languages which are not normally written at all, or which were not written at the time English speakers took words from them, the resulting forms of borrowed English words may be a little unpredictable. English-speaking settlers in North America, in Australia, in New Zealand and elsewhere tried to pick up the local names of new objects and then tried to put these into English in an ad hoc way. Sometimes the results were words that don't look wholly un-English, like *woodchuck* and *squash* (the vegetable), but other examples, like *kiwi, kangaroo* and *canoe*, are decidedly peculiar in form. Vowel-rich Hawaiian has given us an especially large number of words that resemble few others: *poi* (a vegetable foodstuff), *luau* (a feast), *nene* (a goose), *pahoehoe* (a type of lava), *lei* (a garland of flowers), *lanai* (a verandah), and that great favourite of Scrabble™-players everywhere, *aa* (another type of lava).

Some confusions, oddities and blunders

As we briefly saw in the last chapter, the standardisation of English spelling has been a long, slow, gradual process, extending over centuries, and not generally achieved before the nineteenth century. Let's look here at the word *potato*.

This word was taken into English in the sixteenth century, via Spanish from the native American language Taino. In the sixteenth century, we find all of the following spellings in use in English: *botata, batata, battata, potato, potaton, potade, patata, potatoe* and the bizarre *potatus*, a confused Latinism. By the seventeenth century, only some of these were still in use, but then we find the further spellings *partato, potado, potata, pottato* and *puttato*. By the eighteenth century, this variation had been narrowed down to just three choices: *potato, patata* and *potatoe*. By the nineteenth century, only *potato* and *potatoe* were still in the running. The frequency of this second choice is one reason that we require the plural form *potatoes* today, even though we have finally settled on the singular form *potato*.

And this example brings us to another famous uncertainty about English spelling: when a word ends in *-o*, does it form its plural with *-os* or with *-oes*? As everyone knows, this is a chaotic matter. We have *pianos* but *torpedoes*, and *solos* but *heroes*.

Mostly, this is yet another accident. Just as the name of the vegetable was commonly spelled *potatoe* until the nineteenth century, the word now spelled *hero* was commonly spelled *heroe* until not so long ago. Such spellings helped to promote the plural forms *potatoes* and *heroes*, and these plurals in -*oes* were then extended to other words – for example, to *tomatoes*, which was usually *tomatos* in the eighteenth century.

Thanks to the vacillation and confusion of the past, English speakers have now managed to manoeuvre themselves into a position in which hardly anybody feels confident about spelling the plurals of these words. Even if most of them can manage to spell the singular forms, and thus to avoid the obloquy which befell the former American politician Dan Quayle when he embarrassingly offered *potatoe*, not so many of them feel sure about *cargo(e)s*, *fresco(e)s*, *mosquito(e)s* and *veto(e)s*.

Some English spellings are there for no very good reason. For example, *delight*, a word taken from Norman French, was originally spelled *delit*, but in the sixteenth century it came under the spell of all those native English words like *light* and *night*, and so it acquired a completely pointless <gh>.

Likewise, *should* and *would* contain a now-mysterious <l> because these words were once only the past-tense forms of *shall* and *will*, and they really did contain the sound /l/ at one time. But *could* began life as the past tense of *can*; it was never pronounced with the sound /l/, and we now spell it with an <l> merely because of the influence of *should* and *would*.

Some of our strange spellings exist for reasons that are very close to downright silly. A good example is the pair *debt* and *doubt*, both of which contain an utterly mysterious <b>. Why is that <b> there? Well, both these words were taken into English from Old French. The Old French forms were *dette* and *doute*, and originally we took them into English in the spellings *dette* (or sometimes *det*) for the first, and *dout* for the second. But then something strange happened. The two French words are descended from Latin *debita*, the plural of *debitum* 'that which is owed', and from *dubitum* 'doubt'. In the fifteenth and sixteenth centuries, a few writers of English reached the remarkable conclusion that it would be an excellent idea to insert a silent letter <b> into the spellings of these two words in order to remind all of us, ever so helpfully, of their remote Latin origins. Like many other bad ideas, this one prospered, and *debt* and *doubt* have been spelled with their pointless <b>s ever since.

Much the same thing happened with *reign*. This word, of French origin, was formerly spelled *reyne*. But the ultimate Latin source is the word *regnum*: again a few pedants decided that the word had to be spelled with a useless <g>.

Yet another example is *receipt*. The Old French form was *receite*, and the English form was at first about the same. But the Latin source of the French word was *recepta*, and so once again somebody decided, doubtless on the grounds of prestige, that the English word would profit from a <p> in its spelling. In the nineteenth century, this unhelpful spelling led to some confusion, as many writers got the word tangled up with *recipe*, a word which is distantly related to the first one but actually pronounced with a /p/ in it. Very likely you have seen *receipt* written where *recipe* was intended, though this confusion is less common now than it used to be.

As you can probably guess *indict* is one more example. This used to be spelled *indite*, reasonably enough, but the form of the Latin source, *indicere*, had the now predictable effect on our ancestors.

We are lucky that this business never went beyond a handful of words. It could have been a lot worse. After all, *age* derives via French from Latin *aetas*, but self-appointed linguistic arbiters have never decreed that we should spell the word *atge*, or something equally sensible. And, of course, our *rage* derives from Latin *rabies*, which you will recognise in another connection: *rabge*, anyone?

It is not only Latin which has had some strange effects on our spelling. When the Germans discovered a new metal and named it *Zink*, the word was promptly taken into English. But how was it to be spelled? Every other rhyming word in the language is spelled <-ink>: *sink, blink, ink, stink, brink, mink, slink, think, pink* and so on. Naturally, therefore, the metal was spelled *zink*, though some independent souls wrote the word *zinke* or *zinck* on occasion. But then somebody noticed that the French had settled on the spelling *zinc*, and of course anything the French do is elegant by definition, and so the spelling was altered to the unique *zinc*.

Isle was taken over bodily from Old French, where it had the same spelling, reflecting its origin in Latin *insula*. But then this borrowed word began to cause trouble. The native English word for the same thing used to be *iland*, as in John Donne's famous line *No man is an iland*. Since *isle* had an <s> in it, sixteenth- and seventeenth-century English speakers decided that so should *iland*, and the spelling of this was arbitrarily changed to *island*. In fact, this went so far that another wholly unrelated word got caught up in it. That word, taken from Old French, meaning the central part of a church, had previously been spelled *aile*, but the mere resemblance in sound was enough to bring about a change in spelling to *aisle*, the unlikely form we are stuck with today.

In some cases, the reason for a particularly eccentric spelling is simply mysterious. A good example is *build*. Now, by all history, logic and parallel, this word ought to be spelled *bild*. And this is precisely the spelling that was used, until the fifteenth century and the introduction of printing to England. For reasons that are absolutely unfathomable, the first English printer, William Caxton, chose to spell this word as *buyld*. In the modified version *build*, this impenetrable spelling has therefore become universal, and nobody has the faintest idea why.

Caxton is also the culprit in the spelling of *ghost*. This used to be spelled *gost*, just like *gold*. But Caxton preferred the spelling *ghost*, with a useless <h>. Practically all reference sources propose that Caxton did this because the related word was written *gheest* in Dutch – and Caxton had worked for a while in the Netherlands.

We have room for one last example of such tampering. There used to be a word spelled *rime*, applied to poetry; a few people still prefer this spelling today. But several centuries ago this word came under the spell of the unrelated word *rhythm*, of Greek origin, and so it acquired the bizarre spelling *rhyme*, which is the norm today.

Finally, let's turn our attention to a small set of words which share a peculiarity. Among them are *come, some, son, among, honey, money, monkey, love* and *glove*. What is strange about these words is that they all contain a vowel sound which is normally spelled with a U in English, as in *cut* and *buck*, but in all of them this vowel is spelled with the letter O. How did this happen? After all, the Old English spellings were quite different: *sum* for *some*, *sunu* for *son*, *lufu* for *love*, and so on.

The explanation, unexpectedly, involves medieval handwriting. In the Middle Ages, European handwriting was decidedly 'spiky' by our standards. Figure 7.1, for example, shows what a certain English word would have looked like in a typical medieval hand. It is difficult to make out the word because the lower-case versions of the letters <i u n m> (and also <v>, which at the time was not distinguished from <u>) were all produced with a series of angular strokes – one, two or three. When two or three of these letters happened to occur in sequence, the result typically looked like the example in Figure 7.1. The word is in fact 'mummy'.

Medieval readers found such outcomes just as vexing as we do, and various steps were taken to deal with them. One move was to mark out the small letter <i> by placing a dot above it – a custom which we still follow today, even though it no longer serves any purpose (except when writing Turkish). In the same vein, it became customary to place a little curve over a <u>. This custom has not survived in the English-speaking world, though you can still see it in some German handwriting today, to avoid confusion with <n>.

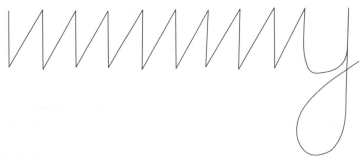

Figure 7.1 A mystery word

But in England, starting from the thirteenth century, writers came up with one further device. When a <u> came next to one of the other troublesome letters, then very often the writer replaced the <u> with a nice round <o> – which stood out clearly on the page in the middle of the spikes. And so, even after English speakers abandoned spiky handwriting in favour of the smoothly rounded styles most of us prefer today, we kept the quaint spellings with <o> in quite a few of these words, because people were used to them by then.

So, every time you type the strange spelling *come* or *love* into your keyboard, you are doing so because some medieval scribes decided to do it in the hope of making their angular hands a little more legible.

A recent complication

At the beginning of the twentieth century, English spelling was already about as eccentric as any spelling on earth. But since that time new complications have been built upon these complications.

In the last few decades, we have become inordinately fond of creating new English words by a variety of procedures which were formerly rare to non-existent. We have become especially fond of clipping, the process which gives us words like *bra* (from *brassière*), *bi* (from *bisexual*), *tache* (from *moustache*), *bus* (from *omnibus*) and *croc* (from *crocodile*). The resulting words often have orthographic forms which are rather peculiar, even by the relaxed standards of English. There are not so many established words which are spelled like *bi*, or like *recce* (a British word for *reconnaissance* or *reconnoitre*), or like *deli*, or *flu*, or *prof*, or *veg*, or *tech*, or the now little-used *hi-fi*, or so many others in this vein.

Sometimes clipping bumps into the existing peculiarities of our spelling. The word *busy* has a weird spelling which hardly suggests a rhyme with *dizzy*. The weirdness is retained in its derivative *business*, and therefore in the compound *show business*. This compound is commonly clipped, but apparently nobody considers that the orthographic form *show bus* is in any way tolerable, and so we have chosen to write the result as *show biz*, giving us yet another unusual written form.

And it is not only clipping that gives us orthographically odd forms. English spelling now make considerable use of several other non-traditional devices for coining new words, devices which give us such orthographically unusual items as *NASDAQ* (the name of the stock market), *op ed* (the page opposite the editorial page in a newspaper) and *OD* (meaning 'overdose'). When these things are inflected, and most especially when they are used as verbs, then all sorts of awkward outcomes may occur, as in *He OD'd on drugs*, which is routine in speech but not so easy to write. In the USA, *Federal Express* is the name of a parcel delivery service, commonly clipped to *FedEx*. This too can be used as a verb, producing yet other surprising looking forms: *I FedExed them the samples*.

All this activity is having noticeable consequences for the written form of English. Let's look briefly at just one development.

In the year 1900, there was perhaps no English word spelled with the letter <v> at the end, save only for the ethnic label *Slav*. And even this one was a recent addition to the language. For centuries, the word had been spelled *Sclave* or *Slave*; the spelling *Slav* was first recorded only in 1866, and it did not become usual until late in the nineteenth century.

Otherwise, words ending in the sound /v/ were spelled with <ve>. This was true even in cases like *give*, *live* and *have*, where the presence of the final <e> violates a familiar rule of our spelling: compare *hive*, *dive* and *cave*, and note cases like *bit* and *bite*, *whit* and *white*, *hat* and *hate*. The sole exception was the grammatical word *of*, whose spelling is wholly unsystematic and without parallel.

But, in the early years of the twentieth century, word-final <v> began to creep slowly into English spelling. In 1913, we find the first printed example of *lav* as a clipped form of *lavatory*. This was followed in 1920 by *rev* as a verb, as in *He revved the engine*. The American word for a fighting knife was recorded as *shive* in 1915, but from 1926 it was usually written *shiv*, its modern form. The British word *spiv* for a crooked businessman in flashy clothes is recorded from 1934. For the famous Cockney term of address, *gov*, I have been unable to locate a first attestation, but the word does not appear to be recorded very early.

Bit by bit, then, words with final <v> have been percolating into our dictionaries. Perhaps this development has been aided by the familiar forms of several given names: *Viv* for *Vivian*, *Bev* for *Beverly*, *Trev* for *Trevor*, and so on. Perhaps the growing use in English of words and names from other languages, like the Hebrew *mazel tov* 'good luck', *Liv Ullmann*, the Norwegian actress, and *Kapil Dev*, the Indian cricketer, has smoothed the way a little bit. Perhaps even opera chipped in, since the two short operas *Cavalleria Rusticana* and *Pagliacci*, which are commonly performed together, are affectionately known to opera buffs as *Cav and Pag*.

Whatever the reason, English speakers no longer seem to object to word-final <v>. In Britain, diesel oil for road vehicles is called *derv*, originally from *diesel-engined road vehicle*. The board game Trivial Pursuit™ is known to its fans as *Triv*. In the city of Brighton, where I live, our most celebrated building, the Royal Pavilion, is sometimes called simply the *Pav*. Whatever has happened, word-final <v>, which not so long ago was unknown and impossible in English, is no longer even especially rare.

Why don't English speakers reform their spelling?

Despite its obvious eccentricity, there are a number of reasons why English spelling reform is unlikely.

First, there exists a colossal amount of material written in English, both on paper and now on the Internet, and the volume of that material grows substantially every day. If we were to change our spelling greatly, then future generations who had learned only the reformed spelling would find all this existing material far more difficult to read and use. In practice, they would have to learn our old system as well as their new one – and this is not progress.

Second, we human beings are conservative creatures, and nowhere is our conservative nature more prominent than in language matters. Once you have spent years painfully mastering the intricacies of the English standard spelling system, you are hardly likely to take kindly to someone who tells you that you should abandon the spellings you have sweated blood to master, and learn a whole load of ignorant-looking new spellings.

Crazy as these spellings are, would you really like now to abandon *debt* and *doubt* in favour if *det* and *dout*? Or, if these don't bother you, what do you think about changing *honest* to *onest*? Or *bread* to *bred*? Or *scythe* to *sithe*? Or *phlegm* to *flem*?

How about changing *eye* to *i*? Or how about changing *buy* to *by*? Or *eight* to *ate*? Or *torque* to *tork*? No double-takes when you see Winston Churchill's famous words written as *We will fite them on the beeches*? Well, you may or may not take a benign view of such a rearrangement of English spelling, although I'd guess that you probably hate the very idea. Most people do. Exasperating as English spelling is, once we have finally learned it, most of us cannot even contemplate any significant fiddling with it. And, even if you are a rare person who finds spelling reform appealing, what do you suppose will happen if you start writing your work in a reformed spelling which other people refuse to accept? Do you think you'll make a good impression on them by writing *Pleez retern the form befor the dedline*? I'm sure you won't.

So, there are substantial reasons why a reform of the English spelling system is most unlikely to be carried out, now or ever. But by far the most important reason we cannot rationalise English spelling is this: we do not all pronounce the language in the same way. So, a reformed spelling that matched your pronunciation would not match mine at all well.

A few years ago, a British journalist, reflecting on chaotic English spelling, proposed an improvement. 'Let's re-spell *thought* as *thort* ', she suggested, 'because that's the way it's pronounced.' She had a typical southeastern-England accent, and, in the southeast of England, *court* is pronounced just like *caught*, and *short* does indeed rhyme perfectly with both of them. So, if you have this kind of accent, re-spelling *thought* as *thort* makes a good deal of sense.

But not every English speaker has this kind of accent. No more than about 3 per cent of native speakers of English come from the southeast of England, and the other 97 per cent of speakers do not speak with the same kind of accent – in other words, they do not use the same kind of pronunciation. For example, in

Table 7.2 *Some pairs of English words*

(a) *court/caught*	(b) *cot/caught*
(c) *farther/father*	(d) *whine/wine*
(e) *horse/hoarse*	(f) *poor/pour*
(g) *dew/do*	(h) *pull/pool*
(i) *buck/book*	(j) *toe/tow*
(k) *hair/air*	(l) *three/free*
(m) *threw/through*	(n) *stir/stare*
(o) *higher/hire*	(p) *marry/merry/Mary*
(q) *missile/missal*	(r) *ant/aunt*

my American accent, *court* sounds completely different from *caught,* and the same is true in all the accents of Canada, Scotland and Ireland, as well as in the accents of the southwest of England, in some Caribbean accents, and elsewhere. For about 80 per cent of the world's native speakers of English, *thort* would be a much crazier spelling of the word than is the conventional spelling *thought*.

And the same is true for almost any other change you might propose to improve our mysterious spelling. Table 7.2 shows a list of pairs of English words, with an interesting property. For each pair of words, the two words are pronounced identically by some native speakers of English, but differently by other native speakers. (One set has three words, usually pronounced all identically or all differently, though I have met one speaker who pronounced two the same but the third differently.) Take a look at the list, and decide in each case whether you pronounce the words identically or differently. There are no right or wrong answers here, of course: the answers you give will merely reflect the kind of accent you have.

You may be surprised to learn that some people make a distinction you don't make, or fail to make one you do make, but there is no doubting the facts: all of these pairs are pronounced identically by some speakers but differently by others. Moreover, these pairs are not oddities: each pair in fact represents two whole classes of English words. For example, pair (d) stands also for the other pairs like *where* and *wear*, *which* and *witch*, *whales* and *Wales*, *whether* and *weather*, *wheel* and *weal*, *whet* and *wet*, *whirled* and *world*, and others. And there is more, much more. Table 7.3 provides another list of pairs of words. For each pair, the words are perfect rhymes for some native speakers of English, but do not rhyme at all for other native speakers.

In all likelihood, it is too late to reform English spelling in any very sensible way. We might, if we liked, adjust a few of the really eccentric spellings that match no one's pronunciation. We could change *debt* to *det*, and *bread* to *bred*, and *buoy* to *boy*, and *people* to *peeple*. But it is hardly likely that the elimination of a few dozen oddities would be enough to overcome the howls of outrage from those who cannot bear to see our established spellings tampered with. Once you

Table 7.3 *Some more pairs*

(a) *singer/finger*	(b) *harass/embarrass*
(c) *granary/tannery*	(d) *felony/miscellany*
(e) *fertile/turtle*	(f) *vagary/fairy*
(g) *garage/carriage*	(h) *says/rays*
(i) *mobile/global*	(j) *often/soften*
(k) *evolution/revolution*	(l) *beta/cheetah*
(m) *one/bun*	(n) *never/sever*
(o) *codify/modify*	(p) *lever/fever*

have learned the erratic spelling *people*, then the orderly and regular *peeple* just looks ignorant and wrong, and that's the end of it – for most of us.

Meanwhile, of course, our pronunciation, like every aspect of English, continues to change. My young niece's pronunciation of the word *how* sounds very little like my pronunciation of the same word but much more like my pronunciation of *Hugh*. So, even if we could agree on a spelling that worked well this year, that same spelling might after a while be as ridiculous-looking as is our spelling of *knight* – which at one time made perfect sense.

It appears, therefore, that we are drifting slowly towards a writing system rather like the one the Chinese use. In the Chinese script, there is no attempt to write down the pronunciation of a word at all. Instead, each individual word is conventionally represented by an arbitrary set of symbols, and learning to be literate in Chinese means learning the particular set of symbols associated with every word in the language. (It is true that the Chinese characters *historically* included an element of pronunciation, and to some extent that historical information is still detectable, but it does not play a crucial role in Chinese writing.)

In our case, we will simply have to learn that squiggles like *reign* and *missile* and *doubt* stand for particular words with particular meanings, and we will stop worrying about how those words are pronounced or whether they do or do not rhyme with any other words. Those speakers in England for whom *tyre* and *tower* are both pronounced like *tar* (and also *ta* 'thanks') will just have to master the squiggles required for each of the four meanings, much as Chinese speakers have to learn the different squiggles that represent words of identical pronunciation but different meanings.

Textspeak

As a postscript, I must add that a form of reformed English spelling *has* appeared in recent years: *textspeak*. This combination of abbreviations (*u* 'you'), quasi-phonetic spellings (*luv* 'love') and rebuses (*gr8* 'great') which was produced by the new technology of SMS-texting in the late 1990s quickly developed rules of its own – a statement which might come as something of a surprise to its critics, many of whom seem to see its use as evidence that the barbarians are at the gates. A spelling like *4* for 'for', for instance, makes sense for some speakers of English, but not all: for most Scots, for instance, *for* and *four* are not homophones. Yet Scottish texters still use this convention. It's too early to say how far textspeak will spread, but it's very likely to be here to stay.

Conclusion

Given the diversity of eccentricity found in the English spelling 'system', a conclusion is very difficult to reach. What we can say, however, is that the present mess is the result of the engagement of the language's speakers with the language across at least six centuries. To a historical linguist this is, of course, very attractive: unlike most other languages, English as it is written today acts as a witness to the linguistic habits of 500 years ago. At the same time, Latinate or pretentious spellings tell us a great deal about social attitudes over the modern period, just as similar processes provide us with understandings of these attitudes now. The English spelling system is a linguistic treasure trove; that doesn't make it any less maddening, however.

In the next chapter we will move far from these highly detailed concerns, instead concentrating on when languages begin and what age they are.

8   Which is the oldest language?

A common question

I belong to the panel of an Internet service which offers to answer questions on language and languages. One of the questions we receive most often is: 'Which is the oldest language?' Sometimes we get variations on this theme. 'Is Hebrew the oldest language?' 'Is Sanskrit the oldest language?' 'Is French older than English?' 'Is it true that Basque is the oldest language in Europe?' Clearly there is a great deal of interest in these matters. But it is actually very difficult to find this answered in a clear but scholarly way. In this chapter I'll try to do so. But let's begin with another question, one which is just about as basic as anything can be in the study of languages.

Where do languages come from?

We need to ask this question in order to talk about the ages of languages. You have a mother tongue, which you learned in early childhood. That mother tongue may be English, or it may be something else: this makes no difference. Where did you get your mother tongue from?

Very likely you don't remember all that much about the early stages of acquiring your first language, but fortunately a considerable number of linguists have studied children learning their mother tongues, and we now know a great deal about what happens. The answer is not very surprising: you learn your first language from people who already know it, or who at least know a little more than you. You learn it from your parents, of course, but you also learn a great deal from friends, neighbours and siblings who are a few years older than you and who know just a bit more language than you do. This is not a startling statement.

But consider the consequences: where does *everybody* get that first language from? Well, everybody gets it in the same way you did: by learning it from people who already know it. That's how your parents learned their mother tongue, and that's how your grandparents learned theirs, and your great-grandparents, and your great-great-grandparents, and so on. Generations ago, tens of generations ago, hundreds of generations ago, children were learning their mother tongue from older people who already knew it.

How else can a child learn a language? Where else can a child turn in order to learn a first language other than to somebody who already knows it? In fact, there *are* a few other possibilities, but they are neither obvious nor usual, and we will leave them until the end of this chapter. For now, I can safely say that *normally* – and by 'normally' I mean in the huge, vast, overwhelming majority of cases – every child learns its first language in the same way you did: by learning it from people who already know it.

So, let's suppose your first language is English. You learned English in childhood from older people who already knew English. Those people had already learned English in their own childhoods from still older people who already knew it, and those still older people had likewise learned English in their yet earlier childhoods from even older people who already knew it. And so on, back and back.

Think of the consequences of what we are saying. We appear suddenly to be trapped in an infinite regress: it seems that we require an endless chain of ever-older speakers of English extending back to the beginning of time, or at least back to the beginning of human speech in the very distant past, perhaps 100,000 or 200,000 years ago or more. And, of course, the same is true for every other language: we also require an endless chain of French speakers running back to the beginning of language, and an endless chain of speakers of Swahili, and Chinese, and Norwegian, and so on. Is this plausible? Has something gone wrong with our reasoning?

What we have so far certainly seems logical. It appears that the very first human beings to speak a language at all must simultaneously have been speaking English, and French, and Swahili, and Chinese, and Norwegian, and everything else, since all humans are descended from them. This conclusion sounds deranged.

In fact, there is nothing wrong with our reasoning at all. Moreover, there is nothing really wrong with our conclusions, either. It is merely that we have overlooked one critical detail, which has made our perfectly reasonable conclusions look preposterous: the fact that *languages change*. It is changing all the time, every moment in fact. It is always changing in every possible way: in pronunciation, in vocabulary, in grammar.

As a result, as we saw earlier, the English that you learn is not *quite* the same English your parents learned several decades earlier. It is already conspicuously different from the English learned by the young Marilyn Monroe around 1930 – remember all those familiar words that Marilyn never heard? It is even more different from the English learned by the infant Humphrey Bogart about a century ago. It is increasingly different from the English learned in childhood by Winston Churchill (born 1871), by Oscar Wilde (born 1854), by Charles Darwin and Abraham Lincoln (both born 1809), by Jane Austen (born 1775), by George Washington (born 1732), by Alexander Pope (born 1688), by Jonathan

Swift (born 1667), by Robert Boyle (born 1627) and by William Shakespeare (born 1564).

As we have already seen, Shakespeare's written English is already very strange to us, and his speech might be incomprehensible to us if we could hear it. Just a couple of centuries earlier, the written English of Geoffrey Chaucer (born 1343) is already at the very limit of comprehension or even a little beyond, while Chaucer's speech would be wholly unintelligible. As we keep moving back in time, the language keeps growing steadily more different from our own – or, to put it more sensibly, the English of later times has been growing steadily more different from earlier English.

If King Alfred the Great could be brought back to life today, he would understand not one word of English speech or writing – and King Alfred lived not much more than a thousand years ago. So long as English does not die out, this constant change will continue for ever, and the English of the future will grow ever more different from ours, until eventually there will be not a single word or form left that we can recognise. And that raises an interesting question: at this point, will the language still be 'English'? This question brings us to the naming problem.

The naming problem

Once upon a time, in the days of King Alfred the Great, there was a language that looked like this:

He cwæð, Soðlice sum man hæfde twegen suna. Þa cwæð se gingra to his fæder, Fæder, syle me minne dæl minre æhte þe me to gebyreð.

And its speakers called it 'English'. Centuries later, the language had changed substantially, and the same sentence now looked like this:

And he seide, A man hadde twei sones; and the ʒonger of hem seide to the fadir, Fadir, ʒyue me the porcioun of catel, that fallith to me.

The speakers of this variety also called their language 'English'. Today, centuries later again, the same sentence looks like this:

And he said, 'There was a man who had two sons; and the younger of them said to his father, 'Father, give me the share of property that falls to me.'

How long can we go on doing this? How long *should* we go on doing it? Recall the little joke about George Washington's axe: 'This is the very axe that George Washington used to chop down that cherry tree. Of course, since then, it's had two new handles and three new heads.'

Suppose King Alfred's language is reasonably called English. When a day finally comes when not a single word or grammatical form still survives from

King Alfred's speech, is it still reasonable to call the result 'English'? Are we still looking at the 'same' language? How can we tell? Does the question make any sense anyway?

There are several possible answers to such questions, and they are all plausible.

The first point is that King Alfred's language has evolved into just *one* modern language – by the most usual reckoning, anyway. King Alfred was quite satisfied that there was just one language called 'English' in the Britain of his day, even though he knew perfectly well that English was spoken somewhat differently in different places. Today most of us are equally satisfied that there exists just one English language, even though we all know that English is spoken rather differently in different parts of the world. So long as we agree that there is only one language involved, there is no particular obstacle to calling it 'English', today and at all periods.

Of course, King Alfred's English was so immensely different from ours that, for some purposes, we really need to make some distinctions in our labelling. We do this in the following arbitrary but convenient manner. From the arrival of English in Britain to the year 1100, we call the language *Old English*. From 1100 to 1500, we speak of *Middle English*. From 1500 to 1700, the language is *Early Modern English*. And, finally, from 1700 to the present we recognise *Modern English*.

You can see that this set of names is not going to work for ever. After a few more centuries, the English of 1700 will be as incomprehensible to future speakers as King Alfred's English is to us, and so they won't be able to continue calling it 'Modern English'. But, for the time being, this set of labels is as good as anything we can think of.

But suppose we lost our consensus that English is a single language? There are already a few people who don't agree about this. In the 1920s, the American writer H. L. Mencken argued that the language of the United States was no longer English, but a quite distinct language which he proposed to call *American*. It is perfectly possible that the several regional varieties of English – in England, in Scotland, in the USA, in Australia and elsewhere – may drift apart to the extent that it no longer makes much sense to regard all them as the same language, or to give all them the same name.

Indeed, the Germanic variety of Scotland – Scots – is considered to be a variety separate from Modern English by a great many people in that country. On this occasion, the fact that the variety had a written standardised form in the Renaissance, is associated with a country with a strong sense of its separate identity and is not at all easy for most speakers of English to understand helps this argument. On the other hand, Scots is presently *dialectalised* under Standard English and no one would deny that it is a very close relative – the closest relative – of English in existence.

Exactly this state of affairs has come about countless times in the past. Around 500 BC, Latin was the language only of a small community in central Italy. Within a few centuries, however, its speakers – the Romans – had carved out a vast empire stretching from Britain and the Atlantic coast of Europe to modern Iraq. In much of this territory, their Latin language displaced the earlier languages and became the mother tongue. For a while, a more or less uniform version of Latin was spoken throughout this territory. But, of course, spoken Latin, like every spoken language, was continuing to change, and it changed in different ways in different places.

After a few centuries, there were enormous differences among the regional varieties of Latin. There were no sharp boundaries, of course, and everybody could easily understand other speakers who lived within twenty or thirty miles, but beyond that things became difficult, and nobody could understand another Latin speaker who came from 300 miles away. Finally, it no longer made much sense to keep applying the name 'Latin' to this welter of local varieties which were no longer mutually comprehensible. Instead, people found themselves speaking of 'Leonese' and 'Tuscan' and 'Provençal' and so forth. Much later, some of these local varieties succeeded in becoming the national languages of large nation-states, and so we began to speak of 'Spanish' and 'Italian' and 'French' and so on – as we still do today.

Latin is not really a dead language. It has several hundred million native speakers today. But those speakers speak Latin in a form that would be wholly incomprehensible to Julius Caesar – just as Modern English would be incomprehensible to King Alfred. In addition, though, they speak modern Latin in quite a number of very different regional varieties, varieties which are not mutually comprehensible. So, instead of adopting such cumbersome labels as *Parisian Latin*, *Florentine Latin* and *Castilian Latin*, we just speak of *French*, *Italian* and *Spanish*.

If we ever find it necessary, we can one day do the same with English. We can abandon the name *English*, and speak instead of regional languages like *American* and *Australian*. So far, however, this has not been necessary, and we can keep the label 'English' for all the many regional varieties.

But now let's take the name backwards in time. How *early* was it appropriate to apply the label 'English' to ancestors of our speech?

As we saw in an earlier chapter, English is descended from a group of Germanic dialects we call North Sea Germanic, which in turn was descended from an unrecorded language we call Proto-Germanic, which in turn was descended from a much earlier unrecorded language we call Proto-Indo-European, which in turn was descended from … a language we know nothing about and do not even have a name for.

Also descended from North Sea Germanic are Frisian, Dutch, Afrikaans and some varieties of Low German. All these we want to count as separate languages from English, and so we don't want to call any of them 'English'.

Also descended from Proto-Germanic, apart from the ones just named, are Norwegian, Swedish, Danish, Icelandic, Faeroese, High German, Yiddish and quite a few extinct languages, such as Gothic. These too we want to count as separate languages from English.

Also descended from Proto-Indo-European are very many languages: Irish, Spanish, Lithuanian, Russian, Albanian, Greek, Armenian, Kurdish, Bengali and many others, including several extinct ones like Hittite, Tocharian A, Illyrian and Dalmatian. We certainly don't want to count any of these as varieties of English.

So, at what point can we reasonably start using the label 'English'? I hope the answer is becoming obvious: we are happy to call an ancestral form 'English' if that ancestor is the ancestor of *only one* modern language: Modern English.

We can't call Proto-Indo-European 'English', because PIE split up into a huge number of quite distinct languages, most of which cannot possibly be regarded as varieties of English. We can't call Proto-Germanic 'English', because Proto-Germanic split up into quite a number of distinct languages, most of which we cannot sensibly call 'English'. We can't even call North Sea Germanic 'English', because North Sea Germanic has split up into several quite distinct modern languages, of which English is only one.

But the version of North Sea Germanic that was introduced into Britain has given rise to only one uncontested descendant: Modern English. Therefore, we now have a reasonable answer to our question. We can safely apply the name 'English' to the ancestral forms of English from the moment those first Germanic-speaking settlers stepped ashore in Britain.

Naturally, those invaders would have been astonished to be told that they were speaking a different language the moment they got their boots wet in the British surf. In reality, of course, they were still speaking the same language as their cousins who had stayed home, and whose speech would eventually evolve into varieties of Frisian, Dutch and (Low) German – all which we now count as languages distinct from English and from one another. But we have to make a decision about how to use our label, and the arrival of those first Germanic speakers in Britain gives us the perfect opportunity to introduce the label 'English'. The Germanic speech of these settlers took root in Britain, and it eventually developed into the Old English of King Alfred, the Middle English of Chaucer, the Early Modern English of Shakespeare, and English today.

Naturally, most cases are not quite as simple as the English one. Latin, as we have just seen, was spoken over a large area of Europe for centuries, but it gradually began to break up into a number of regional varieties, some of which eventually came to be important languages.

Take the speech of Paris. In AD 100, the Romans in Lutetia (as Paris was then known) were undeniably speaking Latin, practically the same Latin that was being spoken by other Roman citizens in Italy, in Spain and elsewhere. Today, however, the people of Paris undeniably speak the language we have agreed to call 'French'. We have to use a different name, because Latin has developed into quite a number of different modern languages, and not only into French. But at what point in time should we start applying the label 'French' to the speech of Paris?

This time there is no discontinuity that we can seize upon, nothing like the Germanic speakers' crossing of the North Sea. So, we must appeal to a convention, a convention which we have invented for our own convenience: we have decided that we will apply the name 'Latin' to the speech of Paris until AD 900, while after that date we will apply the name 'French'. But nothing happened in Paris in AD 900, and this decision does not correspond to an event in the world: it is a purely arbitrary decision.

This decision is a scholarly convenience, no more. Latin was never displaced from Paris by a different language: instead, Latin has just evolved in place into French, and there is no discontinuity we can point to. So, the 'beginnings' that you may sometimes see declared for particular languages are not really beginnings at all, but only scholarly conventions invented for convenience. Languages do not have beginnings.

Another interesting example is provided by Afrikaans. Dutch immigrants began to settle in what is now South Africa in the seventeenth century. Naturally, the Dutch spoken in the Cape Colony and the Dutch spoken in Europe began to diverge, and in this case the interesting social conditions in the colony helped to accelerate this divergence. By the late nineteenth century the European and African varieties of Dutch were already very different. But the Dutch speakers in Africa continued to accept standard European Dutch as their own standard, and educated people in the colony learned to read and write only European Dutch. The very different spoken language of the colony was called 'Cape Dutch', and it was generally regarded as no more than an unusual local variety of the 'mother tongue'.

Then in 1875 an association was formed to promote the writing of Cape Dutch in a form which was close to everyday speech. The association's movement prospered, and before long Cape Dutch was increasingly being regarded as the 'proper' language of the Afrikaner community in South Africa. Finally, in 1925, the Union of South Africa withdrew recognition from European Dutch, and accepted instead that Cape Dutch, now renamed 'Afrikaans', was a real language and an official language of the country.

So, Afrikaans officially came into existence in 1925, but again there was no linguistic event in that year, only a political decision to recognise two languages where before only one language had been recognised.

We are now in a position to answer the question which forms the title of this chapter: which is the oldest language? First, though, we must lay aside a few exceptional languages, languages which are special cases, languages which have not come into existence in the 'ordinary' way. We will talk about these special cases in the next chapter. Leaving the special cases aside, however, we can answer the question very simply and bluntly, as follows:

> No language is 'older' than any other language, and there is no 'oldest' language.

We can sensibly ask about the age of something only when that something has an identifiable beginning. We can ask about your age, because you have a beginning: you were born. We can ask about the age of the Wimbledon tennis championships, or of the United States, or of agriculture, because these things all had beginnings. We can even ask about the age of the Hawaiian islands, because there was a point in time when these islands were first pushed above the surface of the Pacific by volcanic activity. But languages do not have beginnings, and therefore we cannot ask about the 'age' of a language. There is no point in time at which a language that formerly did not exist suddenly pops into existence. Therefore, no language can be 'older' than any other, and there can be no 'oldest' language. Asking whether one language is 'older' than another is a foolish waste of time.

If this troubles you, just think about the consequences of denying it. Suppose you maintain that language A is older than language B. You are therefore claiming that there was a time in the past when language A already existed but language B did not yet exist. So where did language B come from? You are claiming that, at some later time, there came into existence a first generation of speakers of language B, and that these speakers learned a language that did not exist. And this, I hope you will agree, is absurd.

Languages do not appear out of nothing. All that ever happens is that the regional varieties of a language become so different that we eventually find it convenient to invent some new names. But the invention of a new name is not a linguistic event. A child who learns English or French or Afrikaans today represents just one more generation in an unbroken chain of learners stretching back to the beginning of human speech, and the differing names we may choose to apply to different historical periods are nothing but conveniences we have invented to please ourselves: there was never any point at which children were learning a language different from their parents' language.

Which languages were recorded first?

Human beings have been speaking languages for tens of thousands of years, and probably for hundreds of thousands of years. But, until very recently by these standards, our ancestors had no way of making records of their speech. Countless languages arose, were learned by children, were spoken by smaller or larger groups of people for who knows how many generations, before changing into quite different descendants or being displaced by other languages. Of all these thousands of languages we have no records, and we will never know anything about them.

Only very late in human ancestry did somebody think of a technique for recording languages. That technique was not sound recording, which was invented only at the end of the nineteenth century, but something a little less direct: writing.

Writing is a way of transferring pieces of language into a more or less permanent form, by making marks on a solid surface, using a conventional system of marks which represent small pieces of a language. It is important to realise that, in a true writing system, *every utterance* of a language can be adequately written down – everything from *On this day the King destroyed his enemies* to *I love you, Snugglebunny*. If you cannot write down every utterance of your language in a way that is immediately readable by someone who knows the system, then you do not have a writing system.

Long before writing was invented, people were making marks with particular meanings. Sometimes the owner of a valuable artefact would scratch his mark onto it, to show that it was his, much as cattlemen in the Old West used to brand their cattle. Some urban societies developed systems of marks or tokens for keeping track of certain kinds of information, such as taxes owing and taxes paid. But these arrangements are too limited to record anything beyond the special purposes for which they are designed, and they are not writing: we call them *precursors of writing*.

Another point to bear in mind is that a writing system can only allow the writing down of a particular language. The characters of the writing system must, in one fashion or another, represent units of the language, such as speech sounds, syllables or words. It is not possible to construct a writing system which bypasses the language and represents 'thoughts' or 'ideas' directly. Quite a few philosophers have tried to invent such systems, but these absolutely don't work. Failure to understand this blunt fact has at times been a headache in linguistic work. For example, the decipherment of the ancient Egyptian writing system – the hieroglyphs – by European scholars was badly obstructed and delayed because so many of the scholars working on the problem assumed that Egyptian hieroglyphs, with their picturesque characters, could not simply represent the ordinary Egyptian language, but must instead constitute some kind of esoteric symbolic system which conveyed ideas directly, without the mediation of a human language. Without the effects of this confused nonsense, the hieroglyphs might have been deciphered decades earlier than they were. The decipherment was finally achieved in the 1820s by Jean-François Champollion, a young French linguist who realised that the fascinating-looking symbols of the Egyptian monumental texts were nothing more than a system devised for writing down pieces of speech in the ancient Egyptian language (it helped that he knew its descendant, Coptic, which only died out as an everyday language in the sixteenth or seventeenth century). Having understood that much, he needed only a few years of work to decipher the hieroglyphs and read the texts.

Why was writing invented so late? For most of the time of human existence, our ancestors didn't bother to invent writing because they had no need for it. Most of our ancestors were foragers – hunter-gatherers – and even today the remaining foragers do not bother to write anything down. Anything that needs to be remembered can be passed on orally, from one generation to the next. There is nothing that foragers need to keep permanent records of, and anyway such people lead a nomadic existence, moving from place to place with the seasons, and they must keep their physical possessions to a bare minimum (although, of course, hunter-gatherers were able to produce permanent art of the level of sophistication of the cave paintings at Lascaux).

Even when some of our ancestors switched to farming as a way of life, and therefore settled down in one place, there was still nothing that needed to be written down. The first farming communities arose about 10,000 years ago – about 8000 BC – and the farmers flourished and spread for thousands of years without any writing. They had no use for it.

The pressures that led to the invention of writing arose only after people had first invented something else: cities. Urban societies need something that for-agers, pastoralists and farmers don't need: administration. Urban societies have kings, priests, armies and merchants to keep track of. Taxes have to be levied and collected. Armies have to be equipped, and soldiers and officials have to be paid. Laws have to be introduced, explained and of course recorded. They also have to be enforced, and so an urban society needs police, courts, judges and what Americans euphemistically term a 'correctional system'. And all this activity calls for the keeping of records. For a little while, our first urban ancestors managed to make do with notches, scratches and tokens, but such primitive devices are really not adequate for providing the extensive records that soon came to be necessary. And so writing was finally invented.

Writing was not invented in order to preserve literature or religious texts. It was invented by and for bureaucrats. Writing was invented in order to make possible the blizzard of activity that today we call 'paperwork' – though paper was not invented until much later, and the earliest writing was inscribed on clay tablets, on slabs of stone, or on sheets of pressed vegetable fibres.

So far as we know, the first people to invent writing were the Sumerians, who lived in what is now southern Iraq. The Sumerians were a remarkably talented and energetic people, and they developed the world's first elaborate urban civilisation. Before long, they realised they needed a way to keep records, and so they invented the world's first writing system, around 3200 BC. This they used to write down their Sumerian language, which is related to no other known language. This first writing system was complex and cumbersome, by our standards: it employed some hundreds of characters, some of which represented speech sounds while others gave clues to the meanings of words. We call the Sumerian writing system *cuneiform*, which means 'wedge-shaped', but this label denotes nothing more than the shapes of the marks on the clay tablets, and it in no way reflects the nature of the system.

The Egyptians appear to have invented their own writing system no more than a century after the Sumerians. This is the system of monumental writing which we call *hieroglyphs*, a label which means only 'sacred carvings'. Like the Sumerian cuneiform, the Egyptian hieroglyphs were a complicated system involving hundreds of characters with varying functions.

Also around 3200 BC, an unidentified ancient language of Persia began to be written in a script adapted from the Sumerian script. These inscriptions, termed 'Proto-Elamite', lasted only for about two centuries, after which the practice died out.

For some centuries, then, with a short-lived exception in Persia, the Sumerian and Egyptian writing systems were the only ones in use anywhere, and no other languages were written. Eventually, however, the speakers of several other Near Eastern languages began to adapt the Sumerian system for writing their own languages. At the time, there were quite a few Semitic languages spoken in the area, and several of these, such as Kassite, Amorite and Eblaite, began to be written in a modified form of the Sumerian cuneiform around 2500 BC. Around the same time, the cuneiform began to be used to write Elamite, a language of Persia, and Hurrian, an ancient language of eastern Turkey, whose only known relative, Urartian, is extinct, like Hurrian. At this time, however, writing was still unknown outside the Near East and Egypt.

Then, again about 2500 BC, another writing system was invented in the valley of the River Indus, in what is now Pakistan. Here a spectacular urban civilisation suddenly flourished. The unknown people who built the Indus Valley cities created their own writing system, utterly distinct from the Sumerian and Egyptian ones – although possibly inspired by knowledge of the former. Sadly, this script has never been deciphered and we have no idea what language lies concealed within it.

After flourishing for nearly a thousand years, the Indus Valley civilisation declined and finally collapsed – possibly as a result of an invasion by the speakers of Indo-European languages on their way into India. The script dropped out of use, and writing disappeared from the Indian subcontinent for another millennium or more.

Around 2350 BC, the Sumerian cuneiform system began to be used to write Akkadian, the Semitic language of some up-and-coming peoples of Mesopotamia. Akkadian was the language of both the Assyrians and the Babylonians, and these peoples, one after the other, succeeded in establishing formidable empires in the Near East. For many centuries, these peoples wrote their own language in the borrowed Sumerian script with considerable success. The volume of the texts left to us by their bureaucratic states is enormous.

For many centuries after its invention, writing remained largely confined to the Near East. But there were developments. The cumbersome early systems, with their hundreds of characters, began to give way to newer and more efficient systems, with a much smaller number of characters, each of which represented a unit of pronunciation.

One of the first examples of this new approach is found in Crete. From about 1800 BC, the Minoan civilisation of Crete began writing its Minoan language in one of the simple new systems: the first European language to be written. This script, which we call Minoan Linear A, has never been deciphered: once again we have no idea what language (or languages) lies buried in the script. But it seems clear that Linear A is what we call a *syllabary*, in which each character represents the sound of a syllable: one character for *ma*, another for *be*, another for *tu*, and so on.

From the seventeenth century BC we find in what is now Turkey the first written records of Hittite, an ancient and long extinct language of the Indo-European family. Hittite was thus the first Indo-European language to be written.

Around the same time, the speakers of some Semitic languages in the Near East took a momentous step forward: they invented the first alphabetic writing system. This first alphabet was defective, in that it provided letters only for consonant sounds and not for vowel sounds, and some specialists prefer to class this system as an *abjad*, an exclusively consonantal alphabet. Versions of this abjad came to be widely used for writing Semitic languages, such as Ugaritic and Canaanite.

About 1550 BC we find a greatly modified version of the Cretan Linear A script being used to write a quite different language in Crete and in mainland Greece. This new script, *Linear B*, was deciphered in the late 1950s by the English architect and amateur linguist Michael Ventris, who demonstrated to general satisfaction, and also to general astonishment, that the language concealed in the Linear B texts was an early form of Greek – a form which we now call *Mycenaean Greek*. Greek was thus the first language to be written on the mainland of Europe. But the Linear B writing system did not endure for long: around 1200 BC the Mycenaean Greek civilisation collapsed, and all knowledge of writing was lost in Greece for centuries.

So, as we approach the year 1200 BC, we find the use of writing confined to a small area not much greater than the territory of the Near East and Egypt where writing had first been invented 2,000 years earlier. Writing had spread eastward to the Indus Valley and to Persia, but it had survived only in Persia. It had also spread westward to Crete and Greece, but it was about to disappear also from those territories. Writing was in established and continuing use nowhere but in the little triangle of land whose corners were the modern countries of Egypt, Turkey and Iran.

Thus, by 1200 BC, writing was unknown in by far the greater part of the globe, and it has probably crossed your mind that some very prominent languages have not yet been mentioned. But it was at just this time, thousands of miles away, that an important new writing system was invented: the Chinese writing system. By this date speakers of an early form of Chinese had already been settled in north China for perhaps millennia. The system which they invented is in fact the direct ancestor of the modern Chinese script, which has thus been in continuous use for over 3,000 years. Greek was written a few centuries earlier than Chinese, but the temporary loss of writing which occurred in Greece about 1200 BC means that Chinese has the longer uninterrupted tradition of writing.

Meanwhile, back in the Near East, writing was still spreading from language to language. Around 900 BC, we find the first written texts in a language that would later come to be of great importance to western civilisation. Hebrew was a member of the Northwest Semitic dialect cluster, and it had probably emerged as a language recognisably distinct from its relatives by about 1500 BC, but only about 900 BC did the speakers of Hebrew begin to write their language, using a form of the Semitic abjad probably borrowed from their neighbours the Phoenicians. The vast antiquity sometimes imputed to Hebrew is therefore no more than a legend: Hebrew was first written down centuries later than Greek or Chinese, and millennia later than Sumerian or Egyptian. This early Hebrew script was quite different in form from the one that everybody knows today; this later form developed only a few centuries after the Hebrews acquired writing.

Around 750 BC (very roughly, since this date is not known with any accuracy), the Greeks re-acquired writing. They did this by borrowing the Semitic abjad from their trading partners the Phoenicians, but they made one great modification: they added letters for vowels. With letters for both vowels and consonants, the resulting Greek script was thus the world's first true alphabet.

This new alphabet began to spread. A modified version of the Greek alphabet was adopted by the Etruscans, an influential people of northern Italy, who used this to write their Etruscan language, beginning in about the seventh century BC. The Etruscans in turn passed on the alphabet to their southern neighbours the Romans, who modified it further in order to write their own language, Latin. The first known Latin inscriptions date probably from the sixth century BC, while the first Latin literature is found in the third century BC.

Meanwhile, both the Greeks and the Phoenicians had been exploring and colonising much of the Mediterranean, and wherever they went they took their writing systems with them. As a result, indigenous writing systems had appeared in Spain no later than the sixth century BC; these systems were clearly influenced by both the Greek and the Phoenician systems, but were distinct from both.

Writing was finally beginning to spread to places far from its origins in Sumer and Egypt, though only some 2,500 years after its invention. About 500 BC, a new writing system was created in Persia and used to write a form of the Persian language. About the same time, but very much farther away and almost inevitably independently, the first writing in the New World appeared in Mexico. Somewhat later, in the third century BC, a writing system was invented by the speakers of Meroitic, a language which was then prominent in the part of Africa which today we call Sudan.

All this time, India had been wholly without writing ever since the collapse of the ancient Indus Valley civilisation. But finally, in the third century BC, the Mauryan conqueror Aśoka introduced a new writing system, based upon developed versions of the Semitic scripts, the first ever seen in what is now India, and using it to write down his north Indian language, which was related to such modern languages as Hindi-Urdu, Bengali and Gujarati. Very soon after this, and still in the third century, writing was adopted by the speakers of the south Indian language Tamil. Eventually the Mauryan Brahmi script gave rise to a great number of varied writing systems, including all those used in the Indian subcontinent (except the Arabic script, used for Urdu and other languages mainly written by Moslems, and the scripts used in the Maldives), as well as the scripts used for Burmese, Thai, Lao, Khmer, Tibetan and a number of now-extinct scripts once used in central Asia.

In the first century AD, some speakers of Germanic languages in northern Europe encountered the Romans and their alphabet. Intrigued, the Germanic speakers decided to adopt writing, but, instead of taking over the Roman alphabet bodily, they constructed their own alphabet, which we call the *runic* alphabet, or the *futhark* (its first six letters were <f u þ [th] a r k>). They used their runes for short inscriptions from the first century onwards, though apparently they never wrote any longer texts in runic script.

Around AD 250, the Mayans in Guatemala began to write their Mayan language in a graphically stunning script which has only recently been deciphered. The Mayan script was not perfected until about 900, however, to the extent that early examples might be described as 'proto-writing'.

Arabic was first written in the fourth century AD, as were some of the languages of Ethiopia. Armenian began to be written in AD 406, and Georgian (a Caucasian language) in AD 430. We find the first inscriptions in Irish in the fifth century AD, using the distinctive Ogham alphabet devised locally under the inspiration of the Roman alphabet; Irish literature, written now in the latter, followed in the eighth century. Written literature in Welsh began in the sixth century. English and German were written down for the first time in the eighth century, as was Tibetan, half the globe away. The first Slavonic language to be written down was Old Church Slavonic, recorded in a distinctive alphabet from the ninth century.

Sometime between the fifth and tenth centuries – the time is not known with any precision – the speakers of Korean and of Japanese began to write their own languages in scripts derived from the Chinese writing system, although in both cases it took centuries before effective and standardised systems were achieved.

Hungarian was first written in the thirteenth century, and the European languages Finnish, Lithuanian, Albanian and Basque were first written down in the sixteenth century. The North American languages Cherokee and Cree were first written in the nineteenth century, as were several West African languages. Some of the languages of India and many of the languages of South America were only written for the first time in the twentieth century.

Writing has thus existed for a little over 5,000 years. For the first two millennia of its existence, writing was scarcely found outside the Near East. Since then, it has gradually spread across the globe, so that today there is probably no inhabited place anywhere on earth which is devoid of writing. Even so, only a minority of languages are normally written: of the world's 7,000 or so mother tongues, it is unlikely that as many as 10 per cent are regularly written, and most of them are never written at all.

But now let's get back to the point. If Chinese was written down earlier than Hebrew, this fact in no way makes Chinese 'older' than Hebrew. It does mean, of course, that the *earliest written records* of Chinese are older than the earliest written records of Hebrew, but this is a very different matter. The languages and their ancestors were being spoken all the time, whether anybody was writing them down or not, and Hebrew did not suddenly spring into existence only when somebody decided to write it.

If this troubles you, think of your own ancestors. You can only trace your ancestors back so many generations. Perhaps you can only find records of your family going back to your great-grandparents, or perhaps you can get back to some of your great-great-great-grandparents, or perhaps you can trace a branch of your family back to the Norman Conquest or even the restoration of the Jerusalem Temple. But you can only trace your ancestors back in time so far before the written records run out. Before then, you know nothing about them. But do you suppose that you *had* no ancestors before the first ones appear in the records? Like everybody, you have a string of ancestors stretching all the way back to the first appearance of human beings on earth. Your ancestors were always there, whether anybody was keeping records of them or not.

And languages are no different. They have always been there, whether anybody was writing them down or not, ever since our remote ancestors first began to speak. When a language has acquired a written form, we can often date the introduction of that written form with some accuracy. We know that Chinese began to be written approximately 1200 BC, and we know that Armenian began

Table 8.1 *The spread of writing*

	Sumerian, Egyptian, Proto-Elamite
3000 BC	
2500 BC	Semitic, Elamite, Hurrian, Indus Valley language
	Akkadian
2000 BC	
	Minoan Linear A
	Hittite, Semitic alphabet
1500 BC	Greek Linear B
	Chinese
1000 BC	
	Hebrew
	Greek alphabet, Etruscan, Latin
500 BC	Persian, first Mexican writing
	Meroitic, Indian languages
AD 1	Germanic runes
	Mayan
	Arabic, Ethiopian languages
AD 500	Armenian, Georgian, Irish
	Welsh, Korean, Japanese
	English, Tibetan, German
AD 1000	Old Church Slavonic, French, Italian
	Old Norse, Occitan, Serbo-Croatian, Dutch, Tuscan
	Spanish, Catalan, Czech, Danish, Swedish, Hungarian, Turkish
AD 1500	Cornish, Breton, Scots, Yiddish
	Finnish, Estonian, Latvian, Lithuanian, Polish, Slovene, Albanian,
	Basque
	writing widespread
AD 2000	

to be written in AD 406 exactly. Written forms have beginnings, sometimes very sharp ones; Table 8.1 presents a timeline for the spread of writing But languages, once again, have no beginnings.

As ever, when dealing with humans and language, there are, however, a few exceptions to this general tendency.

The possibility of a beginning

I mentioned at the start of this chapter that a few exceptions exist: languages that really do have identifiable beginnings. Where would we find these?

One obvious case is *artificial languages* – languages which are invented by individuals or groups. At least dozens, and perhaps hundreds, of artificial languages have been constructed over the years. Most of them have never left the pages of their designers' notebooks, but a few have attracted some measure of support. Perhaps the most famous – and linguistically sophisticated – artificial language is *Esperanto*, invented in the 1880s by a Polish oculist, Dr L. L. Zamenhof. Other artificial languages which have enjoyed some measure of success are *Volapük*, a predecessor driven out of business by Zamenhof's creation; *Interlingua*, a form of simplified Latin which has found some use for scientific purposes; and *Klingon*, invented by the linguist Mark Okrand for the Klingon characters in the *Star Trek* films, and now perhaps being learned by more Americans than French or German. I might also mention the several artificial languages invented by J. R. R. Tolkien for his own amusement and then built into his books. These languages have also been learned by a significant number of people.

But an artificial language is not a natural language: that is, it is no one's mother tongue. Moreover, there is no artificial language which serves, or has ever served, as the principal language of a community, or even as one of the chief languages of a community. At best, an artificial language plays an auxiliary role, allowing conversation between people who have no other language in common. Otherwise, an artificial language is no more than a toy which can provide some entertainment to those who enjoy such things. There are, however, 'new' languages which *do* have a speech community.

Pidgins

Very often, two or more groups of people have found themselves obliged to deal with one another even though they have had no language in common. There are various ways of dealing with this problem. If time permits, a few people can learn the other group's language well enough to serve as interpreters. Otherwise, perhaps a few gestures, supplemented with smiles and frowns, will get the job done.

In many cases, however, the solution adopted has been another one: the people involved create a *pidgin*, a kind of auxiliary language created in just such circumstances of contact between people with no language in common. A pidgin is no one's mother tongue. If I may simplify things considerably, we may classify pidgins into two types: unelaborated and elaborated. By the standards of any mother tongue, an unelaborated pidgin is a rudimentary affair. It typically has a tiny vocabulary, just enough to permit everyday matters to be handled adequately. And it may have very little in the way of a grammar. Some unelaborated pidgins, in fact, appear to have almost no grammar at all, though no pidgin is entirely devoid of grammatical conventions, and it is never true that 'anything goes' in a pidgin. Others have a recognisable collection of grammatical rules and grammatical elements, but the resulting system is seldom comparable to the rich grammar we can find in any mother tongue.

A good example of an unelaborated pidgin is *Russenorsk*, a pidgin used in the nineteenth century between Norwegian fishermen and Russian merchants. Russenorsk is no longer used, but we have some moderately substantial records of it. Those records contain a total of 390 words, about half of which are recorded only once each. We may therefore surmise that the everyday vocabulary of the pidgin consisted of no more than about 200 words. Of these, nearly half were taken from Norwegian, and almost as many from Russian, with a scattering of words from five or six other languages.

Russenorsk seems to have had almost no grammar at all. Norwegian and Russian both distinguish singular forms of nouns from plural forms, but Russenorsk had no such distinction. Russian has a rich case system, but Russenorsk had no cases. Norwegian and Russian both have elaborate systems for inflecting verbs, but verbs in Russenorsk were invariable: there wasn't even any tense-marking. Interestingly, however, almost every Russenorsk verb ended in the syllable *-om*, of uncertain origin, apparently just to show that it was a verb. Examples are *betalom* 'pay' (from Norwegian) and *robotom* 'work' (from Russian). But some verbs taken from Russian lacked this syllable.

Both Russian and Norwegian have a fair number of prepositions, but Russenorsk had just one: the all-purpose *på* (primarily Norwegian, although there are similar Russian prepositions). Some examples: *klokka på yu* (literally 'watch på you') 'your watch'; *principal på syib?* ('captain på ship?') 'Is the captain on the ship?'; *på morradag* ('på tomorrow') 'tomorrow'; *moya tvoya på vater kastom* ('me you på water throw') 'I will throw you in the water'; *stova på Kristus spræk* ('house på Christ speak') 'church'.

Russenorsk seems to have lacked subordinate clauses. When necessary, clauses were simply juxtaposed or linked with the word *så* 'so'. An example: *Moya på anner skip nakka vin drikkom, så moya nakka lite pyan* ('me on other ship some wine drink, so me some little drunk') 'I drank some wine on another ship, and then I got a little drunk'. Yes–no questions were marked by rising intonation only: *Tvoya fisk kopom?* ('you fish buy?') 'Will you buy fish?'.

The existence of Russenorsk was first noted in 1785, which is probably not long after it first began to be used. The pidgin continued to be used until 1914, when the outbreak of war in Europe destroyed the commerce which it had serviced. During its brief existence, Russenorsk apparently achieved and maintained a measure of stability, though there was always some fluctuation. Notice the occurrence of both *syib* and *skip* for 'ship' above, and note that 'good' could be expressed by any of *bra* (from Norwegian), *good* (from English) or *dobra* (from Russian). The pronunciation was highly variable, depending very much on the linguistic background of the speaker. But it seems clear that the pidgin always remained very narrow in function: it never underwent any significant expansion or elaboration in order to serve a greater variety of functions.

Many other pidgins likewise remain small and limited like Russenorsk. But some pidgins meet a different fate. Let us turn to another case, one of the world's most celebrated pidgins, Tok Pisin.

Papua New Guinea occupies the eastern half of the huge island of New Guinea. Something like 500 indigenous languages are spoken within its territory, and no one of these languages can claim to be vastly more important than any other. This linguistic diversity poses huge practical problems, and the citizens of Papua New Guinea have responded with several different solutions. So far, the solution which has proved to be the most successful is the creation of a pidgin, which is usually called *Tok Pisin* 'Language Pidgin'. Tok Pisin is one of the official languages of the country; it is known and used by all educated people, and it is widely spoken right across the country, including all official contexts.

Before independence, Papua New Guinea was governed by English-speaking Australia. Tok Pisin is therefore a pidgin based on English: almost the entire vocabulary of the language is taken from English, though there are a few words taken from other languages. This, in fact, is the most usual state of affairs with a pidgin. Russenorsk is slightly unusual in taking its words almost equally from two different languages, though we find some other pidgins which have done the same. We say that English is the *lexifier language* for Tok Pisin.

Below is a passage taken from the Tok Pisin newspaper *Wantok*. You should note that the vowels represent 'continental' pronunciations rather than English:

Ol meri gat bikpela wari yet
Helt na envairomen em bikpela samting ol meri long kantri tude i gat bikpela wari long en.

Bikos dispela tupela samting i save kamap strong long sindaun na laip bilong famili na komyuniti insait long ol ples na kantri.

Long dispela wik, moa long 40 meri bilong Milen Be provins i bung long wanpela woksop long Alotau bilong toktok long hevi bilong helt na envairomen long ol liklik ailan na provins.

It is unlikely that you made much of this story, although you may have caught a few glimmerings of what is being talked about. This illustrates a general rule about pidgins: a pidgin is not mutually comprehensible with its *lexifier language*.

Under these circumstances, the best thing to do is break down the text into smaller units and compare with Standard English. Each word is accompanied by its English source word (which does not always have the same meaning), or by an English translation in italics (if the word does not come from English).

> *Ol meri   gat bikpela   wari   yet*
> All *woman* got big-fellow worry yet
>
> *Helt   na   envairomen   em   ol   bikpela   samting*
> health *and* environment him all big-fellow something

ol meri   long kantri   tude i   gat bikpela
all *woman* along country today he got big-fellow

wari   long en.   Bikos   dispela   tupela   samting   i
worry along him. Because this-fellow two-fellow something he

save kamap   strong long sindaun na   laip bilong
know come-up strong along sit-down *and* life belong

famili na komyuniti insait long ol ples na kantri.
family *and* community inside along all place *and* country.

Long dispela   wik,   moa long 40 meri   bilong
Along this-fellow week, more along 40 *woman* belong

Milen Be   provins i   bung long wanpela   woksop
Milne Bay Province he *meet* along one-fellow workshop

long Alotau bilong toktok   long hevi   bilong helt   na
along Alotau belong talk-talk along heavy belong health *and*

envairomen   long ol liklik ailan na   provins.
environment along all little island and province.

We might get more of an understanding of the passage, at least at a small-scale
level, from this treatment. A full understanding would still escape us without a
great deal of work, however. Let's look at an English translation of the passage:

Women still have big worries
Health and environment are two of the major things which women in the country today
have big concerns about.

Because these two things often have a strong effect on the situation and life of families
and communities within villages and in the country.

This week, more than 40 women from Milne Bay Province are meeting in a workshop
at Alotau in order to talk about the difficulties of health and environment in the small
islands and provinces.

Tok Pisin is a success story. It has more speakers than perhaps any other
pidgin on the planet, and it is one of the very few that are regularly written. It has
become what we call an *elaborated* or *extended pidgin*. That is, it is no longer
merely a rudimentary auxiliary speech-form. Its vocabulary is large and growing steadily, and its grammatical elaboration is already well beyond what we
find in most pidgins.

For instance, in the 1890s, the language possessed an adverb *baimbai*,
meaning 'later', 'after a while'. This adverb was derived from English *by and
by*, and it was optional, of course; when it was used, it came first in its sentence.
But then several things began to happen to this word.

First, it has been steadily reduced in form. Over time, the recorded forms have
been these: *baimbai, b'mbai, b'bai, mbai, bai, ba* and *b'*. Today the original
form *baimbai* is almost never heard, and the common forms are *bai* and *ba*.

Second, the word has moved: it no longer occurs at the beginning of the sentence, but instead it immediately precedes the verb. Third, it is no longer optional: when a speaker is talking about future time, then this item *must* be used, even if the sentence contains another word explicitly expressing futurity, such as *bihain* 'later' or *klostu* 'soon'.

In short, this item has been *grammaticalised*. It is no longer an ordinary word, but it has become an obligatory grammatical marker attached to the verb to express future tense. This is a particularly effective example of the way in which languages acquire grammar: what has happened here in Tok Pisin is very similar to what has happened in thousands of other languages, and not only in pidgins.

Another factor in the development of Tok Pisin is that, not infrequently, people in Papua New Guinea with no language in common other than that language get married. Their children will quite possibly learn the mother tongues of both their parents, but they will *certainly* learn to speak Tok Pisin. In fact, they may acquire Tok Pisin as their mother tongue, or as one of their mother tongues. And that makes a very big difference indeed.

Creoles

When a pidgin has become widely used in a community, it is not at all rare for children to begin acquiring the pidgin as a mother tongue. This is a deeply momentous development. A pidgin may be strictly an auxiliary speech variety, rudimentary and severely limited. But no mother tongue on earth is ever rudimentary or limited. Every mother tongue has both a large and expressive vocabulary and a rich and complex system of grammar. So what happens when children begin acquiring a pidgin as their mother tongue?

In the space of a single generation, the children can invent all the vocabulary and all the grammar they need to make their new mother tongue a normal language: a *creole*.

Many of the creoles spoken today are descended from pidgins that were created as a result of the large population movements brought about by the European expansion that started in the fifteenth century. For example, the wholesale carrying of Africans as slaves to the Caribbean produced a number of pidgins in this region, some of which gave rise to creoles which are still widely spoken today.

Here we will look at Sranan, a creole which is the mother tongue of about a third of the population of Suriname, a country on the north coast of South America, and which is spoken as a second language by practically everybody else in the country. Sranan is an English-based creole, meaning that it developed out of an English-lexified pidgin. This may seem surprising, since the colonial language of Suriname was Dutch for some 300 years before independence in 1975. But before the Dutch settlement there were English planters in the country for several decades, and the presence of these English speakers was enough to produce an English-based pidgin among the Africans imported as slaves.

The following is a song in Sranan. The abbreviation 'FUT' labels a marker of future tense; 'PL' is 'plural'; and 'ASP', which stands for 'aspect', represents a rather subtle grammatical marker which is hard to translate into English.

> *Wi na den   uma   fu Sranan*
> we be the-PL woman of Suriname
> 'We are the women of Suriname'

> *Wi na den   mama fu a   kondre*
> we be the-PL mother of the country
> 'We are the mothers of the country'

> *Na wi e   wasi den   pikin*
> be we ASP wash the-PL child
> 'It's we who wash the children'

> *Den mangri anu nanga fesi*
> them thin   hand with face
> 'Their thin hands and faces'

> *Dan wi e   luku in den   bigi ay fu wi pikin*
> then we ASP look in the-PL big eye of we child
> 'Then we look into the big eyes of our children'

> *Pikin nanga angri*
> child with   hunger
> 'Hungry children'

> *En wi e   pramisi:*
> and we ASP promise:
> 'And we promise:'

> *'Dyonsoro mama sa   tyar' a   nyan'*
> just-now   mother FUT carry the food
> 'Soon Mama will bring the food'

> *Go prey now, go prey now*
> go play now go play now
> 'Go play now, go play now.'

Though it will probably not be obvious from these brief extracts, Sranan has a much richer grammatical system than does Tok Pisin – although Tok Pisin is now catching up rapidly, since it too is becoming a native language for some speakers. Again, a speaker of English can understand only so much of this language, and complete understanding is impossible without first learning it. However, in spite of its strange appearance to our eyes, Sranan is just one more of the world's 7,000 or so mother tongues, and it is every bit as rich and expressive as the others. It is in no way deprived or deficient, and there is nothing of importance which other languages have but which Sranan lacks.

Once a creole comes into existence, it is a language like any other language. In the case of a creole created only in the last several centuries, like Sranan, we can still identify the language as a creole and work out quite a bit about its origins and history. But what about a creole that was created several thousand years ago?

After several thousand years of undergoing the ordinary processes of linguistic change, a language that started life as a creole derived from a pidgin would be most unlikely to look much like an obvious creole any more. The accumulated weight of countless changes in vocabulary, pronunciation and grammar would undoubtedly produce something that was indistinguishable from Russian or Zulu or Quechua: complicated pronunciation and grammar, words of obscure origin. For all we know, Japanese or Sumerian or even English might be descended from an ancient creole whose origins are now far beyond our powers of recovery. Some languages really *do* have beginnings.

Mixed languages

The term *mixed language* has often been applied very broadly and loosely to just about any language which has been significantly affected by another language. For example, English is a Germanic language, but its vocabulary, as we have seen, has been immensely affected by Norman French, and substantially influenced by Latin, Greek and Modern French. Some people would therefore say that English is a 'mixed language'. But linguists do not use the term in such a broad way. The problem with this broad use is that there are practically no languages which have not been strongly affected by other languages, and therefore, in this broad sense, there are practically no 'unmixed languages'.

In linguistics, the term *mixed language* is used in a much narrower and more specific way. For linguists, a mixed language is a language which is constructed by combining large chunks of material from two (or more) quite distinct languages, in such a way that we cannot reasonably say that any one language is the direct ancestor of the resulting mixture. English does not qualify as a mixed language, because, in spite of the high levels of borrowed vocabulary, we can easily trace the ancestry of English in a continuous line back through Middle English, Old English, North Sea Germanic, Proto-Germanic and so on, all the way back to Proto-Indo-European. With a truly mixed language, we could not do this. (In fact, because of the troubled history of the label *mixed language*, some linguists now prefer to speak instead of *intertwined languages*, but I'll avoid that label here.)

At least since the late nineteenth century, linguists have wondered whether any true mixed languages exist. One difficult language after another has been put forward as a candidate mixed language, but in almost every case the awkward language has eventually been shown to be a language with a clear ancestry. For example, a number of languages spoken in and near New Guinea exhibit complicated mixtures of features taken from the Papuan languages of New Guinea and from the far-flung Austronesian family, which stretches from Madagascar to Hawaii and Easter Island. For a while, linguists suspected that these 'difficult' languages might have originated in the not-too-distant past as genuine mixtures of Papuan and Austronesian elements. Today, though, there is general satisfaction that every one of these problem languages can be shown to be either a Papuan language heavily affected by Austronesian or an Austronesian language heavily affected by Papuan. The point is that, in each case, we can work out which one of these possibilities is the right answer, and so we have no need to appeal to a hypothetical 'mixing' process some time in the past.

Other cases are more difficult. In Ecuador, there is a language called *Media Lengua*, which consists of vocabulary taken almost entirely from Spanish embedded in a grammar taken entirely from the local language Quechua; in the Bering Strait, we find *Copper Island Aleut*, in which the verb-forms are taken almost entirely from Russian but the rest of the language is taken from the local language Aleut, a relative of the Eskimo languages; in Tanzania, we find *Ma'a*, which consists of vocabulary taken mostly from the local Cushitic languages embedded in an almost wholly Bantu grammar. These languages, and several others like them, really do look like genuine examples of mixed languages: they seem to have been assembled, apparently deliberately, by combining large chunks of material from two quite distinct languages in a more-or-less orderly manner.

But there have been a few quibbles raised about each of these examples, so I will pass over them here to another language. A few years ago, linguists discovered a language which is beyond any dispute or quibble an ironclad example of a truly mixed language: Michif, spoken along the border between the United States and Canada, in Saskatchewan, Manitoba and North Dakota.

The speakers of Michif call themselves the *Métis*, and Michif is the mother tongue of some hundreds of people. It is learned in childhood as the first language, and it is the everyday language of the home in its community, but today all adult speakers of Michif are fully fluent in English, which they use in talking to outsiders.

Michif consists almost entirely of a mixture of sounds, words and grammar taken from just two languages: a local Canadian variety of French, and the Algonquian language Cree. But the mixture could hardly be more orderly. All the verbs and verb-forms are taken from Cree, while all the nouns, adjectives and articles are taken from French. (Grammatical words like 'this', 'what?', 'many' and 'behind' are taken from both languages, however.) All the Cree elements are constructed from a set of Cree consonants and vowels. But all the French elements are constructed from a quite different set of French consonants and vowels. So, for example, the distinctive French front rounded vowels, as in *lune* 'moon' and *deux* 'two', and the French nasal vowels, as in in *bon* 'good' and *vin* 'wine', occur in the French parts of the Michif vocabulary, but not in the Cree parts, because Cree doesn't have them – though Cree has a *different* set of nasal vowels, which occur in the Cree part of the vocabulary. This observation points to the heart of the mixed origins of Michif: there exists no unmixed language on earth in which half the vocabulary is built from one set of speech sounds and the other half from a different set of speech sounds.

But this is only the start. French nouns have grammatical gender. Each French noun must be assigned to one of the two genders, called 'masculine' and 'feminine', and words connected grammatically to a noun, such as articles and adjectives, must agree with the noun in gender. All this is imported into Michif: a Michif noun must bear a French gender, masculine or feminine, and other words must agree with a noun in French gender.

Cree, like all Algonquian languages, also has grammatical gender, but the Algonquian system is quite different from the French one. Cree has two genders, traditionally called 'animate' and 'inanimate', and every Cree noun must be assigned to one or the other. Although the noun elements in Michif are French-based, Cree verbs must agree in gender with their subject or object – and all the verb-forms in Michif are Cree. So, in order for the verb agreement to be achieved in Michif, every noun must be assigned a Cree gender as well as a French gender. This fact makes Michif perhaps the only language in the world in which every noun must be assigned two unrelated and independent genders, each required for different grammatical purposes.

But how is all this gender assignment done? One thing is clear: the Cree gender of a Michif noun is not predictable from its French gender, and vice versa. The two gender assignments are independent, and clearly a speaker of Michif must learn each of the two genders of a noun separately. Predicting the French gender of a Michif noun is easy: with just a handful of exceptions, the French gender of a Michif noun is the same as its gender in French. But, since the nouns in Michif are all taken from French, and not from Cree, how do they get their Cree gender? This is still something of a mystery.

Below I present some example sentences in Michif, in a rather 'rough-and-ready' orthography of my own invention (Michif is not normally written; the transcription system used by scholars is too complex for these purposes.) The nasal vowels I have marked with a superscript tilde, as in <ã>. The Cree parts of a Michif sentence are printed in italics, while the French parts are in roman type. Since you probably don't know any Cree, I haven't explained the Cree parts in much detail, but you may know some French, so I've provided a few comments for the French elements.

(1) *kiimichimineew aatiht* larzhã
he-held-it   some money
'He kept part of the money.' (French *l'argent* 'the money')

(2) *kiiteepishkam*   *ee*-la-mitres-*iwit*
she-succeeded-at-it that-the-teacher-was
'She succeeded in becoming a teacher.' (French *la maîtresse* 'the teacher')

(3) *kii*-li-fu-*iwiw*   *ee*-li-pchi-*iwit*
was-the-crazy-he-was that-the-little-he-was
'He was crazy when he was little.' (French *fou* 'crazy' and *petit* 'little')

(4) *bakwataawak* li   mũd   *kaakimutichik*
I-hate-them   the people that-they-steal
'I hate people who steal.' (French *le monde* 'the world')

(5) li   bon   mark a likol   *mishimiyustamihikuw*
the good mark at the-school make-him-very-happy
'Good marks in school make him very happy.' (French *bon* 'good', *à* 'at',
l'école 'the school')

(6) *aatiht manisha* li   brash dã li   zaabr *uhchi*
some cut-off! the branch on the tree   from
'Cut off some of the branches from the tree!' (French *les branches* 'the
branches', *dans* 'in', *les arbres* 'the trees')

(7) la   zhymãã *kiiayaaweew* ã pchi pulã
the mare   she-had-it   a little foal
'The mare had a foal.' (French *la jument* 'the mare', *un petit poulain* 'a little
foal')

How did Michif come into existence? There is really only one explanation that makes any sense: Michif was deliberately created, some generations ago, by a group of people who were fluently bilingual in French and Cree. Though these people had two languages, each of those languages was spoken also by quite a few other people, and the early Métis had no language of their own. So they decided to create one, in order to give themselves an identity. But they weren't content to change just one word, or just one feature of grammar or pronunciation. Instead, they constructed a new language, one which could not possibly be spoken or understood by anyone outside their community. They began speaking this constructed language exclusively, and they taught their construct, and nothing else, to their children, who acquired it as their mother tongue. This account is confirmed by the oral traditions maintained by today's Métis. This decision was final and irreversible: few Michif speakers can speak French today, and almost none can speak Cree.

Michif is therefore a language – a mother tongue – which does not descend in the 'ordinary' way from an unlimited string of ancestors extending back into the past without limit. Given the facts, we cannot reasonably describe Michif as a variety of French heavily influenced by Cree, nor as a variety of Cree heavily influenced by French. Michif was deliberately and self-consciously constructed by the early Métis, at a date which is not known for certain, but was most likely around two centuries ago.

Sign languages

There is one more circumstance we know of in which mother tongues have been created, without descending from any earlier languages, but this case is very different from the others, because it doesn't involve spoken languages.

Deaf people cannot hear speech, and so they find it very difficult, or even impossible, to learn and use a spoken language. A deaf person isolated among speakers may fail to acquire any language at all – a tragedy which has been repeated countless times in human history. But, when a group of deaf people can somehow manage to get together, the outcome is very different. The deaf people can create a *sign language* – a language which is expressed through the medium of signs produced with the hands, the face and other parts of the upper body.

We need to clarify this notion of a sign language a little. Many people have assumed – and most professional linguists, to our embarrassment, shared this ignorant prejudice until only a few decades ago – that the sign languages used by deaf people are no more than crude and clumsy auxiliary systems, lacking in expressive power and probably derivative of spoken languages. Well, such crude and derivative auxiliary systems really do exist. A good example is Signed English, or Manually Coded English, a system for converting English into manual gestures. Signed English is a kind of halfway house: it is no one's mother tongue, and it is not a real language, but it is easier for English speakers to learn than is a real sign language, and it is easier for deaf people to learn than is English, and so it finds a place as a gadget allowing communication between English speakers and deaf people. But Signed English is not what we are interested in here.

True sign languages are created by communities of deaf people, when they get the opportunity to form them. True sign languages are the mother tongues – if you will pardon the inappropriate metaphor – of their users. True sign languages are real languages in every sense.

A true sign language has a large and expressive vocabulary, and it has ways of creating new words whenever new words are called for. A true sign language has a rich and elaborate grammar, just as rich and elaborate as the grammar of any spoken language. A true sign language permits anything that a spoken language allows: statements, commands, questions, requests for help, the expression of emotions such as joy, anger and excitement, the telling of stories, jokes, puns, insults, obscenities – anything you can think of. And, like any spoken language, of course, a true sign language is constantly changing, as its users keep modifying it to suit their purposes, and so after a while it develops regional dialects.

Several dozen true sign languages are known to exist, though it seems likely that there are many others which we have not yet discovered. Very few of these have so far been studied in any detail at all, and our knowledge of sign languages is woefully behind our knowledge of spoken languages. Among the best studied at present are American Sign Language (ASL), used in the USA, and British Sign Language (BSL), used in Britain. ASL and BSL have different origins, and users of one can understand the other only about as well as they can understand Chinese Sign Language. Neither of them is related in any way to English. Both of them have grammars which are about as different as can be from the grammar of English, and in fact it has often been remarked that they are grammatically rather similar to certain indigenous languages of North America, such as Hopi.

Let's look at a typical example of sign-language grammar, from BSL. Figure 8.1(a) shows the ordinary sign for 'walk'. To express 'walk' in BSL, you push one hand forward in three little jerks while simultaneously waggling two fingers of that hand. So far, this is easy.

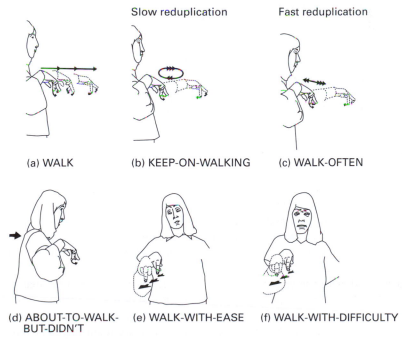

Figure 8.1 The BSL sign for 'walk'

But now comes a bit of grammar. If you repeat ('reduplicate') the 'walk' sign slowly, the resulting sign means 'keep on walking', as in Figure 8.1(b). If, however, you repeat the 'walk' sign quickly, the result means 'walk often', as in Figure 8.1(c). In BSL, you can do this with any sign of suitable meaning in order to express 'keep on doing' or 'do often'. This is how the grammars of sign languages typically work: where English adds extra words to obtain extra meaning, sign languages simply modify the signs.

Figure 8.1(d) shows another grammatical modification of the 'walk' sign. This time the 'walk' sign is produced just once, and briefly. At the same time – and crucially – the eyes are directed sideways or down, and the mouth is opened abruptly. All this produces what sign-language grammarians call the 'inhibitive aspect' of the sign. The meaning of this aspect, applied to the 'walk' sign, is 'about to walk but didn't'. So, where English requires something like *Susie was about to walk out of the door but then she stopped abruptly*, BSL needs only to attach the appropriate grammatical modification to the 'walk' sign.

Note in particular the crucial role of the face in producing this piece of grammar. In every sign language so far examined, the face is at least as important as the hands, and in fact it is the face which carries a great deal of the sign language's grammar. Interestingly, when two signers are having a conversation, they do not look directly at each other's hands: they look at each other's faces.

Figures 8.1(e) and (f) illustrate two more grammatical modifications of the 'walk' sign. The first shows the sign meaning 'walk easily'. Although the picture doesn't show this well, the face is again central: the head and the face are relaxed; the eyes are wide and the eyebrows are slightly raised; and the head tilts from side to side in rhythm with the walking movement of the fingers. The second figure shows the expression of 'walk with difficulty'. This time the head is held rigid; the mouth is tense with the lips spread and pulled back; and the eyebrows are lowered.

Why, then, are there apparently no large families of sign languages comparable to the Germanic or Celtic families of spoken languages? Well, there is no reason in principle why such sign-language families should not exist, but there are formidable difficulties in practice. In order to be used and maintained, a sign language requires a community of users – in practice, deaf users – who interact with one another every day. However, because of indifference and prejudice on the part of the hearing majority, deaf people have typically found it next to impossible to maintain their own communities and to use their sign languages regularly. As a result, there is no known sign language in use today whose roots can be traced back more than a couple of centuries, at best.

Sign languages, like spoken languages, can in principle give rise to pidgins, creoles and mixed languages. Only seldom, however, are circumstances favourable to such developments, but cases do exist.

One good example of a pidgin sign language is *International Sign Language*, or *ISL*, formerly known as *Gestuno*. ISL is not quite a canonical pidgin, since it largely results from decisions taken consciously by committees, but structurally and functionally it is a pidgin.

ISL is no one's mother tongue. Its grammar is limited and far from fixed. It is primarily a collection of agreed individual signs, and it is intended to permit basic communication among signers who have no language in common – just like any pidgin. At present, its degree of standardisation is modest, and signers from different countries often use it in ways that are different enough to produce a measure of difficulty in understanding. Nevertheless, it finds considerable use at international gatherings of signers, even though some signers dislike it greatly, finding it more of a headache than simply learning somebody else's sign language.

But we do know one spectacular case of a sign language creole: Nicaraguan Sign Language, or NSL. The story of NSL is breathtaking and inspiring.

For decades, the hapless Central American republic of Nicaragua was the personal fiefdom of a local gangster named Anastasio Somoza. Somoza's corrupt, brutal and thoroughly criminal regime was dedicated only to maintaining his grip on power and to stuffing as much of the country's wealth as possible into his Swiss bank account. The Nicaraguan educational system was starved of money, and the hundreds of deaf children in the country were ignored – shut away in back rooms and forgotten.

Then, in 1979, a popular revolution toppled the regime and drove the hated Somoza into exile. The new government tackled the huge job of repairing the incalculable damage done to the country by decades of criminal control. Discovering the existence of the deaf children, the government decided to collect these children and to bring them together in a special school.

The plan was to teach the children to lip-read and to speak Spanish. But this plan, well-meaning though it was, was a failure – as such plans usually are. However, the failure didn't matter – because the authorities, almost by accident, had already done the one thing that really needed to be done: they had brought the deaf children together.

In no time, the children began creating a set of signs and using these new signs to communicate among themselves. Before their teachers had realised what was happening, the children were gesticulating feverishly. Like any group of people who need to communicate without having a language in common, the children had invented a pidgin – in this case, a pidgin sign language. But the new invention did not remain a pidgin for long.

Further deaf children arrived at the school. Finding the pidgin in use, these new arrivals at once adopted the pidgin as their mother tongue. And, as always happens in such cases, the new native users at once expanded and elaborated the language, with a host of new grammar and new vocabulary, so that they could chat effortlessly about anything they liked.

Today NSL has several hundred native signers, and the number of these signers is growing. And the world has a new language. In 1979, Nicaraguan Sign Language did not exist in any form at all, not even in the form of a rudimentary pidgin. The deaf children of Nicaragua were isolated from one another, and they had nothing resembling a common language. But now NSL exists and is used every day, just like any other language – and, to its native signers, it is every bit as important as English or Chinese.

As one grinning little boy confessed to a BBC camera, 'Before, I had no language, and I couldn't talk. Now, I have a language, and I can talk to my friends.' If the Nicaraguan revolutionaries never achieved anything else, they can take credit for this little contribution to human happiness.

NSL is therefore a very rare case of a brand-new language which we have almost managed to watch coming into existence. Not quite, because it was a few years before anybody realised that there was something remarkable going on, and before linguists arrived on the scene to see what was happening. But never before have we come so close to seeing a wholly new mother tongue spring into existence before our eyes. The truly striking point of this is that is very likely that processes of this kind have happened repeatedly for deaf people.

Summary

We have looked at the several special cases of languages that do have beginnings: artificial languages, pidgins, creoles, mixed languages and sign languages. Not all these are mother tongues, but some of them are, and so we are obliged to acknowledge that, in certain circumstances, a mother tongue can have a beginning, and we can therefore sensibly ask of that language 'How old is it?' The creole Sranan was apparently born in the seventeenth century; the mixed language Michif was probably created in the first half of the nineteenth century; and Nicaraguan Sign Language was very definitely constructed in a matter of years after 1979. But these are special cases, and they are exceptions. The overwhelming majority of human languages are, as far as we can tell, of the same age. *None is any older than any other.*

Some final thoughts

Language change is inevitable

There is nothing anyone can do to avoid it: the only unchanging language is a language without native speakers, such as Classical Latin or Sanskrit. Languages of this type may be of considerable importance within certain cultures, but they are retained as a heritage item, rather than an integral part of everyone's experience from early childhood. Moreover, there was a time when languages of this type *were* true languages: at that time, these languages were as given to change as any other natural language: we need only consider the differences between early varieties of Latin and the Classical Latin many of us learned at school to recognise this truth.

Language change is everywhere

As I hope I have shown in this book, everywhere we look we will find evidence of language change. We can hear it in our own linguistic behaviour and in that of people younger and older than us. We can see it in the names of places, whether we understand them or not. We can perceive it in the books we read and the reasons why we choose *not* to read books or plays which were once fashionable and current. All we need to do to begin to do this is to 'tune' our inner ear to recognise change; with further study, it becomes very difficult *not* to concentrate on change in the past and the present.

We can often trace languages back into pre-history

As we have seen, the overwhelming majority of languages have 'bloodlines' in the same way humans do. Like humans, some languages are blessed in having three to four thousand years of recorded history behind them; most humans and languages have a very limited recorded history. The time-depth is the same, however. With sufficient experience of how languages can change, it is possible to establish at least close relationships even between languages with few written records. Sometimes, as has been the case with the geographically widespread

Na-Dené family of western North America (which includes Apache and Navaho), much has been achieved with practically no availability of earlier varieties.

But even with the better-charted language families, such as the venerable Indo-European, much needs to be done to make sure that we fully understand how one language became so many very different ones. The techniques upon which this type of work is based are not secret: with some training they are open to anyone interested. I want to stress this training again, however.

Many people with an interest in these matters have not studied how to use the comparative method and therefore fall into the error of seeing coincidence as being equivalent to relationship. As we have seen again and again, this is a dangerous presupposition. Sadly, there are also some published writers who have political or personal agendas which either encourage them to obscure inconvenient truths or to build large theories – such as (to take particularly unusual but expressed views) the origin of all human languages in the drowned civilisation of Atlantis or in contact with advanced alien cultures – based upon misunderstood and often singularly peripheral similarities between languages. Naturally, the growth of the Internet has only encouraged the visibility of these views by giving those interested greater exposure.

Humans lie at the centre of all change

When we discuss language change, it is sometimes convenient to speak about changes or languages as if they were entities independent of speakers. This can be misleading, however. The processes involved in most – probably all – change are human-centred (even if individuals are not completely conscious of taking part in change). Certainly, when we look at evidence for present-day linguistic variation and change, we can actually see that choosing a particular variant instead of another is normally triggered by the desire of a speaker to be identified with a particular grouping within society, whether this is the *overt prestige* of middle-class respectability or the *covert prestige* of working-class solidarity and teenage in-group identity. If enough people make this type of variant choice, the language *will* change. There is no reason to assume that this was not the case in the past. While it is true that the ways in which societies construct themselves differ markedly across time, humans probably change little. Language change will always be a result of how individuals and groups perceive themselves and their relation to others.

Further reading

A great deal of ground has been covered in this book; it would be very easy to fill twenty pages or more with references and suggestions for further reading. I have decided, however, to confine myself to suggesting a few studies which are readily available and transparent to non-specialist readers. Further references can be derived from the bibliographies of any of the books cited here.

HISTORICAL LINGUISTICS

There is a *vast* amount of literature discussing language change, most of it fairly impenetrable to non-specialists. A good introduction to the field is

Aitchison, Jean. 2001. *Language Change: Progress or Decay?* 3rd edn. Cambridge: Cambridge University Press.

More advanced, but still approachable are:

Campbell, Lyle. 2004. *Historical Linguistics: An Introduction*. 2nd edn. Edinburgh: Edinburgh University Press.
McMahon, April. 1994. *Understanding Language Change*. Cambridge: Cambridge University Press.
Millar, Robert McColl. 2007. *Trask's Historical Linguistics*. London: Hodder Arnold.

INDO-EUROPEAN AND THE INDO-EUROPEANS

With the Indo-European languages and the origins of the Indo-Europeans, there is an unfortunate gap between highly erudite works which require a considerable amount of specialist knowledge and books whose populism blended with a lack of knowledge of recent scholarship is deeply unfortunate. The following two books are approachable to the non-specialist, however:

Clarkson, James. 2007. *Indo-European Linguistics: An Introduction*. Cambridge: Cambridge University Press.
Giacalone Ramat, Anna and Paolo Ramat (eds.) 1998. *Indo-European Languages*. London and New York: Routledge.

ETYMOLOGY

There are a number of very good etymological dictionaries available for English and other languages. If you want to get the full story of how an English word's meaning developed over time, the first place to look is the *Oxford English Dictionary*. Most larger libraries in the English-speaking world will have a reference copy of this multi-volume work. Many will also subscribe to the online version (www.oed.com), which is being continually updated. Bear in mind, however, that, no matter how authoritative the explanation of the origin of a word is, there is often room for scholarly disagreement. An excellent one-volume introduction to the etymology of English lexis can be found in

Hughes, Geoffrey. 2000. *A History of English Words*. Oxford: Blackwell.

PLACE NAMES

There is no one scholarly resource which can give you the origin of all place names. Most countries – or even regions within countries – will have had some kind of scholarly survey carried out. Many works which you will find in libraries have been written by independent scholars. This does not mean that they are by their nature flawed – indeed, often the dedication given to their task by these scholars is humbling. It does mean that the authors may not always be equipped with the same level of linguistic knowledge as are professional scholars (although the latter inevitably make mistakes as well). As a general rule, *beware of easy explanations*.

HISTORY OF THE ENGLISH LANGUAGE

There are a plethora of books on this subject, most of them of a good standard. Perhaps the best known and most used is

Baugh, Albert C. and Thomas Cable. 2002. *A History of the English Language*. 5th edn. London: Routledge.

There are also a considerable number of books which discuss different stages in the language's history. Particularly good are the following introductory texts from the same series:

Hogg, Richard M. 2002. *An Introduction to Old English*. Edinburgh: Edinburgh University Press.
Horobin, Simon and Jeremy J. Smith. 2002. *An Introduction to Middle English*. Edinburgh: Edinburgh University Press.
Nevalainen, Terttu. 2006. *An Introduction to Early Modern English*. Edinburgh: Edinburgh University Press.

A good – although now somewhat dated – history of English spelling is

Scragg, D. G. 1974. *A History of English Spelling*. Manchester: Manchester University Press.

HISTORY OF WRITING SYSTEMS

There are many excellent surveys of the history of writing systems. Two I would strongly recommend are:

Coulmas, Florian. 1989. *The Writing Systems of the World*. Oxford: Blackwell.
Rogers, Henry. 2005. *Writing Systems: A Linguistic Approach*. Oxford: Blackwell.

LANGUAGE CONTACT, 'NEW LANGUAGES', PIDGINS AND CREOLES

Probably the best introductory discussion of language contact is

Thomason, Sarah Grey. 2001. *Language Contact*. Edinburgh: Edinburgh University Press.

In recent years, there has been much discussion of the nature of pidgin and creole genesis, meaning that there is often considerable disagreement over processes and results. Nevertheless, a good (fairly conservative) introduction is

Holm, John A. 2000. *An Introduction to Pidgins and Creoles*. Cambridge: Cambridge University Press.

A discussion of Michif can be found in

Bakker, Peter. 1997. *A Language of Our Own: The Genesis of Michif*. Oxford: Oxford University Press.

The birth of Nicaraguan Sign Language is discussed in:

Senghas, Ann. 1995. *Children's Contribution to the Birth of Nicaraguan Sign Language*. Cambridge, Mass.: Massachusetts Institute of Technology.

Index